# The Subverting Vision
# of Bulwer Lytton

"The Trial." Frontispiece to Edward Bulwer, *Eugene Aram: A Tale* (London: Richard Bentley, 1933). Courtesy of the Department of Special Collections, Young Research Library, UCLA.

# The Subverting Vision of Bulwer Lytton

## Bicentenary Reflections

Edited and with an Introduction
by Allan Conrad Christensen

Newark: University of Delaware Press

Associated University Presses
2010 Eastpark Boulevard
Cranbury, NJ 08512

The paper used in this publication meets the requirements of the American National Standard for Permanence of Paper for Printed Library Materials Z39.48-1984.             .

Library of Congress Cataloging-in-Publication Data

The subverting vision of Bulwer Lytton : bicentenary reflections /
    edited and with an introduction by Allan Conrad Christensen.
        p.   cm.
    "Most of the articles in this volume originated as papers presented at a
    three-day conference entitled "Bulwer Lytton 2000," held at the
    Institute for English Studies, University of London, in July
    2000"—Introd.
    Includes bibliographical references and index.
    ISBN 0-87413-856-6 (alk. paper)
    1. Lytton, Edward Bulwer Lytton, Baron, 1803-1873—Criticism and
interpretation.   2. Literature and history—Great Britain—History—
19th century.   3. Historical fiction, English—History and criticism.
I. Christensen, Allan Conrad.
PR4938.S83   2004
823'.8—dc22                                                    2003019433

PRINTED IN THE UNITED STATES OF AMERICA

To

Lady Hermione Bulwer Lytton,
Dowager Baroness Cobbold of Knebworth,
in her ninety-ninth year

For some twenty-five years
the gracious and capable custodian of the family heritage,
she has generously welcomed
scholars and admirers of her illustrious forebears into the family,
a tradition magnificently continued since her retirement
by her son and grandson.

# Contents

# Introduction

MOST OF THE ARTICLES IN THIS VOLUME ORIGINATED AS PAPERS PRE-
sented at a three-day conference entitled "Bulwer Lytton 2000,"
held at the Institute for English Studies, University of London,
in July 2000. The conference demonstrated to the satisfaction of
its participants that the works of Edward Bulwer Lytton deserve
the serious attention of scholars and a larger public.

Studies of his works in recent decades have gone far towards
reestablishing him as a significant exponent of Victorian culture.
It is hoped that the present volume will contribute in a decisive
way, on the occasion of the bicentenary of his birth in 1803, to
this process. The texts of Bulwer Lytton—or Bulwer, as he is
more often referred to in these articles—repay attention in the
light of contemporary critical theories and methods. The emergence of common themes in the conference papers has also made
it increasingly clear that beyond the generic diversity of the individual works a unifying coherence informs Bulwer's whole career.

Somewhat paradoxically, perhaps, that coherence emerges particularly in repeated patterns of antitheses or subversion. Components exist in their relationship to counter-components; and in
the articles of this volume, the components that may seem to be
negative or antithetical often preponderate or elicit a greater interest. Our attention to the negating elements that are more or
less hidden in texts may betray, of course, our own subverting
optics, even as it discovers those elements within the texts. Still,
in our first article, Andrew Brown observes convincingly just how
self-subverting Bulwer's entire career actually was. The meteoric
success of the Bulwerian phenomenon was always preparing its
own posthumous decline: "Bulwer's [immense] reputation in his
own day . . . carried within it the seeds of his subsequent fall from
grace." In many ways he may seem to have been the quintessential figure of his age, to the extent that, in Brown's citation of
Chesterton, "You could not have the Victorian Age without him."
Yet the age itself possessed self-subversive tendencies, of which

we have since become more aware, and as the representative of his times Bulwer naturally exemplifies such tendencies as well. The articles that follow examine these tendencies, I suggest, in three principal areas—in Bulwer's constructions and deconstructions, namely, of psychological, cultural, and generic identities.

On the psychological level, Bulwer was conscious at the outset of his career of a certain self-division, a consciousness that underlies the frequent motif, from *Pelham* and on, of the mirror image. (The subtitle of our volume alludes, indeed, to the continuing operation of Bulwer's "reflections" in our own responses to him.) The self-division receives expression too in the omnipresence in his works of alter egos or doubles.

Worth consideration in this context is a hitherto neglected long poem of 1831, *The Siamese Twins*, which C. C. Barfoot analyzes in an article that could not, unfortunately, be included in this volume. Beyond its satiric purpose, the poem possesses an autobiographical relevance to the contradictions between Bulwer's public and private personae. The relationship between the inseparable twins involves love, jealousy, and hatred until the poet imagines a surgical separation, not of their own choosing, and the disappearance of the darker, more wildly passionate twin. In Lawrence Poston's discussion of the case of the brothers Morton and Aubrey, whose bond in *Devereux* is even more intensely erotic, the lonely survivor remains "a permanently wounded spirit." Poston also traces relationships of passionate recognition and repulsion between alter egos in the tale "Monos and Daimonos" and in *Pelham, Eugene Aram, Ernest Maltravers*, and *Lucretia*. In the last work, Gabriel Varney suffers the fate of being chained in prison forever to Grabman, "the *Doppelgänger* [of one's own creation] from whom one can never be divorced and in whose brutish lineaments one detects [as in a mirror] the debased features of the self." While Bulwer associates Grabman, the "Grave stealer," with the "Oulos Oneiros—the Evil Dream of the Greeks," Poston describes the "fascination with this deadly symbiosis" as Godwinian—there being parallels in Mary Shelley too. Self-identification would seem in any case to require confrontation with a fearful version of oneself and the risk of self-annihilation.

Outside the covers of his books, Bulwer's wife Rosina became a version of the haunting antagonist or Nemesis to whom he was fearfully bound. Their descendant Lord Cobbold describes him as subject to "continuous provocation from an ever present tormentor," for the desire to avenge herself on him became the ruinous fixation of her life. A mutual hostility between the sometime lovers was also actively fought out, as Marie Mulvey-Roberts indicates, within the covers of their books. Rosina "us[ed] her novels as conduits for entering his texts." She parodied and sought to undermine his novels, and he fought back by putting her unpleasantly into episodes of his own works. The obsession with one another, "both in real life and as a literary subject, maintained their co-dependency."

In going beyond psychological to cultural identities, Bulwer tended similarly to define any zeitgeist, for which he shared the characteristic Victorian fascination, with respect to its intrinsic dependence upon oppositions. Catherine Phillips thus mentions—in connection with his unfinished history of ancient Athens—the importance of constructing the Athenian identity in opposition to that of Sparta. And in writing his own history, Bulwer was essentially writing it "against" the accounts of Gibbon and Hume.

The treatment of ancient Pompeii too, as Angus Easson shows, brings into relief two starkly contrasting principles. On the one hand, the sense of the quotidian normality of life in the ancient city intrigued Bulwer, and Easson emphasizes especially this "domestic," somewhat Biedermeier quality of the narrative. The story abounds in references to the objects of everyday use that had so caught Bulwer's fancy at the archaeological site and in the museums, and the action occurs in seemingly real domestic interiors. Yet this environment is not so solid as it seems, and there is, on the other hand, the hint of dark subterranean energies, associated both with violent, imperfectly domesticated instincts in human beings and with the impending eruption of the volcano. Besides being a domestic novel, which may prefigure those of the Caxton series, *Pompeii* is designed as we know from the start to tell a story of horror and spectacular catastrophe. The domestic and the apocalyptic dimensions seem, indeed, to require one another, as Easson shows with respect to "the tension between life and cataclysmic ending" that defines the essential mood of the novel. The city that Bulwer felt himself to be recalling so fully to life was also very much for him, as it had been for Sir Walter Scott, "The city of the Dead." The possibility for recovering the domestic life of the inhabitants depended precisely on the violent extinction of their life under the weight of the lava that preserved the evidence: "For us to know them living, they had to die."

With respect to *Pompeii* again and to *Rienzi*, Esther Schor traces further connections between the zeitgeist of earlier ages

and that of nineteenth-century Italy and England. She finds that
the treatment in these novels of the plebeian classes with their
convulsive, instinctive energies reveals his growing uneasiness
about Mazzini and the "Giovine Italia" and his fear of the "mob"
in England. The "people" might prove a more dangerous menace
to social stability than he had thought when campaigning for the
Reform Bill. The antagonistic political positions, as Bulwer speculated at the time of the elections of 1834, might seem to be those
of Tory oligarchy and "ochlochracy" (mob rule), but in this case
there was a dangerous symbiosis between the apparent oppositions: "The extremes meet," he wrote in the famous *Letter to a
Late Cabinet Minister* that may have been responsible for the
Whig victory in the elections, "or as the Eastern Proverb informs
us, when the serpent wants to seem innocent, it puts its tail in its
mouth!"

Bulwer hoped for a more productive symbiosis in the cultural
sphere that regarded relationships between mother country and
colonies. As Charles W. Snyder has indicated, the logic of the underlying tensions between the potential antagonists did also
strike him. During his tenure as Colonial Secretary, it was therefore his concern to elaborate and put into practice a theory of colonialism that would encourage colonists to identify their
interests and their culture with those of the mother country. The
object was "to ensure the endurance of their connection with
Britain." The complexity of the rapport between "'home' country and . . . its colonial margins" similarly engages Peter W. Sinnema's attention in his study of the Caxton novels as "domestic
fiction." The terms of the oppositions also become "hearth" versus "public sphere" and "female" versus "male." In the gendered field of such novels, each side "may be said to presuppose
and rely upon the other for its own sense of identity and the containment of its distinct values." The parallels between the colonial endeavor and the relationship between the sexes may also
imply analogies between wild Australian spaces with their mysterious inhabitants and women as "eternal Others" to be colonized.

"A contrastive approach," according to Joachim Mathieu, "is
an essential characteristic of Bulwer's *England and the English*"
as well. Here the best aspect of the English cultural identity is
defined in its opposition to the "aristocratic" spirit that has been
corrupting England. But as Mathieu indicates, France constitutes in Bulwer's perceptive analysis another very important
"Other" against which the English "Self" may measure and define itself. Far from chauvinist in his patriotism, Bulwer sees this

French Other not so much as a hostile antagonist but as an interesting protagonist from whom the English may learn valuable
lessons. Indeed, Bulwer imaginatively reverses the positions. The
English are encouraged to look through French eyes at themselves as the Other: "it is important," in Mathieu's understanding of the lesson, "to see oneself through foreign eyes in order to
understand oneself and to observe models from abroad in order
to reform oneself." As occurs in the novels discussed by Jonathan
H. Grossman, too, Bulwer provides in *England and the English* a
new or double point of view that usefully defamiliarizes the material.

In *The Parisians*, at the end of his career, Bulwer will once
more undertake a definition of the cultural identity of a nation by
opposing, implicitly in this case, England and France. Philip
Rand studies the oppositions as well, however, through a construction of Zola's treatment of the same events as a foil or
French Other against which to evaluate Bulwer's English vision.
What Bulwer seems particularly to see in the last days of the Second Empire is a catastrophe that recalls those of the last days of
Pompeii or of Rienzi. In *Rienzi*, as Schor suggests, the tribune
calls into being the "people" that become the instrument of his
downfall. The pattern resembles that noticed by Poston in other
works by Bulwer too whereby a Frankenstein's monster turns
against his creator. The nemesis of the French, therefore, is less
the Prussian forces than one, Rand maintains, of their own making. The conspiratorial Vicomte de Mauléon, for example, "has
set forces in motion that he has not reckoned upon," which, in
the form of his creature Monnier, "cost him his own life . . . [and]
threaten the fabric of the entire society." He and the classes of
French society with which he is associated have "drawn down"
the deserved deluge.

*The Coming Race*, another late treatment of cultural identity,
proposes particularly complex patterns of opposition. The Other
is now the subterranean, inhuman, antidemocratic race of the
Vril-ya, but they themselves typify, in Lillian Nayder's analysis,
many self-contradictory possibilities: "an odd composite of the
very old and the very new, the imperial and the aboriginal," they
also constitute a threat to both Americans and Britons, who are
otherwise seen in counter-position. The menace emerges finally,
in a paradigm like that defined by Sinnema with reference to the
Caxton novels, in terms of gender and of domesticity: "Bulwer
reiterates his theme," Nayder concludes, "that Britons and
Americans face a common threat but he does so with a significant

variation: the greatest danger to both empires may lie at home . . . among women uncivilized enough to hunger for the rights of their fathers and husbands."

In the last area (for our purposes) of his creativity, Bulwer has seemed fruitfully to transgress the supposed boundaries between literary genres and thus to define new ones. Phillips discusses the "hybrid technique" of his *Athens* whereby the historical narrative easily introduces fictional details to "contextualize" the facts and impart a "warmer" human interest to them. The point is that historical events occur not only because of objective material factors but also as a result of subjective human elements, which need to be imaginatively recovered. Ultimately there is a difference not in kind but only in degree between the genres of history (like that of *Athens*) and of historical romance (like that of *Pompeii* and *Rienzi*, which were being composed in the same period).

According to Richard Cronin, Bulwer was reacting in *Pelham* to the historical romances of Scott. Supposedly antithetical to the historical romance, the silver-fork genre nevertheless submitted to the influence of Scott in its self-conscious concern with the present as a peculiar, fleeting historical moment. *Pelham* also came to exist, in Carlyle's appropriation of the work, in a fascinating symbiosis with *Sartor Resartus*: "Carlyle defines himself in opposition to the fashionable novelists, but he also recognizes himself in them. They are, in however distorted a manner, a reflection of himself." A tension of ambivalent oppositions has been created as well within *Pelham*. The structure of this novel and its immediate successors "offered [Bulwer] what he most needed, the means to reconcile his avid social ambition with . . . principled political radicalism." And "in working out his own dilemma," Cronin concludes, "Bulwer happened on a structural principle that was to inform the novel of social criticism throughout much of the nineteenth century."

In Bulwer's practice, the silver-fork novel is brought into a dialectical relationship not only with the historical romance and the novel of social criticism but with the Newgate novel. The frivolous world of high society and the criminal underworld become inverted reflections of one another. The emphasis of Heather Worthington, however, is upon Bulwer's "transgression" of the laws of the silver-fork genre when he introduces the criminal element into *Pelham*. In *Eugene Aram*, he would then transgress the conventions of another genre by attempting to make the criminal into the hero of romance. Such generic transgressions are nevertheless appropriate in novels like these and *Paul Clifford* that are designed to attack the laws of the state as well: "Subversive in politics and literature, . . . Bulwer brought into visibility, in Foucauldian terms, that which had been concealed." What had lain darkly underground were not only "inequities and iniquities in the law, [but] also the potential for a new genre of fiction."

Focusing primarily on the courtroom scenes in *Paul Clifford* and *Eugene Aram*, Jonathan H. Grossman notices other symmetries of opposition. In the earlier novel, there is, in Bulwer's own words, the confrontation in court of "the hunted son and the honoured father, the outcast of the law, the dispenser of the law—the felon, and the judge." Here, though, the point is not so much the felon's and the judge's recognition of one another as the spectators' recognition of them as doubles: "instead of seeing criminal and judge as opposites, they see analogues, likeness not only of external qualities but of internal ones. And so of course do we, whose changed perspective has all along been Bulwer's target." *Eugene Aram* too provides an "epiphany of perspective," as shown in the illustration reproduced for the frontispiece of this volume. We watch Aram being watched in court, seen from the perspective of Madeline as a hero and from the simultaneous perspective of the judge as a criminal. He is, as we are thus able to see, both hero and criminal at once, and Bulwer's great achievement in these novels, Grossman argues, is his construction of this double perspective. The significance of the Newgate novels lies less in their criminal content than in their technical innovations, their "sculpting [of] a new narrative perspective." The new double or self-subverting vision, which also aligns the omniscient third-person viewpoint of the narrator with the criminal's own first-person view, probably shocked the early readers even more than the lurid material. It implied that the criminal, who had been made by circumstance, might be a man like any other. The greatest shock might then derive from readers' recognitions of the potential criminal, the subversive double, within themselves.

In the later novels, literary genres that imply contrasting perspectives upon reality coexist or transgressively menace one another in still other ways. Aggressive confrontations like those that Mulvey-Roberts observes between the books of Edward and Rosina, or like those that Worthington defines against preexisting genres, are prosecuted entirely within the covers of some of the novels. Allan Christensen perceives the hostilities in the Caxton novels and *A Strange Story* as a process of writing that unwrites other writing. Bulwer's narrators describe fictitious narratives that are being written in the course of their stories—specifically, these are examples of historical and scientific writing that is nevertheless seen to possess a large element of fiction. These narratives are then abandoned, undermined, or exorcised in order to clear ground on which to construct the narratives that we actually read. The resulting narratives emerge as examples of identities that precisely depend on the subversion of their hostile alter egos.

The bildungsroman provides a final example of a genre that Bulwer comes for his own purposes to subvert. *Ernest Maltravers* and its sequel *Alice* have often been seen as one of the most faithful versions in English fiction of the Goethean bildungsroman. Bulwer's last novel, *Kenelm Chillingly*, then follows, in Walter Göbel's analysis, the pattern of the bildungsroman only to "revoke" or, in Christensen's terminology, to "unwrite" it. The hero does not develop to the point of resigning a futile idealism and embracing the practical possibilities for a career of public service that his own age offers. Instead of being "educated," he is "de-educated" and nostalgically alienated from the modern zeitgeist. His conversion is essentially an unconversion to the values of the romantic past, symbolically sealed in a moving reconciliation with his father.

The denouement of *Kenelm Chillingly* may mirror Bulwer's own alienation from his times and from life itself as his subterranean self prompts him to prepare for death. Although he has seemed, to Chesterton and others, to be such a quintessential Victorian, he has always been an opponent of the zeitgeist too. At the beginning of his career, the opposition involved a radical and forward-looking hostility, in Benthamite terms, towards the penal system, the electoral laws, and the other tyrannical aspects of an ancien régime. At the end, when Benthamite considerations of utility had triumphed, he reacted with backward-looking nostalgia against *their* cold and crass insensitivity to human values. This is, in Göbel's analysis, the principal thrust of his last novel. His career therefore demonstrates precisely in its negative and antithetical elements, which include the restlessly experimental transgression of laws of literary genres, a unifying pattern.

The summary offered in this introduction necessarily neglects many aspects of the individual essays, which advance a variety of arguments besides those reported here. In the present selection of essays many aspects of Bulwer's creativity are of course neglected as well. Several novels of his midcareer—*Night and Morning, Zanoni, The Last of the Barons*, and *Harold*—do not receive their deserved attention, since it happened that no essays on them were forthcoming. *King Arthur* and the other poetry is left out too. More serious may be the omission of the plays, including the last, unpublished one, *The Captives*, that received its lively world premiere at Knebworth House during the conference.

Yet this selection may provide sufficient material for a new recognition, beyond the clichés that are still unfortunately repeated about Bulwer, of his achievement with respect to both its restless variety and its coherence. At the time of *Kenelm Chillingly* and his impending death, Bulwer believed that an appropriate recognition of his life's accomplishments would be accorded him in the other world. "The act of dying," he wrote in a passage cited in a note to Göbel's essay, enacted the summoning of the life-traveler to a paternal judgment: "It is to a father's judgment that he is to render the account of his wanderings—it is to a father's home that he returns." As the courtroom scene of *Paul Clifford* reminds us, however, the antithesis of judging father and judged son may also need to be inverted. The bicentenary offers an appropriate moment for reflections upon, and reflections of, the pilgrimage that began in 1803 from the filial perspective of the heirs of Bulwer's considerable achievement.

The editor acknowledges with gratitude the committed support of Warwick Gould, Director of the Institute of English Studies of the School of Advanced Study, University of London. Among the contributors, who have all cooperated industriously to make their essays suitable for this particular volume, Andrew Brown, Marie Mulvey-Roberts, and Philip Rand have offered especially helpful assistance in the editorial task. For the necessary financial backing, our thanks go to the Institute of English Studies for its generous sponsorship of the convention and to John Cabot University, Rome, for its underwriting of the editorial expenses.

# A Chronology:
# Edward George Earle Lytton Bulwer Lytton First Baron Lytton of Knebworth, 1803–1873

(prepared by Andrew Brown, with titles of novels in *relief*)

1803     May 25: born in London, the youngest son of Colonel (later General) William Earle Bulwer and Elizabeth Warburton Lytton of Heydon and Wood Dalling, Norfolk.

1807     His father dies of a stroke, aged fifty-one.

1810     His mother inherits the Lytton family estates at Knebworth in Hertfordshire and changes her surname to Bulwer Lytton.

1812–21     Attends various schools, then from age fifteen studies with a private tutor; his first publication, *Ismael: an Oriental Tale* (verse) issued in 1820.

1822–25     Attends Cambridge University for a term at Trinity College, then as a Fellow Commoner at Trinity Hall, where he becomes President of the Union Debating Society; *Delmour, or the Tale of a Sylphid* (verse) published in 1823; during the summer vacation of 1824 he has an affair with Lady Caroline Lamb, a family friend and neighbor eighteen years his senior.

1826     As a fashionable dandy in London he lives extravagantly at his adoring mother's expense; falls in love with Rosina Wheeler, an Irish beauty of no social standing or wealth; publishes *Weeds and Wild Flowers* (verse).

1827     His first novel, **Falkland**, attracts little attention and sells poorly; marries Rosina (August) despite implacable opposition by his mother, who cuts off his allowance; turns to writing as his main source of income; *O'Neill, or the Rebel* (verse).

1828    ***Pelham, or the Adventures of a Gentleman*** proves a huge commercial success and makes his reputation; his first child, Emily, is born in June; receives £900 for ***The Disowned***.

1829    Lionized by fashionable society, he devotes himself to political networking and further literary endeavor; paid £1500 for ***Devereux***.

1830    Begins a lifelong friendship with Benjamin Disraeli; reconciled with his mother, he grows increasingly estranged from his wife; his novel ***Paul Clifford*** initiates the vogue for "Newgate" fiction.

1831    *The Siamese Twins* (verse); elected M.P. for St. Ives in Huntingdonshire as an independent radical (April), maiden speech (July) in support of second reading of the Reform Bill; in November he becomes editor of the *New Monthly Magazine*.

1832    ***Eugene Aram*** proves another best-seller, though widely criticized in the press for making a hero out of a notorious murderer; his son Edward Robert born in November; elected M.P. for Lincoln in the first postreform Parliament (December).

1833    ***Godolphin*** is less successful, but *England and the English*, his first full-length work of nonfiction, enhances his standing as a social and political commentator; sponsors a parliamentary bill to establish dramatic copyright; ill health and increasing marital friction (the latter exacerbated by his flirtation with Mrs. Robert Stanhope) prompt him to resign as editor of the *New Monthly* in August and to set out with Rosina on a Grand Tour of Italy.

1834    After five months of almost incessant quarrelling, they return home and agree to a trial separation; *The Pilgrims of the Rhine*, a collection of short stories, is followed by his single most celebrated novel, ***The Last Days of Pompeii***; when the king dismisses Lord Melbourne's ministry in November, he writes the progovernment pamphlet *A Letter to a Late Cabinet Minister on the Present Crisis*: within six weeks it runs through twenty-one editions and sells thirty thousand copies.

1835    Following Melbourne's victory at the ensuing general election, he declines the offer of a junior lordship of the admiralty in the new administration; *The Student*, a collection of essays and tales, is followed by another best-selling historical novel, ***Rienzi, the Last of the Tribunes*** (the inspiration for Wagner's opera); his affair with Laura Deacon signals the death-knell of his marriage.

1836   He and Rosina sign a formal deed of separation (he secures custody of the children, she receives an annuity of £400); his first play, *The Duchess de la Vallière*, written as a vehicle for his friend the actor-manager William Macready.

1837   His history *Athens, Its Rise and Fall* appears in April, his Germanic bildungsroman ***Ernest Maltravers*** in September.

1838   ***Alice, or the Mysteries*** (the sequel to ***Ernest Maltravers***) and the hugely successful play *The Lady of Lyons* both published in March, the novella *Leila, or the Seige of Granada* in April; in July, Lord Melbourne recommends him for a baronetcy in Queen Victoria's coronation honors list; from March to October he edits the *Monthly Chronicle*, in which he publishes his influential essay "On Art in Fiction."

1839   Publishes two more plays, *The Sea-Captain* and *Richelieu, or the Conspiracy*, the latter of which includes the most famous words he ever wrote: "Beneath the rule of men entirely great / The pen is mightier than the sword." Rosina's novel *Cheveley, or the Man of Honour* ridicules thinly veiled representations of himself and his mother.

1840   Rosina's novel *The Bubble of the Budget Family* presses home the attack; his single most lasting play, *Money* (most recently revived at the National Theatre in London in 1999) has its first performance.

1841   ***Night and Morning***, another sensational story of crime and criminality; in July he loses his parliamentary seat to a Tory at the general election.

1842   ***Zanoni*** reflects his growing interest in the occult; *Eva, a True Story of Light and Darkness* (verse).

1843   ***The Last of the Barons***, set during the Wars of the Roses; his long campaign against the monopoly of London's patent theaters (Covent Garden and Drury Lane) finally leads to the abolition of the royal patent; on his mother's death in December he inherits the Lytton estates at Knebworth.

1844   Changes his surname by royal license to Bulwer Lytton; publishes a translation of *The Poems and Ballads of Schiller*.

1845    *The Crisis, a Satire of the Day* (verse).

1846    *The New Timon, a Romance of London* (verse); **Lucretia, or the Children of Night**, based on the true story of the forger and poisoner Thomas Wainewright.

1847    His daughter Emily dies of typhus fever aged 19.

1848    **Harold, the Last of the Saxon Kings**.

1849    *King Arthur* (an epic poem in twelve books); **The Caxtons, a Family Picture**, the first in a successful trilogy of Sternean "domestic" novels, serialized in *Blackwood's Magazine* (April 1848 to October 1849).

1851    The comic play *Not So Bad As We Seem*, written to raise funds for the "Guild of Literature and Art"—which he and his friend Charles Dickens had established to support impoverished authors—is given its inaugural performance before the Queen and Prince Albert.

1852    Having changed his political allegiance under Disraeli's influence, at the general election in July he re-enters Parliament as Tory member for Hertfordshire.

1853    **"My Novel"**, the second in the Caxton series, completes its serialization in *Blackwood's* (September 1850 to January 1853).

1854    Following his support for the Crimean campaign, he becomes a government front-bench spokesman in Parliament.

1855    Stamp duty on newspapers (the so-called "taxes on knowledge"), of which he had been a prominent opponent for twenty years, finally repealed.

1857    Rosina issues the pamphlet *Lady Bulwer Lytton's Appeal to the Justice and Charity of the English Public*.

1858    Prime Minister Lord Derby offers him the post of Secretary of State for the Colonies following a successful outcome to the general election in June; at an eve-of-poll meeting at Hertford, Rosina publicly denounces him for mistreating his wife and murdering his daughter; he reacts by having her consigned to a private asylum, but public opinion soon forces him to release her and to increase her annuity; as Colonial Secretary he establishes the new Canadian colony of British Columbia.

1859  ***What Will He Do With It?***, the last of the Caxton trilogy, concludes its serialization in *Blackwood's* (June 1857 to January 1859); his celebrated ghost story "The Haunted and the Haunters" is published in *Blackwood's*; he presides over the establishment of the new Australian colony of Queensland; increasing deafness and ill health force him to resign his office in December.

1860  *St Stephens* (verse).

1861  Dickens invites him to publish the occult-scientific novel ***A Strange Story*** in the weekly journal *All The Year Round* (August 1861 to March 1862); as a quid pro quo for editorial advice on his own novel he persuades Dickens to alter the ending of *Great Expectations*.

1863  *Caxtoniana: a Series of Essays on Life, Literature, and Manners*.

1864  *The Boatman* (verse).

1866  Raised to the peerage as Baron Lytton of Knebworth in recognition of his public service; *The Lost Tales of Miletus* (verse).

1868  *The Rightful Heir* (drama).

1869  *Walpole* (drama), *The Odes and Epodes of Horace* (translation).

1871  ***The Coming Race***, one of the earliest English examples of science fiction, runs through eight editions in eighteen months.

1873  January 18: dies at Torquay of a cerebral abscess and is buried in Westminster Abbey; his novel ***Kenelm Chillingly*** is published a few days later.

1874  ***The Parisians,*** his novel about the end of the Second French Empire, concludes posthumously its serialization in *Blackwood's* (October 1872 to January 1874).

1876  His unfinished novel of ancient Greece, *Pausanias the Spartan*, is published by his son (who in 1880, as Viceroy of India, was created Earl of Lytton).

1882  March: Rosina dies in obscurity, still obsessed by her ill-treatment at her husband's hands.

The grave of Edward Bulwer Lytton in Westminster Abbey with plant placed by his descendants for the bicentenary, 25 May 2003. Photograph taken by Philip Rand. By courtesy of the Dean and Chapter of Westminster.

# Note on Citations and Editions

THE DATES OF THE FIRST EDITIONS OF THE WORKS OF BULWER LYTton are given in the chronology above. Unless otherwise indicated, the references in the articles of this volume are to the publications of his works in *Lord Lytton's Novels* and *Lord Lytton's Miscellaneous Works: Knebworth Edition*, 37 vols. (London/ New York: George Routledge and Sons, 1873–77). These references, given parenthetically in the text of the articles, are in Roman numerals that refer not to pages but to the number of the book (or part) and/or the chapter of the particular work. Since the Knebworth edition is not always readily available, it is hoped that such references to book (or part) and chapter will enable readers to locate the particular passages in any of the many other editions of the works.

# The Subverting Vision
# of Bulwer Lytton

# Bulwer's Reputation

## Andrew Brown

WHEN EDWARD BULWER LYTTON DIED IN 1873 HE WAS BURIED IN Westminster Abbey and obituaries marked the passing of England's foremost man of letters. Posthumously, too, he remained a pillar of the Victorian literary establishment, with no fewer than twenty-five separate collections of his complete novels issued in Britain and America between 1874 and 1901. The twentieth century, however, witnessed a precipitous decline in his reputation and popularity alike. By 1944 V. S. Pritchett could fairly describe him as "the totally unread Victorian";[1] fifty years later not a single one of his books was in print in his native land. No other Victorian writer of note has suffered so total an eclipse. How could things have come to quite such a pass? To answer this, my aim in this essay is to examine the nature of Bulwer's reputation in his own day, and to suggest how this carried within it the seeds of his subsequent fall from grace.

The first thing to establish is that virtually none of his contemporaries had as far to fall. Reviewing the state of English fiction in 1855, Margaret Oliphant placed Bulwer above Dickens and Thackeray as "the first novelist of his time,"[2] while in 1859 W. E. Aytoun's entry on "Romance" in the eighth edition of *Encyclopaedia Britannica* judged him "now unquestionably the greatest living novelist of England."[3] To an extent, these (representative, middlebrow) claims for his literary preeminence were probably influenced by his status as a perennial best-seller. As early as 1834, two years after the death of Scott, he was hailed by the *American Quarterly Review* as "without doubt, the most popular writer now living."[4] Two decades, a baronetcy, and numerous blockbusters later his commercial valuation remained undiminished, and in 1853 George Routledge paid him the unprecedented sum of £20,000 for a ten-year lease to the copyrights of his nineteen existing novels. Of the various formats in which these were then reissued, the 1s. 6d. "Railway Library" proved the most successful, and in 1857 W. H. Smith reported that Bulwer was the most requested author at his station bookstalls.[5] The pattern was to repeat itself right to the end of his career: of his occult-scientific novel *A Strange Story* (1861–62), which followed *The Woman in White* and *Great Expectations* as the principal serial in *All the Year Round*, the *Times* noted, "It appears to be the greatest of all the successes achieved by [the magazine]. Hundreds of thousands of readers rush to read . . . Sir E.B. Lytton";[6] in 1873 his final three-decker, the bildungsroman *Kenelm Chillingly*, sold out its first impression of 3,150 copies (at one-and-a-half guineas the set) on the morning of its publication. Next to Dickens, he was the most consistently successful novelist of his generation, while his total *earnings* were even higher. As Edmund Gosse was to put it, "Everything he wrote sold as though it were bread displayed to a hungry crowd."[7]

The bread, it should be noted, was of an unusually rich recipe. Like many thoughtful young men in the 1830s, Bulwer was troubled by the materialist ethic scorned by Carlyle, in a memorable phrase, as "virtue by Profit and Loss."[8] Where he singled himself out from the post-Byronic crowd was in his contention that the *novel*, as the most popular and powerful mode of communicating ideas, should play a key role in countering this tendency—by seeking "to inculcate a venerating enthusiasm for the true and ethereal springs of Greatness and Virtue . . . the noble aspirations that belong . . . to the diviner excitation of the soul."[9] A delineation of man's spiritual life, he claimed in 1838, was "the appointed destiny of the Romance of the Nineteenth Century,"[10] and this, with varying degrees of emphasis, is what he sought to accomplish in his own work—if in practice for the most part by means of rhapsodic asides, moralizing commentaries, and self-consciously learned quotation from the leading (mostly German) philosophers of the previous generation.

From the outset of his career appreciative reviews paid tribute to the originality of this ambition and to the salutary effect of its realization. "The volumes of Mr Bulwer," as one notice observed in 1832, "are imbued with a deeper tone of philosophy, and possess more pretensions to thought and reflection than those of his great contemporaries."[11] Recalling his reading experience in the 1830s, the American diplomat Henry Wikoff noted: "It was the vein of philosophy that pervaded [Bulwer's novels] that attracted me, and aroused a habit of reflection vastly beneficial. I believe I derived more instruction in this way from Bulwer than any author I ever read."[12] Wikoff's judgment was endorsed by no less a commentator than Ruskin, who remarked in 1836 that the perusal of Bulwer's works "must always refine the mind to a great degree, and improve us in the science of metaphysics."[13] With a single drop of ink, the *Monthly Magazine* pronounced in 1837, he could make thousands reflect, for he was "the metaphysician-novelist of England."[14] Time and again, in seeking to distinguish Bulwer's fiction from that of his peers, such commentators stressed the high-minded intellectual conception of his work—its (erudite) philosophical idealism and its (didactic) moral tendency—whose result was, according to G. P. R. James in the *Dublin University Magazine*, that "from what we have read for amusement at first, we at length derive instruction and profit."[15] Bulwer's were novels that, according to Poe, were sure to enkindle "the most profound of our thoughts . . . and the most ennobling and lofty of our aspirations,"[16] and which, according to L. E. Landon (writing as early as 1831), had revolutionized the genre by basing it on "a vast mass of moral investigation and truth."[17]

Other commentators, however, took a very different line. Hostility towards Bulwer's fiction in the periodical press (notably in the *Quarterly Review* and *Fraser's Magazine*, led by Lockhart, Maginn, and the young Thackeray) was initially motivated for the most part by prejudice against his radical politics, and by a thoroughgoing personal dislike of his aristocratic airs and graces. *Pelham*, Lockhart reported to Scott in 1828, "is writ by a Mr. Bulwer, a Norfolk squire and horrid puppy. I have not read the book, from disliking the author."[18] To Thackeray, the most implacable of these early assailants, he was the insufferable "Bulwig"— "bloated with vanity, meanness, and ostentatious exaltation of self."[19] Underlying the gratuitous cruelty of such attacks was a strain of more serious criticism, which took increasing hold as his career progressed: namely, that while he posed as a great thinker he was in fact merely a charlatan and impostor. "Everybody has a spite at Bulwer," Ruskin noted in his diary in 1840, "because the public think him clever, and they don't."[20] "Tinselled truisms feature as new discoveries," the *Athenaeum* complained in 1842, "and obscurity of meaning passes for elevation of thought."[21] His philosophizing, the Irish novelist Gerald Griffin remarked, seems "as deep as the sky in a lake, / Till the mud at six inches reveals your mistake."[22] His vaunted thoughtfulness, according to Kingsley, was little more than "washy and somewhat insincere *blague*."[23]

That the middlebrow reading public did indeed regard him as

"clever" is undeniable, though not necessarily complimentary. When George Eliot, in her celebrated essay "Silly Novels by Lady Novelists" (1856), defined the *"oracular* species" of the "mind-and-millinery school" of fiction as a type of novel in which emptily sententious passages are "doubly and trebly scored with the pencil,"[24] we can be fairly sure, even leaving aside the gender-specificity of her title, that she was not thinking of Bulwer (for whom she, like Dickens, had considerable respect). Others, though, were less favorable in their judgment, and particularly in their estimate of the sort of (mostly female) readers who were most impressed by his works. Twenty years earlier, for example, the *Gentleman's Magazine* accused him of pandering to "Duchess-dowagers . . . ladies' maids, governesses at Kensington-gore, dress-makers, and sentimental and single virgins in town and country."[25] By the 1850s even the appreciative Margaret Oliphant felt obliged to acknowledge that Bulwer's novels were irrevocably associated with the "grand passions which appeal to the boudoir and to the milliner's shop with an irresistible fascination."[26] Though the evidence may be circumstantial and anecdotal, the conclusion that the majority of his readers were women is inescapable. One recalls Isabel Sleaford, the eponymous heroine of Mary Braddon's novel *The Doctor's Wife* (1864), who longs to be swept off her feet by "Ernest Maltravers, the exquisite young aristocrat, with violet eyes and silken hair," or by "Eugene Aram, dark, gloomy, and intellectual, with that awkward little matter of Mr. Clarke's murder preying upon his mind."[27] One might equally consider the numerous private letters he received from similarly impressionable (and occasionally infatuated) female admirers. "Dearest much beloved Lytton," wrote a certain "Helena B." in 1839, "who can read your soul subduing works and not love your glorious Rienzi, your noble Maltravers. Will you then meet me next Saturday at a quarter past ten [in Hyde Park]?"[28] (History fails to relate whether he kept the proposed assignation.) "If there is one spark of poetry in my soul," confided Miss Martha Griffith of Baltimore, Maryland in 1850, "'tis to you I am indebted. Magician of Beauty! You are my mind's benefactor."[29]

It seems clear that for a large number of his readers (of whichever gender) Bulwer's great attraction was his interweaving of romantic idealism and (at least what passed for) deep philosophical thought with the more conventional features of the popular thriller, thereby elevating novel-reading to a more respectable status. A letter to him from the young Mary Braddon about her own aspirations as a novelist serves nicely to define the twin goals (and twin successes) of *his* fiction. "I want to serve two masters," she wrote; "I want to be artistic and to please *you*. I want to be sensational, and to please Mudie's subscribers."[30] That he too wanted to have it both ways is unremarkable, and unsurprising given his intensely ambitious nature. What enraged Bulwer's critics, above all, was his habit of patronizing the common reader as a means of asserting his own intellectual and artistic superiority. For example, in the dedicatory epistle to the 1845 edition of *Zanoni* (a dedication by an "Artist in words" to the sculptor and "Artist in marble" John Gibson) he announced that the book had been "little understood, and superficially judged by the common herd," adding loftily "It was not meant for them." A review in *Punch*, though equally patronizing in its own implications, threw these words straight back in his face—

> NOW, SIR EDWARD, this is not fair to the circulating libraries. It's all very well to talk of the "common herd" and say "it was not meant for them," with a curl of your fine lip; but you know it was meant for everybody who could pay threepence for a perusal of the volumes— and very popular it has been, especially with ladies'-maids and milliners.[31]

With staggering nerve, Bulwer sought to turn this admonition to his own advantage in his pamphlet *A Word to the Public* (1847)— written in response to moralizing critical attacks on his novel of criminal lowlife *Lucretia* (1846)—in which he defended himself by pointing to the book's huge success with the generality of the reading public and observing, "These poor circulating library readers are a little too superciliously treated [by the metropolitan reviews]. Say what we like about them . . . they certainly cannot be said to exclude the refined and scholastic few, while they as certainly do not embrace the lowest orders in mental cultivation."[32] In 1862, his own superciliousness transferred from Mudie's subscribers to the readers of *A Strange Story* in Dickens's two-penny weekly *All the Year Round*, we find him complaining about the "blockheads" who are likely to lack the imagination and wit to appreciate the complexities of his novel.[33] When the serialization was completed (having proved a resounding success with the paying public), Bulwer rounded indignantly in a letter to John Forster on the *reviewers* who had misunderstood the symbolic purpose of the story and had therefore branded as "un-artistic the highest reaches of Art the Book possesses," commenting with characteristic haughtiness, "of art I ought to know something after 30 years practice and incessant study."[34]

Bulwer was not an easy man to like. Though he craved the recognition of his peers as much as the admiration of the "common herd," his pronounced sense of social hauteur, allied to his habitual pose of intellectual superiority, instead provoked merely envy, offense, and outrage in the critical press. Toward the end of his career, when his status as a leading politician, popular bestseller, and arbiter of literary taste was well established, it became increasingly commonplace to debunk him as a tired poseur—the "Knebworth Apollo," as Thackeray put it, dispensing "very dexterously brewed and bottled small beer."[35] Even his early triumphs were thus retrospectively dismissed as well-dressed impostors, in which the adventures of the conventional romantic hero were apparently invested with profounder significance simply by association with windy propositions about the life of the soul. As one posthumous review observed, "He was never weary of making sententious reflections of the kind that look profound to people who are not in the habit of reflecting themselves."[36] Or, as another commented, "the grandest ornaments of his most philosophical orations . . . often turn out to be of the Brummagem variety."[37]

By any standards, Bulwer's claims to literary fame were remarkable. During a career spanning five decades he published two dozen best-selling novels (including, in *The Last Days of Pompeii*, one of the most famous titles in all of nineteenth-century fiction); nine plays, two of which (*Money* and *The Lady of Lyons*) proved among the most resilient of the Victorian era; fifteen volumes of poetry, including an epic in twelve books (*King Arthur*) and translations of Horace and Schiller; a history of Athens, a pioneering sociological survey of the national character (*England and the English*), four volumes of essays and enough uncollected prose to fill a dozen more. Samuel Smiles, the high priest of Victorian industriousness, noted in 1859 that "there are few living English writers who have written so much, and none that have produced so much of high quality."[38] That, taken as a whole, his reputation in his own time was so partial, so fraught, and so grudging is mostly due to circumstances of his own making, for had he been less arrogant in his own pronouncements of his artistic worth and intellectual standing he would surely have attracted less critical opprobrium. We should not be surprised, for example, to find his lifelong friend Disraeli glossing a description of Charles Greville as the vainest man who had ever lived with the remark, "and I don't forget Cicero and Lytton Bulwer" (a telling historical conjunction).[39] Or indeed that Trollope, when commenting that Disraeli's own works "smelt of hair oil," added that since they took their savor from Bulwer "the original compound was at least the very finest Macassar."[40] With his ornately rhetorical style and lofty moralizing manner, Bulwer was pre-eminently a writer for his own time, and as that time passed so did his special attraction. When he ceased to appeal to the common reader, his star sank almost without trace. *Critically*, the writing had long been on the wall. W. C. Roscoe's jibe, in the *National Review* in 1859, that Bulwer's style was not so much "polished" as "French-varnished" prefigures Joseph Conrad's later dismissal, in (*The Nigger of the "Narcissus"*), of his "elegant verbiage," his "polished and so curiously insincere sentences,"[41] while Thackeray's objection to his "premeditated fine writing" nicely anticipates Q. D. Leavis's scorn of his "pseudo-philosophic nonsense and preposterous rhetoric."[42]

His general neglect today is well attested by his omission from the series of literary "classics" issued by Penguin and OUP (though located alphabetically in their lists between Charles Brockden Brown and Samuel Butler, he would scarcely have been upstaged by his neighbors). Notwithstanding, and as this volume indicates, there are clear signs of renascent academic interest in Bulwer as a new generation of scholars sets out to re-map the parameters of Victorian literary culture. It seems improbable that he will ever be restored to the forefront of the canon alongside his now more celebrated contemporaries, whether as a novelist, playwright or poet, essayist, critic or social historian. It is, however, entirely reasonable that his unrivalled ubiquity and remarkable breadth of reference—the *fact* of his innovative contribution to so many genres and the extraordinary success he enjoyed in each of them (his unique claim to be considered Victorian England's most complete *man of letters*)—should reestablish him as a pivotal figure in the literary culture of the age. One thing is certain: simply to ignore Bulwer is crucially to mistake and anachronistically to misrepresent the nature and reception of Victorian letters, for he epitomizes that category of writers who, in his own words (written in the year of Victoria's accession), "form a link in the great chain of a nation's authors, which may be afterwards forgotten by the superficial, but without which the chain would be incomplete. And thus, if not first-rate for all time, they have been first-rate in their own day" (*Ernest Maltravers* III:iii). In this instance at least, his own formulation was right on the mark. Or, as G. K. Chesterton was to put it some eighty years later (offering an incontestable summary of Bulwer's place in literary history), "You could not have the Victorian Age without him."[43]

## NOTES

1. V.S. Pritchett, "Books in General," *New Statesman and Nation*, 15 April 1944, p. 259.

2. Margaret Oliphant, "Bulwer," *Blackwood's Edinburgh Magazine* 77 (1855): 223.

3. *Encyclopaedia Britannica*, 21 vols. (Edinburgh: Adam and Charles Black, 1853–60), 19: 283.

4. "Novel Writing," *American Quarterly Review* 16 (1834): 507.

5. See J. A. Sutherland, *Victorian Novelists and Publishers* (London: Athlone; Chicago: University of Chicago Press, 1976), p. 34.

6. Eneas Sweetland Dallas, review of *Great Expectations*, *Times*, 17 October 1861, p. 6.

7. Edmund Gosse, *Some Diversions of a Man of Letters* (London: William Heinemann, 1919), p. 128.

8. Thomas Carlyle, *On Heroes, Hero-Worship and the Heroic in History*, in *Works*, ed. H. D. Traill, 30 vols. (London: Chapman and Hall, 1896–99), 5:76.

9. Bulwer, *England and the English*, Knebworth ed., p. 195.

10. Bulwer, "Lady Blessington's Novels," *Edinburgh Review* 67 (1838): 357.

11. "Monthly Review of Literature," *Monthly Magazine* 13 (1832): 233.

12. Henry Wikoff, *The Reminiscences of an Idler*, 2 vols. (London: Robson and Sons, 1880), 1:25.

13. John Ruskin, "Essay on Literature," in *Works*, ed. E. T. Cook and Alexander Wedderburn, 39 vols. (London: George Allen, 1903–12), 1:371.

14. "Monthly Review of Literature," *Monthly Magazine* 24 (1837): 541.

15. G. P. R. James, review of Bulwer's *Harold*, *Dublin University Magazine* 32 (1848): 277.

16. Edgar Allan Poe, "Bulwer as a Novelist," *Marginalia*, in *Works*, ed. John Ingram, 4 vols. (Edinburgh: Adam and Charles Black, 1874–75), 3:363.

17. Letitia E. Landon, *Romance and Reality*, 3 vols. (London: Henry Colburn and Richard Bentley, 1831), 1:201.

18. *The Life and Letters of John Gibson Lockhart*, ed. Andrew Lang, 2 vols. (London: John Nimmo, 1897), 2:37.

19. W. M. Thackeray, "Mr Yellowplush's Ajew," *Fraser's Magazine* 18 (1838): 196; "High-Ways and Low-Ways," *Fraser's Magazine* 9 (1834): 725.

20. *The Diaries of John Ruskin*, ed. Joan Evans and J. H. Whitehouse, 3 vols. (Oxford: Clarendon Press, 1956–59), 1:82.

21. Review of Bulwer's *Zanoni*, *Athenaeum*, 26 February 1842, p. 182.

22. See Daniel Griffin, *The Life of Gerald Griffin Esq.* (London: Simpkin and Marshall, 1843), p. 275.

23. Charles Kingsley, "Sir E.B. Lytton and Mrs. Grundy," *Fraser's Magazine* 41 (1850): 111.

24. George Eliot, "Silly Novels by Lady Novelists," *Westminster Review* n.s. 10 (1856): 448.

25. Review of Bulwer's *The Last Days of Pompeii*, *Gentleman's Magazine* n.s. 3 (1835): 174.

26. Margaret Oliphant, *Annals of a Publishing House*, 2 vols. (Edinburgh and London: William Blackwood and Sons, 1897), 2:418.

27. Mary Braddon, *The Doctor's Wife*, 3 vols. (London: John Maxwell, 1864), 1:164.

28. Unpublished letter in the Hertfordshire County Record Office [hereafter Hertford] ref D/EK C2 103.

29. Unpublished letter, Hertford D/EK C23 19.

30. Hertford D/EK C12 124 [undated: ? May 1863], quoted by Robert Lee Wolff in "Devoted Disciple: The Letters of Mary Elizabeth Braddon to Sir Edward Bulwer-Lytton, 1862–1873," *Harvard Library Bulletin* 22 (1974): 14.

31. "Letter to Sir E. Bulwer Lytton, Bart.," *Punch* 9 (1845): 91.

32. Reprinted as appendix to 1853 ed. of *Lucretia* (London: Chapman and Hall), p. 308.

33. See Andrew Brown, "The 'Supplementary Chapter' to Bulwer Lytton's *A Strange Story*," *Victorian Literature and Culture* 26 (1998): 158.

34. Hertford D/EK C27 (March 1862), quoted by Brown, "Supplementary Chapter," p. 164.

35. *The Letters and Private Papers of William Makepeace Thackeray*, ed. Gordon N. Ray, 4 vols. (Cambridge: Harvard University Press; London: Oxford University Press, 1945–46), 3: 181, 248.

36. Edith Simcox, review of Bulwer's *Kenelm Chillingly*, *Academy* 4 (1873): 164.

37. Review of *Kenelm Chillingly*, *Saturday Review*, 5 April 1873, p. 457.

38. Samuel Smiles, *Self-Help* (London: John Murray, 1859), p. 19.

39. Quoted in W. F. Moneypenny and G. E. Buckle, *The Life of Benjamin Disraeli*, 6 vols. (London: John Murray, 1910–20), 5:348.

40. See Amy Cruse, *The Victorians and their Books* (London: George Allen and Unwin, 1935), p. 331.

41. W. C. Roscoe, "Sir E.B. Lytton, Novelist, Philosopher, and Poet," *National Review* 8 (1859): 291; Joseph Conrad, *The Nigger of the "Narcissus"* (London: William Heinemann, 1898), p. 6.

42. *The Letters and Private Papers of William Makepeace Thackeray*, 2: 485; Q. D. Leavis, *Fiction and the Reading Public* (London: Chatto and Windus, 1932), p. 164.

43. G. K. Chesterton, *The Victorian Age in Literature* [1916] (London: Williams and Norgate, 1925), p. 136.

# Bulwer, Carlyle, and the Fashionable Novel

### Richard Cronin

IN THE *NEW MONTHLY MAGAZINE* FOR 1 APRIL 1826, HENRY COLBURN inserted a puff for his latest publication: "A new novel to be named Vivian Grey is said to be a sort of Don Juan in prose, detailing the adventures of an ambitious, dashing and talented young man of high life." Disraeli, followed very shortly by Bulwer, were the chief architects of the fashionable novel, the novel set in what Catherine Gore calls "the world, the exclusive world, whose territories are so narrow of limit, and whose population is so easily resolved by the census of Debrett."[1] As Michael Sadleir notes, the sentimental novel of the late eighteenth and early nineteenth centuries characteristically chose its central characters from the aristocracy too, but for him "fashionable novels" are distinguished from earlier novels about fashionable people by their concern for "verisimilitude": the fashionable novel "might be dull and silly, but it must appear correct."[2] It is a very particular kind of verisimilitude, and consists most importantly in references to real people, real clubs, real shops, and real tradesmen. When Vivian Grey's father wishes to speak seriously to his son, he invites him to "step into Clark's and take an ice."[3] In *Pelham*, there is a meeting in Calais with Pelham's legendary predecessor, Beau Brummell (Pelham outdoes Brummell by employing three rather than two tailors to make his gloves), and the two discuss the relative merits of Staub, who tailors in Paris, and Stultz of London, agreeing that Stultz reveals "a degree of aristocratic pretension in his stitches, which is vulgar to an appalling degree" (xxxii).[4]

The novels often accommodate melodramatic plots—there is a rape and a murder in *Pelham*, an attempted murder and a fatal duel in *Vivian Grey*, a suicide in Lister's *Granby*, and in Gore's *Women As They Are* both a suicide and an averted incestuous relationship between a father and his natural child—and they most often incorporate a love story, but these are predominantly novels of conversation. Characters talk at their club, as they stroll through the gardens of a country house, as they endure a rainy day with no shooting, and they talk at dinner. Their conversation has no end other than itself, and for the reader its sole purpose is to identify a community of speakers. One of the pleasures that these novels offer their readers is initiation into the closed world of fashionable slang.

Colburn was able to enlist some genuine aristocrats—Constantine Henry Phipps, Viscount Normanby, for example, soon to succeed his father as Earl of Mulgrave,[5] and, even more exalted, Lady Charlotte Bury, the daughter of the Duke of Argyll—but their novels were far from the most successful of their kind. Colburn's most successful authors were not quite of the "ton" whose doings they described. Disraeli was the son of a retiring Jewish scholar, Catherine Gore's father was a wine merchant, and, although Bulwer, as he always insisted, was of ancient family, it was, even at the time of his birth, a family in reduced circumstances, and he began writing novels only when he was disinherited and wholly reliant on his own earnings. Isaac D'Israeli was surprised to learn that his son's second novel was entitled *The Young Duke*: "But what does Ben know of Dukes?"[6] But in fact Ben's lack of firsthand acquaintance with the upper reaches of the aristocracy makes him a representative fashionable novelist. It was a position that allowed the novelists to mediate between the society inhabited by their characters and the more modest social milieu of the greater part of their readers. It encouraged the cultivation of a perspective at once within and outside, with the result that these novels characteristically satirize the world that they celebrate, or celebrate the world that they satirize.

In its insistent contemporaneity and in its concentration on the ephemeral, silver-fork fiction is a reaction against the historical novel, and in particular the novel as practiced by Scott. And yet the fashionable novel cannot quite free itself from Scott's influence. The novelists retain, but in a new form, the historical sense that Scott had made central to fiction. They become the historians of the contemporary. The novels delight in slang and in fashions in dress precisely because slang and fashion are so completely of their moment, vulnerable not just to the passage of years but of months. For Catherine Gore, fashionable novels are "the amber which serves to preserve the ephemeral modes and caprices of the day."[7] She defends "triflers," because, "like a straw thrown up to determine the course of the wind, the triflers of any epoch are an invaluable evidence of the bent of the public mind."[8]

Triflers, here, seem to comprehend not only the characters of the fashionable novel but their authors. Their popularity lasted for some fifteen years, from 1825 to 1840, but it is somehow fitting that by 1833 Bulwer could speak of "the three-years' run of the fashionable novels" as if it were already a phenomenon of purely historical interest.[9] The novels seem oddly aware of their own obsolescence. Even in *Pelham*, his first attempt of the kind, Bulwer imagines the rapidity with which his novel will become antique: "the novel which exactly delineates the present age may seem strange and unfamiliar to the next" (xvi). The rapidity with which the novels will become obsolete is offered as a guarantee of their verisimilitude, because the society that they represent is defined by the swiftness with which it changes, and in such an age the conscientious novelist must attempt to write novels as ephemeral as newspapers.

It is significant that newspapers are the reading matter to which these novels refer more often than to any other kind except the fashionable novel itself, and the novels recognize the similarity between the two kinds. Catherine Gore's Lord Willersdale says of the "English modern novel, with its my Lord Dukes and Sir Harrys, and caricatures of the beau monde," "I hold its vulgarity and bad taste as secondary only to that of the columns of your newspapers after a drawing room."[10] The column most eagerly scanned is "Fashionable Intelligence," in which the characters can read of the balls that they attended, and their arrival in and departure from town. It is as if they rely on the newspapers to authenticate their existence. But this gives them a peculiarly ephemeral identity, which persists only for the hours or days that a newspaper commands attention. The books that record their doings seem designed to last little longer. In *Vivian Grey* Disraeli solemnly regrets such a state of affairs: "Amid the myriad of volumes which issued monthly from the press, what one was not written for the mere hour?"[11] But these novels, and *Vivian Grey* more than most, seem gleefully to accept their own transience as the condition of faithfully representing a society that is fashionable precisely because its commodities so quickly become obsolete. In Lister's *Granby*, Trebeck, a character based on Beau Brummell and at the very center of the fashionable world, "quite one of the recherché few—the pet of the exclusives," abandons the dandyism of his youth, when he is "seriously disgusted" at seeing a style of waistcoat that he had himself devised "adorning the person of a natty apprentice."[12] Literary modes, these novels seem to accept, are subject to the same rigorous law as fashions in clothing, in which the difference between the fashionable and the vulgar becomes a matter not of taste but of time, and the period of time that secures the difference becomes ever briefer, until it is reduced to a matter of a weeks.

The novelists often describe their age as marked by an accelerated process of change. The best of them, *Vivian Grey*, *Pelham*, Theodore Hook's stories in the *Sayings and Doings* series, most of Catherine Gore's fashionable novels, move with an unusual rapidity. "There never was a novel written at such a slapping pace," says R. H. Horne of Catherine Gore's *Cecil*.[13] It is a calculated effect. Gore suggests that "the velocity of steam inventions seems to demand a corresponding rapidity of narrative, dialogue, and discourse," and that the "accelerated velocity" of modern society demands a different kind of novel: "The rapidity of the waltz offers no pause for soft ramblings; and the endless whirl of engagements supersedes the possibility of plots such as endangered Miss Harriet Byron and annihilated Miss Clarissa Harlowe."[14]

Conventionally, the novel deplores societies that whirl like a waltzer, given up to a process of frenetic and purposeless change. In *Women As They Are*, Lord Willersdale is pained to see his teenage bride waltzing with fashionable young men, and the novelists often mimic his disapproval. Bulwer himself defended the fashionable novel as a variety of satire: "Few writers ever produced so great an effect on the political spirit of their generation as some of these novelists, who, without any other merit, unconsciously exposed the falsehood, the hypocrisy, the arrogant and vulgar insolence of patrician life."[15] But satire is itself a disguise for novelists who are as practiced as their characters in "the consummate dissimulation of bon ton" (*Pelham*, lv), and what it disguises is the novelists' own delighted fascination with the fashionable world that they mock.

The fashionable novelists, supported by Colburn their publisher, daringly presented their books as commodities, as items for sale in a world inhabited by people like the characters of these novels, people who are defined by the character of their purchases. "In fact," says Lister, "fashion is not so aristocratic as you may imagine; it may be bought, like most other things,"[16] or, as Vivian Grey explains to the Marquis of Carabas, "Think you not, that intellect is as much a purchasable article as fine parks and fair castles?"[17] The high-spirited cynicism of these novels is itself an expression of the glee with which the novelists confess that they are not, like Robert Plumer Ward in *Tremaine*, writing fictions that soberly protest against the "wide spread of that luxury which is consequent on wealth,"[18] but rather themselves the purveyors of luxury items. Literature is not, for Disraeli, an index of the moral state of the nation, but of its economic prosperity: "There is nothing like a fall of stock to affect what it is the fashion to style the literature of the present day." Literature is "the mere creature of our imaginary wealth. . . . Consols at 100 were the origin of all book societies."[19]

It is because fashionable novels are themselves fashionable items that they so frequently figure in the conversations that the novels record. In *Vivian Grey* Disraeli acknowledges only one precursor, but compensates by the frequency of his references to him, as for example when Grey is surprised by a country house library—"I thought the third edition of Tremaine would be a very fair specimen of your ancient literature"—or when he replies to a young lady who asks him if he knows who wrote it: "O! I'll tell you in a moment. It's either Mr. Ryder, or Mr. Spencer Percival, or Miss Dyson, or Mr. Bowles, or the Duke of Buckingham, or Mr. Ward, or a young Officer in the Guards, or an old Clergyman in the North of England, or a middle-aged Baronet on the Midland Circuit."[20] Pelham's mother responds to his loss of his parliamentary seat by withdrawing to her bedroom where she "shut herself up with Tremaine, and one China monster, for a whole week" (xlvii), and when he goes into Brooke's one evening Pelham recognizes the author himself: "Mr.———, the author of T———, was conning the Courier in a corner" (lv). In Catherine Gore's *Women as They Are*, Bulwer himself becomes a topic of conversation, "And Pelham!—with its sparkling conceits, that blind one, as though the pages were dried with diamond dust."[21] But more often the self-consciousness is self-mocking, as when Pelham hurriedly leaves his uncle, going off "with the rapidity of a novel upon 'fashionable life'" (xxxviii). Or the derision may be keener, and never more so than when challenging the claims of rival novelists to be truly familiar with the fashionable world that they represent.

Bulwer and Disraeli were to become friends, but Pelham seems to have Disraeli in mind when he winces at the use of the words "genteel" and "dashing," "those two horrid words! low enough to suit even the author of '———'" (xl). Most commonly of all, the novelists offer a mocking recipe for the production of fashionable novels. In *Vivian Grey* Disraeli invents a Mr. Thomas Smith, a fashionable novelist; that is to say, a person who occasionally publishes three volumes, one half of which contain the adventures of a young gentleman in the country, and the other volume and a half the adventures of the same young gentleman in the metropolis; a sort of writer, whose constant tattle about beer and billiards, and eating soup, and the horribility of 'committing' puns, gives truly a most admirable and accurate idea of the conversation of the refined society of the refined metropolis of Great Britain.[22]

Bulwer includes in *Pelham* a discussion of the social ignorance of novelists who claim to be fashionable: "Most of the writers upon our little, great world, have seen nothing of it: at most, they have been occasionally admitted into the routs of the B.'s and C.'s, of the second, or rather the third set" (lxii). By 1828 Lord Normanby could include in his *Yes and No: A Tale of the Day*, a more precise description of the requirements of this kind of novel:

Do you know the modern receipt for a finished picture of fashionable life? Let a gentleman*ly* man, with a gentleman*ly* style, take of foolscap paper a few quires, stuff them well with high-sounding titles— dukes and duchesses, lords and ladies, *ad libitum*. Then open the Peerage at random, pick a suppositious author out of one page of it, and fix the imaginary characters upon some of the rest; mix it all up with a quantum suff of puff, and the book is in the second edition before ninety-nine readers out of a hundred have found out that the one is as little likely to have written, as the others to have done, what is attributed to them.[23]

Normanby, as one of the few authentically aristocratic writers of fashionable novels, could afford the gibe, as could Lady Charlotte Bury, daughter of the Duke of Argyll, who included in *Journal of the Heart*, one of the three fashionable novels that she published in 1830, a warning that many such novels are written by those who have had no opportunity "even of seeing or mixing, at whatever distance, and under whatever circumstances, with those they intend to represent; and others again by persons who have only achieved their station among the race apart, and are not of that indigenous stock which alone enables anyone to write of the arcana of ton."[24] But the novels of Lord Normanby and Lady Charlotte Bury have little other than the rank of their authors to recommend them. As Bulwer remarks "gentlemen, who are not writers, are as bad as writers who are not gentlemen" (*Pelham*, lxii). Disraeli, in his scorn for the fictitious fashionable novelist Thomas Smith, is the significant figure, precisely because he is himself so vulnerable to the same charge. The best fashionable novelists—Disraeli, Bulwer, and Catherine Gore—have in common a gleeful effrontery. Their novels are enlivened by the impudence with which they claim intimacy with a world, "the world," into which they were only grudgingly admitted.

*Vivian Grey* and *Pelham* are the most complete examples of the fashionable novel because their heroes so completely mimic the dashing effrontery of their writers. The story of young men in a hurry, young men intent on gaining recognition in the most exclusive society by an astute use of their only talents, impudence and cleverness, is reproduced in novels that are themselves the means by which Disraeli and Bulwer made their triumphant assaults on the world of letters, and the fashionable world that literary success opened to them. "To enter into high society," says Vivian, "a man must either have blood, a million, or a genius."[25] He, like Disraeli, recognizes that he has only the third qualification, but, again like Disraeli, he is quite confident that it will suffice. Pelham, like Bulwer, is luckier—he has blood as well as genius—but he shares fully Vivian's reckless confidence in his own social skills, and in both cases the talents of the heroes are scarcely distinguishable from those of the novelists.

On his first entry into Parisian society, Pelham considers what "character" to assume, and decides that none is more likely to be so "remarkable among men, and therefore pleasing to women, than an egregious coxcomb": "accordingly I arranged my hair into ringlets, dressed myself with singular simplicity (a low person, by the bye, would have done just the contrary), and putting on an air of exceeding languor, made my maiden appearance at Lord Bennington's." There he successfully discomforts a young man whose watch and chain from "Brequet's" he is invited to admire by announcing that he can imagine "nothing so plebeian" as wishing to know the time, and outrages all the other men present by recalling that on the only occasion on which he had ventured on the Parisian pavements "à pied," he had stepped into a gutter, and been forced to stand still and scream for assistance (x). Compare Disraeli at Malta, flushed with the success of *Vivian Grey*, reporting an incident at the garrison when he had watched two young officers playing racquets:

> Yesterday at the racket court sitting in the gallery among strangers, the ball entered, slightly struck me, and fell at my feet. I picked it up, and observing a young rifleman excessively stiff, I humbly requested him to forward its passage into the court, as I really had never thrown

a ball in my life. This incident has been the general subject of conversation at all the messes today![26]

There is a seamless transition from the novels to such letters.

Both heroes end their novels disillusioned with the world that they have so assiduously courted. Vivian Grey retreats to the continent, and Pelham into marriage with Ellen Glanville, whose "pure and holy love could be at once [his] recompense and retreat" (lxxi). Their worldly ambitions are thwarted at the last in a manner that seems to counterpoint rather than echo the careers of their authors. *Pelham* and *Vivian Grey*, after all, made Bulwer and Disraeli famous. But the novels also made them extremely unpopular. In this, too, both novels seem oddly self-conscious. They wantonly provoke their unsympathetic readers in a way that closely corresponds to Pelham's performance at Lord Bennington's Parisian soirée, which prompts one man to mutter to another, "What a damnation puppy" (x). Bulwer provoked a hostile campaign against him, led by *Fraser's*, unexampled for its ferocity and for the length of time that it was sustained, and Disraeli found himself described in *Blackwood's* as "an obscure person for whom nobody cares a straw," who had written a "paltry catchpenny" which had succeeded only by virtue of Colburn's "shameful and shameless puffery."[27]

Both Disraeli and Bulwer were wounded by these attacks.[28] They came to think of the novels that charted the youthful indiscretions of their heroes as themselves constituting a youthful indiscretion. The brittle cynicism of the novels seemed inappropriate to the lofty literary and political careers that both men were anxious to pursue. The oddity is that this retrospective embarrassment infiltrated the novels even as they were being written. *Vivian Grey* ends mournfully, with Vivian in Germany, where he becomes "addicted to field sports" and "feared nothing so much as thought, and dreaded nothing so much as the solitude of his own chamber."[29] When Disraeli continued the novel he transformed it into a solemn bildungsroman modeled on *Wilhelm Meister*. Pelham, even more than Grey, is aware throughout that, however adept he might be at acting the puppy, he preserves underneath this façade a quite different character which is evident to his more perceptive friends such as Lady Roseville: "While you seem frivolous to the superficial, I know you to have a mind not only capable of the most solid and important affairs, but habituated to consider them" (lxvi). By the end of the first volume, Pelham, under the tutelage of his uncle Lord Glenmorris, is preparing studiously for his political career by studying utilitarianism, beginning with "Mr. Mill, upon Government" (xxxvii). They are odd novels in which the novelist seems at once anxious to appear before his readers as a "damnation puppy," and to invite his readers to recognize, like Lady Roseville, a moral earnestness concealed beneath the frivolity. The contemporary who seems to come closest to recognizing this is, strangely, the Fraserian who made the most enduring of all attacks on the fashionable novel, Thomas Carlyle.

*Sartor Resartus* is a parody of the fashionable novel. It was first published in *Fraser's Magazine* (1833–34), and it continued the campaign against the fashionable novel in general and Bulwer in particular that preoccupied William Maginn, the editor of *Fraser's*, throughout the 1830s. It is only in book 3, the tenth chapter, "The Dandiacal Body," that the attack on the fashionable novel is explicit, but it is implied throughout.

Most obviously, Carlyle parodies the style of the novels, "apparently some broken Lingua-franca or English-French," by inventing a rival language of his own, broken between English and German. Second, Teufelsdröckh is designed as the antithesis of the fashionable hero. His English editor is obliged to admit that Teufelsdröckh's style often reveals his "apparent want of intercourse with the higher classes."[30] He lives in scholarly squalor, and spends his evenings in coffeehouses, reading periodicals and consuming huge tumblers of "Gukguk" or beer, a way of life that acts in itself as a satire on such a hero as Pelham—who, in a Parisian café, is apt to choose a glass of lemonade, the most expensive drink available. Third, there is puffing. Fashionable novels, Maginn and others asserted, were wholly reliant for their success on their unscrupulous publisher's skill at puffing, and *Sartor Resartus* is presented by Carlyle as a single, monumental puff, an attempt by Teulfelsdröckh's English editor to boost the sales of his hero Teufelsdröckh's massive volume "Die Kleider, ihr Werden und Wirken (Clothes, their Origin and Influence)," by publishing "Article after Article on this remarkable Volume, in such widely-circulating Critical Journals as the Editor might stand connected with, or by money or love procure access to."[31] The practice of puffing was the clearest evidence of a literature that was offered for sale like any other commodity.

Bulwer introduces into *Pelham* his own recognition that the novel should be useful, not just a luxury item. His hero, after all, abandons his self-indulgent life of gentlemanly leisure to study utilitarianism; but this would not have impressed Carlyle, because utilitarianism; seemed to him itself simply a commodification of ethics. The whole of *Sartor Resartus* is written in earnest protest against the notion that "the Past Forms of Society" may be destroyed and burnt except for "the sounder Rags among them" that may be "quilted together into one huge Irish watchcoat for the defence of the Body only!"[32] Teufelsdröckh's business is with the spirit, not the body. It is a choice that he can afford. His appointment at Weissnichtwo as *"Professor der Allerley-Wissenschaft*, or as we should say in English, 'Professor of Things in General'"* has given him a modest competence, freeing him from the literary marketplace to assume instead the vantage of the prophet, a "wild Seer, shaggy, unkempt, like a Baptist living on locusts and wild honey."[33] But Carlyle's economic position was very different. In 1833, he was still painfully trying to earn enough to keep himself by offering his work to periodicals. To suppose that, in a piece of writing itself published in *Fraser's*, Carlyle could express an uncomplicated contempt for those like Bulwer who wrote for their living is to credit him with an improbable lack of self-awareness. His response to the fashionable novel in *Sartor Resartus* becomes interesting precisely to the extent that we recognize its ambivalence. Carlyle defines himself in opposition to the fashionable novelists, but he also recognizes himself in them. They are, in however distorted a manner, a reflection of himself.

Most obviously, he shares with them a recognition of the supreme importance of clothes. Man, for Teufelsdröckh is "a Tool-using animal . . . of which truth Clothes are but one example," and yet they are the crucial example, for it is clothes that gave us "individuality, distinctions, social polity; Clothes have made Men of us."[34]

It is a point that would have been quickly taken by Pelham, who devotes a chapter of ten pages to the description of a single meeting with his tailor, generalizing from the incident a brief dissertation on "the greatest of all sciences—the science of dress" (xliv). Teufelsdröckh comes close to quoting the sentence when he claims that "the essence of all Science lies in the PHILOSOPHY OF CLOTHES."[35] But, of course, for him there remains a crucial difference. Clothes, having made us men, "are threatening to make Clothes-screens of us," and, in the case of men such as Pelham, the threat has been realized. Pelham's attention is exclusively fixed on "the minutiae of dress, such as the glove, the button, the boot, the shape of the hat, &c," and for Teufelsdröckh this is a kind of fetishism, a worship of a sign independent of its significance. For Teufelsdröckh, clothing is the supreme figure because it figures figuration itself. It is only through figures that the infinite spirit that dwells in us can accommodate itself to the finite world in which we live, only by figuring itself in word or deed that thought can act upon the world, and all such figurings are regarded by Teufelsdröckh as varieties of clothing. So, language is "the Flesh-Garment, the Body of Thought." For Teufelsdröckh clothes are the only guise in which the spiritual can gain entry into the world: "must not the Imagination weave Garments, visible Bodies, wherein the else invisible creations and inspirations of our Reason are, like Spirits revealed, and first become all-powerful?"[36]

Nothing seems further from Pelham in earnest discussion with his tailor. Pelham too chooses his clothing so carefully because it is the only guise in which he can gain entry into the world, but the world he has in mind is "the World," the exclusive world of the twice two thousand. And yet in his obsessive concern with clothing Pelham offers not a contradiction but a compelling instance of the central tenet of Teufelsdröckh's philosophy, so that it cannot be understood as wholly ironic when the editor remarks: "The all-importance of Clothes, which a German Professor of unequalled learning and acumen, writes his enormous Volume to demonstrate, has sprung up in the intellect of the Dandy, without effort, like an instinct of genius."[37]

When he hears of a new school of novelists distinguished by their deep interest in styles of dress, Teufelsdröckh eagerly searches out some examples of their work. Unfortunately, all his attempts to read them are frustrated:

> that tough faculty of reading, for which the world will not refuse me credit, was here for the first time foiled and set at naught. In vain that I summoned my whole energies (mich werdlich anstrengte), and did my very utmost; at the end of some short space, I was uniformly seized with not so much what I can call a drumming in my ears, as a kind of infinite, insufferable Jew's harping and scrannel-piping there; to which the frighfulest species of Magnetic Sleep soon supervened. And if I strove to shake this away, and absolutely would not yield, came a hitherto unfelt sensation, as of Delirium Tremens, and a melting into total deliquium; till at last, by order of the Doctor, dreading ruin to my whole intellectual and bodily faculties, and a general breaking-up of the constitution, I reluctantly but determinedly forbore.[38]

He is forced to rely for his knowledge of the novels on a torn sheet of *Fraser's* that had been used to wrap one of his parcels of books and happened to include the second of Maginn's furious attacks on Bulwer.[39] The alarming physical symptoms that attempts to read the novels induce in Teufelsdröckh seem wittily to continue Maginn's attack, but the joke is far from simple. It was, after all, Carlyle who, as he well knew, was pronounced unreadable by most of his contemporaries, whereas *Pelham*, to quote the novel itself, "went off like a fashionable novel." The mockery of Bulwer in such passages is heavily tinged with self-mockery.

*Pelham* was famous in part because its hero's preference for black rather than blue coats, and his hostility to padding, established a new style in men's clothing. To be fashionable a style of clothing must be new, but it must also have, inherent within it, its own obsolescence, for styles of clothing become fashionable by virtue of being copied, and become unfashionable the moment they have been copied too often. Teufelsdröckh too is a student of fashion: "Thus is the Law of Progress secured; and in Clothes, as in all other external things whatsoever, no fashion will continue." And he too aspires to set new fashions. Churches and religions are to him only suits of clothes, and the existing religion, Christianity, is a coat that is "sorrowfully out at elbows." His second volume, he promises, will treat "the Wear, Destruction, and Re-Texture of Spiritual Tissues, or Garments."[40]

The chief difference between Pelham and Teufelsdröckh might seem to be political and born out of class. Pelham, like Bulwer, is proud of his ancient family name, whereas Teufelsdröckh, like Carlyle, takes pride in his own peasant stock: "Wouldst thou rather be a peasant's son that knew, were it never so rudely, there was a God in Heaven and in Man; or a duke's son that only knew there were two and thirty quarters on the family coach?" Teufelsdröckh, his Editor sorrowfully admits, is in politics an arrant "sansculotte," apt to set the coffeehouse cheering by proposing a toast, "Die Sache der Armen in Gottes und Teufels Namen (The Cause of the Poor in Heaven's Name and——'s)!" He enters into correspondence with the Saint-Simonians, and is rumoured, when he disappears from Weissnichtwo, to have gone to Paris, drawn there by the outbreak of the 1830 revolution.[41]

In "The Dandiacal Body," Teulfelsdröckh begins by deducing from chapter 44 of *Pelham* the dandy's articles of faith, consisting of such precepts as "The good sense of a gentleman is nowhere more finely developed than in his rings." Then, Teufelsdröckh turns from the Dandies to the Drudges, the Irish poor. He gloomily prophesies a nation divided between two sects that are separated even now only by "a foot-plank, a mere film of Land." The two sects are stores of energy, like "two World-Batteries," one positive and one negative, and when they come into contact one with another: "What then? The Earth is but shivered into impalpable smoke by that Doom's-thunderpeal: the Sun misses one of his Planets in Space, and thenceforth there are no eclipses of the Moon."[42] The fashionable novel, it seems, is a symptom of a society increasingly divided between the rich and a poverty-stricken underclass from which the rich, in their daily lives and in their preferred fictions, wish only to avert their eyes.

The chapter represents one of Carlyle's earlier pictures of a Britain divided between the rich and poor, a Britain that has become two nations. The phrase did not become current until 1844, when Disraeli published *Sybil*, and it may seem no more than a coincidence that it was given currency by a writer who was one of the chief architects of the fashionable novel. But *Sybil* itself begins as a fashionable novel. Charles Egremont, whose education into the social realities of class division the novel will trace, is introduced at a grand evening party, where conversation centers on the Derby, which is to be run the following day. Languid wits like Mr Mountchesney say, " 'I rather like bad wine; one gets so bored with good wine.' " It may be that the fashionable novel from the first contained the potential to reproduce the picture of Britain that Carlyle offers in "The Dandiacal Body."

By the 1830s the fashionable novel was losing popularity to a kind of novel that seems its opposite, in its concentration on the low life of thieves and scoundrels. Harrison Ainsworth published *Rookwood* in 1833 and *Jack Sheppard* in 1839, and between them, in 1837–38, came *Oliver Twist*. It was a fashion that Bulwer himself had instigated with his *Paul Clifford* (1830), the tale of a highwayman, and *Eugene Aram* (1832), which tells the story, loosely based on fact, of a murderer. But Bulwer's crucial innovation was to show how the fashionable novel and the Newgate novel might be combined. Already in *Pelham* the final episode of the novel shows Pelham procuring the witness who can prove his friend, Glanville, innocent of murder by assuming a disguise and gaining entry to a thieves' kitchen, where he practices the thieves' cant in which he has been carefully schooled. Similar abrupt transitions between high and low life occur in his next two novels, *The Disowned* and *Devereux* (both 1829).

Just as Carlyle recognizes the Irish pauper as a grotesque parody of the dandy, Bulwer in *Paul Clifford* notices that the highwayman parodies the man of fashion, that thieves' cant is precisely analogous to gentlemanly slang.[43] It was not an original perception, but it was crucial, for it made possible a kind of novel that reproduced the picture of an England divided between the Dandies and the Drudges that Carlyle offers in "The Dandiacal Body," a novel like *Sybil* that represents Britain as an island divided between two nations. It is predictable that it should have been Bulwer, in a novel such as *Paul Clifford*, who first realized this potential, because it offered him what he most needed, the means to reconcile his avid social ambition with the principled political radicalism that he represents Pelham as imbibing from Lord Glenmorris. But in working out his own dilemma, Bulwer happened on a structural principle that was to inform the novel of social criticism throughout much of the nineteenth century. A late Dickens novel such as *Our Mutual Friend* (1864–65) begins with Rogue Riderhood drifting on the oily surface of the Thames as he pulls aboard the boat a corpse that seems a ghastly embodiment of the oozy, unseen depths of the river. The second chapter switches abruptly to the Veneerings' vulgarly ostentatious dinner party, which is seen for much of the chapter as it is reflected in the hard, silver, depthless glass of the "great looking-glass above the sideboard." One reflective surface, the river, darkly parodies the other. It is the structural device that informs a large number of Victorian novels, and its source—perhaps surprising for some students of the period—is Bulwer and the fashionable novel of the 1820s.

## NOTES

1. Catherine Gore, *Women as They Are; or, The Manners of the Day*, 3 vols. (London: Henry Colburn and Richard Bentley, 1830), 1:136.

2. Michael Sadleir, *Bulwer: A Panorama: Edward and Rosina, 1803–1836* (London: Little, Brown, 1931), p. 125. Sadleir offers a helpful introduction to the fashionable novel. For more comprehensive treatments, see Matthew Whiting Rosa, *The Silver Fork School: Novels of Fashion Preceding "Vanity Fair"* (New York: Columbia University Press, 1936), and Alison Adburgham, *Silver Fork Society: Fashionable Life and Literature, 1814–1840* (London: Constable, 1983).

3. Benjamin Disraeli, *Vivian Grey*, 5 vols. (London: Henry Colburn, 1826), 1:33.

4. I quote here and throughout from the first edition of *Pelham; or, The Adventures of a Gentleman*, 3 vols. (London: Henry Colburn, 1828)—a novel that Bulwer revised—because it is the version with which Carlyle would have been familiar, and because the "vulgarisms" to which Bulwer's critics objected are often removed in the revised version. However, chapter numbers refer to the Knebworth edition.

5. Like Disraeli and Bulwer, Normanby was also active in politics. As Earl

of Mulgrave and Lord Privy Seal, he was the addressee of his friend Bulwer's *Letter to a Late Cabinet Minister on the Present Crisis*, the pamphlet that contributed, perhaps decisively, to the Whig victory in the elections of 1834 and thereafter to Bulwer's being awarded his baronetcy. He would later be appointed ambassador to France and created first Marquis of Normanby.

6. Quoted by Robert Blake, *Disraeli* [1966] (London: Methuen, 1969), p. 57.

7. Gore, *Women As They Are*, 2:235.

8. Catherine Gore, *Cecil: or The Adventures of a Coxcomb* (London: Richard Bentley, 1845), p. 102. This is the one-volume edition. The novel was first published in 1840.

9. Edward Lytton Bulwer, *England and the English* [1833], ed. with an introduction by Standish Meacham (Chicago and London: University of Chicago Press, 1970), p. 288.

10. Gore, *Women As They Are*, 2:237.

11. Disraeli, *Vivian Grey*, 2:162.

12. Thomas Henry Lister, *Granby*, 3 vols. (London: Henry Colburn, 1826), 1:281; 1:108.

13. R. H. Horne, *A New Spirit of the Age*, 2 vols. (London: Smith, Elder, 1844), 1:235.

14. Gore, *Women As They Are*, 3:123–24; 1:133.

15. Bulwer, *England and the English*, p. 288.

16. Lister, *Granby*, 1:257.

17. Disraeli, *Vivian Grey*, 1:95.

18. Robert Plumer Ward, *Tremaine* (London: Henry Colburn, 1825), p. iii.

19. Disraeli, *Vivian Grey*, 2:160.

20. Ibid., 1:149–50, 153.

21. Gore, *Women As They Are*, 2:235.

22. Disraeli, *Vivian Grey*, 1:74.

23. Lord Normanby, *Yes and No: A Tale of the Day*, 2 vols. (London: Henry Colburn, 1828), 1:135–36. The adverbial suffix in "gentlemanly" is italicized presumably to mark the word as itself a vulgarism, a low form of "gentleman-like."

24. Lady Charlotte Bury, *Journal of the Heart* 2 (London: Colburn and Bentley, 1830): 93. In fact, this work is a miscellany rather than a novel, a sort of scrapbook for a fashionable novel, and retains a certain interest on that account.

25. Disraeli, *Vivian Grey*, 1:50.

26. *Benjamin Disraeli, Letters 1815–1834*, ed. J. A. W. Gunn, John Matthews, Donald M. Schurman, and M. G. Wiede (Toronto/Buffalo/London: University of Toronto Press, 1982), p. 155.

27. *Blackwood's Edinburgh Magazine* 20, no. 114 (July 1826): 98. Horne took a more jovial view of Colburn's marketing stratagems. He notes, for example, that Catherine Gore's novels "are as sure to come out with the earliest spring and winter advertisements, as the scribe of the mysterious 'Evening Paper' is sure, by some inexplicable means, to anticipate the merits of every one of Mr. Colburn's new publications" (1:232–33).

28. Robert Blake (*Disraeli*, p. 42) persuasively suggests that Disraeli refers to the reception of *Vivian Grey* in *Contarini Fleming*: "With what horror, with what blank despair, with what supreme appalling astonishment did I find myself for the first time in my life the subject of the most reckless, the most malignant, and the most adroit ridicule."

29. Disraeli, *Vivian Grey*, 2:233.

30. Thomas Carlyle, *Sartor Resartus* (London: Ward, Lock, 1891), p. 29.

31. Ibid., p. 17.

32. Ibid., p. 156.

33. Ibid., p. 29.

34. Ibid., pp. 35–36.

35. Ibid., p. 56.

36. Ibid., p. 55.

37. Ibid., p. 177.

38. Ibid., pp. 179–80.

39. "Mr. Edward Lytton Bulwer's Novels; and Remarks on Novel Writing," *Fraser's Magazine* 1 (1830): 509–32. Maginn sent Carlyle this and several other issues of *Fraser's* in 1830, just as he was beginning the first draft of *Sartor Resartus*.

40. Carlyle, *Sartor Resartus*, pp. 39, 144–45.

41. Ibid., pp. 74, 20, 191–92.

42. Ibid., pp. 184–85.

43. Not a perception original to Byron and Bulwer, of course. Both were widely read in eighteenth-century literature, and would have been familiar with *The Beggar's Opera* and *Jonathan Wild*.

# Against the Law:
# Bulwer's Fictions of Crime

## Heather Worthington

> In the delineation of a criminal, the author will take care to
> show us the motives of the crimes—the influences beneath
> which the character has been formed. He will suit the nature
> of the criminal to the state of society in which he is cast.
> —Sir Edward Bulwer, "On Art in Fiction," 1838

Edward Bulwer Lytton was a man of many talents: "novelist, essayist, editor of the *New Monthly Magazine*, reforming Member of Parliament," in the list of one critic, not to mention poet and literary theorist.[1] He was also, particularly in his early career, motivated by a spirit of rebellion, which he articulated in his novels. In his political life, he was committed to the newly emergent process of reform, specifically the reform of the penal system: in his fiction he manipulated the literary conventions of contemporary popular genres in his desire to find a methodology that would permit the expression of social, moral, and political concerns in a palatable form. In both his politics and his writing, Bulwer was against the law,[2] a stance apparent in his choice of subject matter for his early novels. As he said, "In the portraiture of evil and criminal characters lies the widest scope for an author profoundly versed in the philosophy of the human heart."[3]

Crime fiction speaks volumes about the culture by and for which it is produced, and Bulwer, with his aptitude for recognizing and utilizing contemporary popular themes, wrote early fictions of crime. To locate and comprehend these fictions in a historical and cultural context, I have turned to Michel Foucault's *Discipline and Punish* (1975), in which he considers crime, criminality, and punishment in the eighteenth and nineteenth centuries. Foucault posits a realignment of interest from the crime to the criminal, arguing that "curiosity about the criminal . . . did not exist in the eighteenth century, when it was simply

54

a matter of knowing whether the person accused had really done what he was accused of."[4] In the nineteenth century, as punishment became an instrument of the individual subject's reform and recuperation rather than a demonstration of sovereign power, the criminal became the focus of attention. My contention is that three of Bulwer's early texts enact this Foucauldian paradigm. In *Pelham* (1828) Bulwer introduced criminal characters and their crimes into his fiction; in *Paul Clifford* (1830) he considered society's role in the construction of the criminal; and in *Eugene Aram* (1832) he approached the completion of the Foucauldian model in an attempted psychological analysis of the criminal individual. In these texts Bulwer was writing against the law—the laws of literary genre as well as the law of society and the state.

## BLOOD ON THE SILVER FORK:
### *Pelham, or The Adventures of a Gentleman*

The impetus behind *Pelham* was itself the result of Bulwer's going against familial law: in marrying Rosina Wheeler in 1827, he was directly contravening his mother's command. Her response was to cease supporting him financially, and the novel was written in part as a solution to Bulwer's marital financial problems. Seeking monetary reward as well as critical acclaim, he exploited the taste of the contemporary novel-reading audience, and wrote a fashionable fiction of the silver-fork school.[5] This was not difficult for Bulwer; unprepared for any professional career, as Michael Sadleir states, "the production of silver fork fiction was almost the only creative activity for which his hitherto circumstances and inclination qualified him."[6] Drawing on his own experiences, Bulwer produced the requisite text, but moved against generic law, introducing into it what the *Edinburgh Review* described as "a thread of a darker and more tragic interest."[7] This darker thread is concerned with crime, a subject more commonly associated with the *Newgate Calendar* and the broadsides than with the silver-fork novel. In 1828, Bulwer's introduction of a criminal theme into his fashionable narrative was a transgressive act in both a literary and a social sense, contravening the conventions of the genre by bringing crime into its elevated social world and into the lives of its socially elevated readers. As criminality was associated particularly with the urban poor at this time, Bulwer's juxtaposition of generic elements brought high and low society into contact in a literary context, enabling direct comparisons to be made between the two, and drawing attention to the operation of the law within society.

In *Pelham* the established silver-fork genre is gradually superseded by the new genre constructed in the crime fiction narrative: simultaneously, the social norm of fashionable society depicted in the text is penetrated by the deviant criminal underworld that is its inverted image. In Foucault's account of the genealogy of modern power, "strict divisions between texts, genres . . . break down because . . . what lies outside each unity of totality (and which defines it as a unity) also works within it in order to delimit it."[8] The focus on criminality within the text positions Bulwer as an early exponent of what Foucault suggests is "a whole aesthetic rewriting of crime, which is also the appropriation of criminality in acceptable forms."[9] This appropriation of criminality is articulated in *Pelham* in the crimes committed and the characterization of the criminals. To facilitate this articulation, the role of the individual in society, whether high or low, becomes central to the novel, while the crimes depicted in the narrative become signifiers for the dangerous elements within society.

The concentration on the individual in the text is made clear by its author. In Bulwer's own words, he "intended *Pelham* for a description of persons. It was not my aim to paint drawing-rooms, but the people in them."[10] But he also painted portraits of those excluded from the drawing rooms, for example the gin-drinking Mr. Gordon and the clever thief Job Jonson. While these characters are essential to the plot in that they facilitate Pelham's entry into the criminal underworld, the textual space they are allocated outweighs their narrative importance, suggesting a significance that exceeds the demands of plot. However, Bulwer made the social basis of crime complex. Criminality is not confined to the lower classes: the moral crimes within the upper echelons of society make necessary the text's excursion into the criminal underworld, an excursion that culminates in murder. In contaminating the silver-fork genre with bloody murder, Bulwer's satire on the contemporary society creates parallels and makes connections between the rules implicit in silver-fork society and the explicit penal code that governs the poor.

Crime enters the narrative of *Pelham* when Glanville's affair with a woman who is his social inferior breaches the unwritten laws of society, placing him outside his accustomed social milieu and bringing him into contact with the dissolute and amoral Tyrrell and subsequently Thornton, "a person of low birth and character'' (lxxv). Glanville, and implicitly the upper echelon of society that he represents, are criminally contaminated by this contact with lower-class criminality: immorality in high society is a reflex of illegality in the criminal underworld. While Bulwer's own life provided material for his depiction of the upper class, he relied on the contemporary reportage of crime for information about the criminal class. Despite the occasionally overblown rhetoric and the flights of gothic fantasy, there is an element of gritty realism in Bulwer's text, a realism that comes in part from his use of thinly disguised fact in his fiction. In *Pelham*, Bulwer took his material from the real-life murder in 1823 of William Weare by John Thurtell. The killer in *Pelham* is Thornton, a name not dissimilar to Thurtell, and both Weare and his fictional avatar Tyrrell were murdered for their money. The widely disseminated contemporary accounts of the Thurtell case would have provided Bulwer with a rich source of factual information and ensured the reader's recognition of Bulwer's reworking of the details. Although *Pelham* is most frequently discussed as a novel of fashionable society, "large numbers of readers must," as Keith Hollingsworth suggests, "have hastened through Bulwer's demonstrations of integrity in politics and constancy in affection simply to find out who killed Sir John Tyrrell."[11] Pelham as criminal investigator comes to take precedence over the Pelham who is figured as an adventuring "gentleman" in the subtitle of the novel.

Within the crime narrative thus constructed in the text, Pelham functions as an early configuration of the detective, motivated by the desire to solve "a mystery which excited my curiosity more powerfully than anything not relating to himself ought ever to occupy the attention of a wise man" (lvii). In Bulwer's text, Pelham is the ideal detective, asserting that "Nothing is superficial to a deep observer! It is in trifles that the mind betrays itself" (xliv), and *"I observe and I remember"* (xxiv; emphasis in the text), assertions that preempt those of Edgar Allan Poe's proto-detective C. Auguste Dupin and Arthur Conan Doyle's fully-formed detective, Sherlock Holmes. Pelham's detective status, assisted by his skillful use of disguise and his criminal contacts, enables him to move between social milieus in the narrative, revealing and deciphering the criminal underworld for the reader. Further, Pelham evidences what Doyle would term "deductive" thought, and uses forensic methodology in his reading of the crime scene, while the retrospective reconstruction of the events preceding the crime will become standard practice in the detective fiction genre. In *Pelham*, the insertion of a detecting figure into the narrative constructs the text as crime fiction rather than silver-fork novel.

The criminal act is an important feature in *Pelham*, but the introduction of a detective figure to track down the criminal, rather than the contemporary and conventional reliance on Providence to solve the crime, is instrumental in the realignment of focus from the crime to the criminal posited by Foucault. In earlier criminography, most clearly in the *Newgate Calendar*, the crime somehow marks the criminal, either by proximity, difference, or guilt, and, as Stephen Knight notes, "there is no special agent of detection at all."[12] With the introduction of a detecting agent, the character and psychology of the criminal must figure largely in solving the crime; motivation and opportunity replace proximity and Providence. In *Pelham*, attention is focused on both crime and criminal. With reference to the criminal, Foucault suggests that:

> At first a pale phantom . . . this character becomes gradually more substantial, more solid and more real, until finally it is the crime which seems nothing more than a shadow hovering about the criminal, a shadow which must be drawn aside to reveal the only thing which is now of importance, the criminal.[13]

*Pelham* is an early fictional example of the evolving concentration on the figure of the criminal, albeit not yet in fully realized form. It was well received by most of the contemporary critics, although *Fraser's Magazine* deplored "the snobbish and sinister alliance between high life and low."[14] Bulwer's covert advocacy of reform and the attack the novel made on society and the government had an impact upon the right-wing sector of its audience, as Sadleir notes: "in the minds of the Tory critics, [he] was no gifted trifler, but a young man who for all his affected foppery, meant business, and business of a subversive kind."[15] Bulwer's writing against the law, figured in his exposé in *Pelham* of the double standards inherent in the existing legal system, thus received early acknowledgment from his political peers, while his innovative disruption of the silver-fork genre brought crime fiction to the attention of a socially elevated audience. The imagined reality of high society had given way to a broader depiction of society as a whole in a step towards the classic realist fiction of the Victorian period.

Writing against the laws of genre appeared to facilitate, for

Bulwer, writing against the laws of the state. Encouraged by the generally positive reception of the criminalized *Pelham* and motivated by his burgeoning political interest in penal reform, he moved on to consider in *Paul Clifford* (1830) the place of the criminal in society and the role of society in the construction of the criminal.

## BLOOD ON THE STATUTE BOOK: *Paul Clifford*

Now Bulwer was writing explicitly against the law: his avowed intent was "to draw attention to two errors in our penal institutions; viz., a vicious Prison discipline, and a sanguinary Criminal Code."[16] The social contradictions and inequalities exposed by the juxtaposition of high and low society in *Pelham* formed the basis for his fifth novel.

Central to *Paul Clifford* are crime, its causes, and its practitioners, as Bulwer sought to place criminality in the context of contemporary society and the drive towards penal reform. According to Sadleir, the book "as originally planned, was to be a propagandist novel in favour of the reform of the criminal code."[17] To achieve this aim, Bulwer fictionalized social "truth" to make it more palatable to his audience. Paul Clifford, the text's youthful protagonist, is criminalized by the system intended to prevent crime. The text's proposal—that the criminal is a product of society and the law—was radical and transgressive, reversing the conventional view that the criminal was somehow outside society. Bulwer's narrative illustrates Foucault's suggestion that "it is not crime that alienates an individual from society, but that crime is itself due . . . to the fact that one is in society an alien."[18] The ever-multiplying and Draconian laws of the early part of the nineteenth century constructed by social exclusion a growing criminal population.[19] Those who could not conform to the norm of society were by definition aliens, and therefore criminal: in fact, for many, existence within the law was impossible: wages, when employment was to be had, were often insufficient to support the individual, even less the family, and state provision for the destitute was minimal. As Bulwer stated in his preface to the 1848 edition of *Paul Clifford*, it is "the victims of circumstances beyond their control" to whom he gives form and expression in his text.

In a literary climate wherein novelistic heroes conformed to very specific conventions, Bulwer attempted in two ways to overcome the difficulties inherent in making a criminal the hero of *Paul Clifford*. Firstly, Paul's background proves to be firmly upper-middle-class, as his accent and actions reveal; secondly, locating the narrative in the past and making Paul an eighteenth-century highwayman lends the story an air of romance that in turn gives the writer greater latitude in the depiction of his characters. However, while this historical location permits Bulwer's satirical representation of nineteenth-century political figures as members of an eighteenth-century robber band, it detracts from the immediacy of its reforming intent. Furthermore, siting the text in the past did not save it from the accusation that it made criminal life appear glamorous, a charge which, as Hollingsworth states, resulted in the novel's being referred to by "contemptuous critics of the time [as] Newgate fiction."[20]

But the text's historical setting did expose the archaic nature of a penal system, which had changed only for the worse in the years separating the temporal location of the narrative from its nineteenth-century present, thus emphasizing Bulwer's reformist message. The old laws had not appreciably lowered the incidence of criminality; hanging the criminal for the smallest offense was obviously not the solution to the problem. What was required, Bulwer argued, was a consideration of the factors that turned the individual into the criminal, and an examination of the possibility of reversing the process, re-forming the criminal back into the obedient—or as Foucault would phrase it, docile—subject. Bulwer's objection to the existing penal system "was not to capital punishment, but to the promiscuous application of it[;] . . . destruction is irrational . . . where improvement has a balance of practical advantages."[21]

In a movement away from what Foucault suggests was the eighteenth-century "procedure of heroization,"[22] whereby the crime ensures the criminal's fame, Paul's heroism lies rather in his reformation. In Paul's case, this must perforce take place in the colonial margin to which he is transported; the unreformed system in the eighteenth-century England depicted in the text can only punish the crime, not reform the criminal individual. Bulwer's text explores the construction and motivation of the criminal: whereas in *Pelham*, crime and criminals are both essential to the plot, in *Paul Clifford*, Paul's crimes are almost incidental; central to the narrative are his reasons for committing them. Locating the criminal at the center of the text inverts the normative perspective, an inversion that, Foucault suggests, "makes visible what was previously unseen."[23] Full representation of the more usually marginal figure of the criminal brings into focus the causes and construction of his criminality, questioning the normative center and thus facilitating Bulwer's reformist agenda.

The relationship between the law and criminality is made clear in *Paul Clifford* and articulated in the voice of the criminalized protagonist: "The laws themselves caused me to break the laws: first by implanting within me the goading sense of injustice; secondly by submitting me to the corruption of example[;] . . . your legislation has made me what I am!" (xxxv). Paul's intelligence and comprehension of his circumstances permit him to see criminality as a social and cultural construct, recognizing the proliferation of laws that criminalize the poor: "I came into the world friendless and poor—I find a body of laws hostile to the friendless and poor!" (xviii). The law, he (and implicitly Bulwer) argues, is a codified system: "Men embody their worst prejudices, their most evil passions, in a heterogeneous and contradictory code, and whatever breaks this code they term a crime" (xviii).

Such a definition suggests that as the code is not fixed and coherent, and therefore not universally comprehensible, the law becomes an instrument of social exclusion and class oppression. In Foucauldian terms, "the language of the law, which is supposed to be universal, is in this respect, inadequate[;] . . . it is . . . the discourse of one class to another, which has neither the same ideas as it, nor even the same words."[24] Paul is conscious of the fact that " 'under fairer auspices, I might have been other than I am' " (xxi), but his social status makes him the exception rather than the rule. In a reformist message that directly attacks the law, Bulwer uses Paul to speak for those who cannot speak for themselves.

There is no necessity for a detective figure in *Paul Clifford*: rather, it is the reader who is constructed as a detective, encouraged to seek the solution to the mystery of Paul's birth in the clues scattered throughout the text. It is the events that surround Paul's origins that lead him inexorably into a life of crime; his criminality is represented as the result of social and judicial injustice, and he commits his crimes in the spirit of Robin Hood, as a gesture in defiance of the law that makes criminals out of the poor and appears to condone the moral crimes of the ruling classes. While Paul is represented as a victim of the judicial system, his antagonist William Brandon is, in contrast, the product and representative of that same system, dispensing injustice masquerading as justice with a rigid hand and blinkered eye. Their opposing perspectives are clearly articulated in the trial scene which is the climax of the narrative. Despite Brandon's attempts to make central the crimes and not the man, it is Paul's history and motives that compel the interest of the jury and, implicitly, the reader. In its concentration on Paul rather than on the crimes he has committed, the trial scene enacts Foucault's theorization of the relocation of attention from the crime to the criminal. Simultaneously, Paul's long speech in defense of his crimes provides the opportunity for Bulwer to make his case against the law.

More forcibly than in *Pelham*, Bulwer makes in *Paul Clifford* the connection between moral and legal transgressions in terms of social status. The ruling class is shown to abuse its position and responsibilities and to commit crimes against morality; the poor, in contrast, are constructed as criminal by the laws that their so-called betters have made. Apparently above reproach as a member of the upper echelons of society, Brandon is in fact concealing a moral crime in his past: he "sells" his wife to Lord Mauleverer in return for preferment in his chosen profession of the law. It is this moral crime that displaces Paul, who is later revealed as Brandon's son, from his proper social status and relocates him in the criminal class. In Bulwer's texts, the inequity of the judicial system is exposed in terms of the inegalitarian social structure: the law is represented as a control mechanism for the containment of the lower echelons of society, while the crimes of the upper classes are subject to a higher, divine jurisdiction: their moral crimes are without the law, and punishment is effected through Providence, or at the hand of God.

*Paul Clifford* is Bulwer's fictional articulation of his own position on the necessity for penal reform. Paul is not a real criminal; his chivalrous behavior during his criminal activities endears him to his readers, but his actions in fact deconstruct the existing penal and social systems to reveal the gaps and strains in their structure and the essentially inequitable nature of their administration. Bulwer's transgression of the law is more serious in this text than it has been in *Pelham*, where it consisted only in the introduction of "a new kind of socio-political element into the fashionable novel."[25] In *Paul Clifford* Bulwer challenges less the laws of literary genre than statutory laws themselves.

## BLOOD ON HIS HANDS: *Eugene Aram*

After his insertion of crime into the silver-fork world of *Pelham* and his concentration on the construction of the criminal in the reformist *Paul Clifford*, "it was almost the natural progress of reflection," as Bulwer said in his preface to the 1848 edition of that text, "to pass to those [errors] which swell to crime in the solitary human heart." *Eugene Aram* (1832) is the terminus of Bulwer's "natural progression" in his criminal fictions: his attempted psychological analysis of Aram requires that the text concentrate on, as Foucault suggests, "the criminal himself rather than the crime . . . on his reasons, his motives, his inner will, his tendencies, his instincts."[26] Bulwer was fascinated by the capacity for evil within man: as Allan Christensen has noted, Bulwer found " 'a gloomy and profound sublimity' in the notion that each man possessed his evil demon,"[27] or, as Foucault has it, "crime is . . . a potentiality that interests or passions have inscribed in the hearts of all men."[28] In *Pelham*, Bulwer had incorporated a true-crime narrative into the text, but in disguised form; in *Eugene Aram*, undisguised true crime is central to the text: not only is the hero a criminal, but a criminal whose name and crime are precisely those of public record. The focus in *Eugene Aram* is on that criminal individual, the Foucauldian delinquent who is constructed by "the circumstances, . . . the causes of his crime [which] must be sought in the story of his life, . . . psychology, social position and upbringing."[29]

Such a criminal must do more than simply confess his crime. As Foucault states with reference to this final stage in the realignment of focus, in the nineteenth century, from the crime to the criminal: "it is not enough for the accused to say 'I am the author of the crimes before you'. . . . Beyond admission there must be . . . explanation of oneself, revelation of what one is."[30] So Bulwer introduces into the narrative judiciously tailored material from the real Aram's autobiography (published postmortem). The fictional confession, based on the original factual account, constitutes an attempt—the only one, really, in the novel—to analyze and understand the criminal mind.

The confession provides an instance, however, of the generic conflict that informs the work. For in his sensitivity to the possible reception of a novel in which the hero is inescapably a murderer, Bulwer has chosen to transform the actual Aram into the alienated, Byronic hero of romance. Here he was once more writing against the laws of literary genre because such a criminal hero was in direct contravention of the conventions of romance. As a contemporary critical appraisal of *Eugene Aram* in the *Edinburgh Review* stated, romance renders "certain qualities indispensable in its heroes, and the naked and coarse-grained villainy of the real Aram disqualifies him from occupying that position."[31] Possibly Bulwer considered it desirable to effect the maximum distance between his flawed hero and reality and located Aram's narrative in the genre of romance for this reason. But in fact Aram's romantic fictional representation strains credulity. Bulwer has gone too far against the law of genre, and he must make amends for his own authorial transgression. Aram's confession is thereby made to justify not only *his* criminal actions, but also the *author's* penning of a criminal narrative: Bulwer's attempted psychological analysis of the thoughts and events that might drive a man to murder both questions the cultural construction of morality and serves to excuse his own choice of subject matter.

The contradictions in the depiction of Aram's character reveal the textual strains that result from the interweaving of fact and fiction: the gentle Aram who would "step aside to avoid a worm in his path," simultaneously "despised men" (I:iv). The complexities of Bulwer's Aram, intended to offer an insight into his mind and motives, indicate rather the struggle of the author to create a fictional hero from an actual criminal. In Foucauldian terms, the real, eighteenth-century Aram was heroized by his crime—his heroism is the product of his murderous act. Bulwer's rewriting of the historical Aram attempts to dissociate him from crime as the source of his heroism. This follows the paradigm shift posited by Foucault, whereby attention is refocused onto the criminal individual and his or her motivation. But the narrative largely fails to offer a credible substitute construction of heroism for Aram within the romantic fictional frame.

In the case of the real Aram, his crime remained undetected for fourteen years until a series of coincidences led to the discovery of the body of his victim and subsequently to Aram himself. In Bulwer's text, as a substitute for providential coincidence, there is a detective figure. The character of Walter is reminiscent of Pelham in his detective role, but his detection of Aram's crime is incidental to his search for his lost father: Bulwer had to perform textual acrobatics in order to connect his romantic narrative to the historical facts, turning the fictional Walter's father, Geoffrey Lester, into an approximation of Aram's victim, Clark. To reduce Aram's villainy, Clark is depicted in the blackest terms—his rape of an innocent girl supposedly forming part of Aram's motive for murder. For further exculpation, in the early editions of the text Aram claims that "my hand struck—but not the death blow!,"[32] while in the 1849 and subsequent editions, Bulwer absolves Aram entirely, altering the text to "I did not strike the blow[;] . . . my hand raised not to strike but to shield him!"(V:vii). With this romanticized reconfiguration of Aram's intent, the whole objective of portraying a criminal hero is lost, so to speak, at one stroke. Aram is decriminalized and Bulwer exonerated from his own literary crime; yet the novel is damaged by the effort.

Still, *Eugene Aram* was a success, "taking Europe by storm, and [becoming] one of the most abidingly popular of all Bulwer's works,"[33] but critics noticed the strain in the text. *Fraser's Magazine* deplored "this awakening sympathy with interesting criminals,"[34] while the *Athenaeum* "lamented 'the fine powers which the author has squandered on this sad subject.'"[35] In the context of this paper, *The Cab* made the most pertinent comment: "It is the murder of a murderer . . . an attempt to convert a swindler and an assassin into the sentimental love-making, speech-making hero of a sickly romance."[36]

In striving to make Aram acceptable, Bulwer diminished his criminal impact: nonetheless, the criminal is central to the narrative, as is the exploration of his motivation and psychology, completing the shift posited by Foucault from the concentration on the crime to the focus on the criminal individual. In locating a real criminal at the center of a romantic narrative, Bulwer was fleshing out the bones of history with romance. But, as in the text, the bones of Aram's victim are eventually exposed, revealing Aram as a murderer, so all Bulwer's attempts to conceal and soften his protagonist's criminality are inadequate: the reality of the crime is inescapable. In the text, the bones function as a metaphorical representation of Aram's hidden demon—a criminal capacity that, Bulwer suggests, is shared by us all.[37]

The suggestion that respectable people, as Aram appears to be, might also be criminals, while very much in keeping with Bulwer's own ideas, would have been a step too far along the Foucauldian route for the critics. The text's message with regard to the criminal capacity of the ordinary man would not find critical acceptance until it was embodied in the respectable villains of Doyle. Matching the thematic strain, the generic strain resulting from the bold mix of romance and reality also hindered the critical fortunes of *Eugene Aram*. The work contravened the conventions of literary genre too alarmingly for the critics, if not for the book-reading public, with a taste coarser—or perhaps more subtle—than their literary masters.

In *Pelham* Bulwer introduced criminal characters and events into his silver-fork fiction; in *Paul Clifford* he used a fictional criminal as the vehicle for his reformist message; and in *Eugene*

*Aram* he fictionalized and made central the criminal. He thereby completed a textual enactment in fiction of Foucault's analysis of the reformist relocation of the juridical gaze from the crime to the criminal, from the obliteration of the criminal to his or her recuperation and normalization. Although Aram, in fact and fiction, is executed for his crime, Bulwer's text boldly—for many, too boldly—attempts to make the case that Aram has managed to achieve reform and recuperation. His remorse and self-imposed social exile have been punishment enough, and his intelligence should henceforth have been employed in the service of humanity.

Subversive in politics and literature, writing from the margins, against the law and against the conventions of genre, Bulwer brought into visibility (in Foucauldian terms) that which had been concealed: both inequities and iniquities in the law, and also the potential for a new genre of fiction. This innovative early criminography and its urgent use of fact opened up the high road for the later fictional detectives' surveillance of more realistic crime and their authors' creation of a new genre, which, unlike Bulwer's bold experiments, would not be against literary or social law.

## NOTES

1. The list happens to be that of Allan Conrad Christensen, *Edward Bulwer-Lytton: The Fiction of New Regions* (Athens: University of Georgia Press, 1976), p. 55.

2. I use the word "law" here in both the legal sense and the sense of literary convention; genres are collectively recognized forms rather than objects of rigid definition.

3. Edward Bulwer Lytton, "On Art in Fiction," *Monthly Chronicle: A National Journal of Politics, Science and Art* 1 (1838): 47.

4. Michel Foucault, *Power/Knowledge: Selected Interviews and Other Writings 1972–77*, trans. and ed. Colin Gordon, et al. (London: Harvester Press, 1980), p. 49.

5. The term "silver fork" originated in an essay by Hazlitt on the work of Theodore Hook, a writer of novels of fashionable life; it denoted a genre that purported to reveal glimpses of life as it was led by the great or wealthy. Hazlitt mocked Hook for what he derided as the novelist's preoccupation with silver forks. See Alison Adburgham, *Silver Fork Society: Fashionable Life and Literature from 1814 to 1840* (London: Constable, 1983).

6. Michael Sadleir, *Bulwer, a Panorama: Edward and Rosina 1803–36* (London: Constable, 1931), p. 127.

7. Anonymous review of *Eugene Aram, Edinburgh Review* 55 (1832): 210.

8. Simon During, *Foucault and Literature: Towards a Genealogy of Writing* (London/ New York: Routledge, 1992), p. 82.

9. Michel Foucault, *Discipline and Punish: The Birth of the Prison*, trans. Alan Sheridan (Harmondsworth: Penguin, 1997; reprint 1991), p. 68. Foucault locates this aesthetic rewriting and appropriation of crime in the first half of the nineteenth century, giving as early exponents De Quincey and Baudelaire.

10. First Earl of Lytton, *The Life, Letters and Literary Remains of Edward Bulwer, Lord Lytton*, 2 vols. (London: Kegan Paul Tench, 1883), 2:190.

11. Keith Hollingsworth, *The Newgate Novel 1830–1847: Bulwer, Ainsworth, Dickens and Thackeray* (Detroit: Wayne State University Press, 1963), p. 39.

12. Stephen Knight, *Form and Ideology in Crime Fiction* (Bloomington: Indiana University Press, 1980), p. 11.

13. Michel Foucault, "The Dangerous Individual," in *Politics, Philosophy and Culture: Interviews and Other Writings 1977–1984*, trans. Alan Sheridan et al., ed. and intro. Lawrence D. Kritzman (London: Routledge, 1988), pp. 127–28.

14. Cited in Robin Gilmour, *The Idea of the Gentleman in the Victorian Novel* (London: Allen and Unwin, 1981), p. 49. *Fraser's Magazine*, under the editorship of William Maginn, had a long-running feud with Bulwer.

15. Sadleir, *Bulwer, a Panorama*, p. 193.

16. Edward Bulwer Lytton, "Preface" (1840), *Paul Clifford*, Knebworth edition (London: Routledge, 1875), p.vii.

17. Sadleir, *Bulwer, a Panorama*, p. 225.

18. Foucault, *Discipline and Punish*, p. 275.

19. Before the reform of the penal system, there were approximately 233 capital offenses under English law. See Lytton, *The Life, Letters and Literary Remains*, 2: 242–43.

20. John Sutherland, *Victorian Fiction: Writers, Publishers, Readers* (Basingstoke: Macmillan, 1995), p. 107.

21. Lytton, *The Life, Letters and Literary Remains*, 2:242.

22. Foucault, *Discipline and Punish*, p.192.

23. Foucault, *Power/Knowledge*, p. 50.

24. Foucault, *Discipline and Punish*, p. 276.

25. Adburgham, *Silver Fork Society,* p. 160.

26. Foucault, "The Dangerous Individual," p. 137.

27. Christensen, *Edward Bulwer-Lytton,* p. 64.

28. Foucault, *Discipline and Punish*, p. 275.

29. C. Lucas, *De la réforme des prisons* (1836), cited in Foucault, *Discipline and Punish*, p. 252.

30. Foucault, *Politics, Philosophy, Culture*, p. 138.

31. "Eugene Aram: A Tale," *Edinburgh Review* 55 (1832): 214.

32. Edward Bulwer Lytton, *Eugene Aram* (London: King, 1832), p. 371.

33. Sadleir, *Bulwer, a Panorama*, p. 268.

34. William Maginn, "A Good Tale Badly Told," *Fraser's Magazine* 5 (Feb. 1832): 111.

35. Cited in Nancy Tyson, *Eugene Aram: Literary History and Typology of the Scholar-Criminal* (Hamden, Conn.: Archon, 1983), p. 91.

36. This review, which is cited in Sadleir, *Bulwer, a Panorama*, p. 278, was published in *The Cab* on March 3, 1832.

37. Christensen, *Edward Bulwer-Lytton,* pp. 58, 61–64, discusses the caves and graves containing bones in Bulwer's early novels that represent a hidden truth related to that within what *Eugene Aram* terms "that deep cave—the human heart."

# In the Courtroom of Bulwer's Newgate Novels: Narrative Perspective and Crime Fiction

Jonathan H. Grossman

In THE 1830S AND 1840S, A LITERARY CONTROVERSY RAGED OVER THE depiction of criminals in novels. William Makepeace Thackeray shuddered "for the public, whom its literary providers have gorged with blood, and foul Newgate garbage." "Let your rogues in novels act like rogues, and your honest men like honest men," he cried; "don't let us have any juggling and thimblerigging with virtue and vice, so that, at the end of three volumes, the bewildered reader shall not know which is which."[1] Ever since Edward Bulwer had published *Paul Clifford* in 1830, taking a highwayman for his hero, and two years later sympathetically told the story of a near-murderer in *Eugene Aram*, the question of how novels should portray criminals had become an intensely scrutinized public issue. One result would be an identified school of fiction, the Newgate novel.[2]

These Newgate novels were not—as one might think—much concerned with London's infamous Newgate prison and its gallows. Three of the criminals most famously depicted by Newgate novels (Paul Clifford, Eugene Aram, and Dick Turpin) never even stayed there. Nor were the Newgate novels identified primarily by a general concern for imprisonment or capital punishment. Rather, their Newgate name derived from reviewers and satirists who accused novelists of elaborating unhealthily on the genre of *The Newgate Calendar*—that is, on anthologies of criminals' lives (a number of which were named *The Newgate Calendar*) and similar popular collections of state trials, such as George Borrow's *Celebrated Trials, and Remarkable Cases of Criminal Jurisprudence* (1825). Newgate novels portray actual figures found in these books, or they imagine characters who seem to have crept from their pages. And, most important, according to the contemporary critics, these novels inadequately condemned the outlaws they depicted. As an advertisement for Thackeray's anti-Newgate novel *Catherine* (1839) explained, these "popular fictions . . . made heroes of highwaymen and burglars, and created a false sympathy for the vicious and criminal."[3]

This essay returns to the era of this Newgate controversy and focuses on two novels by Bulwer that were absolutely central to the unfolding Newgate debate: the first Newgate novel, *Paul Clifford* (1830), and the most important and controversial one, *Eugene Aram* (1832). Both of these novels culminate in dramatic trial scenes. This is, I believe, no accident, and if we look carefully at these two courtroom scenes, we discover something of a key to the special narrative perspective characteristic of the Newgate novels that Bulwer originated.

In the culminating trial of *Paul Clifford*, the judge is William Brandon, the very man whose false accusation of Clifford for the theft of his watch seven years earlier has precipitated Clifford's career of crime. Armed with this fact and a sense of how "circumstances make guilt" (xxxvi), Clifford constructs his defense speech as a lengthy protest against the criminal justice system. Denouncing publicly the legal institution he holds responsible for making him a thief, the accused accepts his doom and, "revers[ing] the order of things," roundly accuses the court (xxxv). The mishmash of critiques he levels, from his original wrongful conviction to the law's protection of the rich, partly inveighs against those "errors in our penal institutions" that Bulwer raises in an 1840 preface. Yet it is his heroic speech itself—"the boldness and novelty of the words" told in a "deep and firm voice" (xxxv)— that confirms he is not to be slotted into the conventional role of villain and registers Bulwer's larger aim. Not only are Clifford and other criminals produced by circumstances (meaning society in general and the criminal justice system in particular), but by nobly saying so, Clifford underscores that there is no absolute divide between criminal characters and virtuous ones.

Bulwer melodramatically fixes the trial to support this case. The overambitious and corrupt judge Brandon learns from a message delivered in the middle of the trial that Clifford is his son. There will be no *Tom Jones*–like moral shaking out of the good and the bad in this novel. As Bulwer demands rhetorically of his readers in an 1848 preface: "Compare . . . the hunted son and the honoured father, the outcast of the law, the dispenser of the law—the felon, and the judge; and, as at the last, they front each other, one on the seat of justice, the other at the convict's bar, who can lay his hand on his heart and say, that the Paul Clifford is a worse man than the William Brandon?"

Bulwer's problem was how to narrate this collapsed distinction between "the outcast of the law" and "the dispenser of the law" without seeming to sympathize with immorality. Leaving aside the stir caused by *Paul Clifford*'s sidelight of contemporary satire,[4] the moral outrage dogging this novel's wild success arose from its nonjudgmental portrayal of the delinquent Clifford. A guilty criminal protagonist justified his wrongs by laying them at the feet of society, and it was unclear what perspective the omniscient narrator was ultimately providing on this situation. Were readers really to sympathize with Clifford's crimes? Was the legal system itself a villain or merely its officials?

Epitomizing the narratorial opacity is a rare moment when Bulwer's narrator finally opens "more of [Clifford's] secret heart." In the long speech that follows, the novel lacks any defined third-person voice or authorial presence distinguishable from Clifford, who rants: "To those laws hostile to me, then, I acknowledge hostility in my turn. Between us are the conditions of war. Let them expose a weakness—I insist on my right to seize the advantage: let them defeat me, and I allow their right to destroy" (xviii). Seeming merely to concur in his hero's self-defeating, personal duel with the legal system, Bulwer brought down upon himself much righteous fury from the critics. In 1848, he parried with an impatient footnote: "The author need not, he hopes, observe, that these sentiments are Mr. Paul Clifford's—not his."

But what were "his" sentiments? Without a consistent narratorial voice or silent-but-guiding authorial presence, Bulwer creates a novelistic hybrid—the criminal-hero—without the framework for assessing him that his third-person narrative accompaniment implied. From the first, the Newgate novel's critics thus paradoxically protested not only the new extended use of an omniscient narrator to explore and share a criminal character's perspective but also the inadequate performance of this omniscient narratorial perspective. Thackeray, for instance, simply damned Bulwer's Newgate novels outright for "false sympathy," while John Forster complained more technically that Bulwer depicts a "man of crime . . . in whom the limits between good and evil are scarcely marked throughout with sufficient clearness and precision" when precisely "upon these points there should be no possible doubt, for they imply the extreme danger of suggesting a false sympathy with crime."[5]

This question of the novel's perspective upon Clifford animates the trial scene. For ultimately the trial scene isn't merely about Paul Clifford as a sympathetic and self-justifying criminal. By this point in the novel we know full well that Clifford is our hero and a wrongdoer. What we see for the first time in the trial is a mirror of ourselves, an audience, watching Clifford. As a result, the trial scene turns out to be about the reader's perspective upon Clifford, and by extension about the Newgate form's own omniscient third-person viewpoint of its leading criminal character.

The trial's central moment is literally an epiphany in perspective. Judge Brandon is staring at the accused Clifford, who he has just learned is his son. Clifford is staring back. But crucially it is the onlookers, the courtroom spectators, who undergo a recognition scene: "as . . . the judge and the criminal gazed upon each other a thrilling and electric impression of a powerful likeness between the doomed and the doomer . . . struck . . . the audience" (xxxv). Bulwer models a revolution in the third-person perspective of the court spectators. Instead of seeing criminal and judge as opposites, they see analogues, likeness not only of external qualities but of internal ones. And so of course do we, whose changed perspective has all along been Bulwer's target ("Compare the felon and the judge, who can lay his hand on his heart and say, that the one is worse than the other?"). At issue in the trial is thus the third-person perspective through which the sympathetic omniscient vision generally applied to a novel's righteous hero might be extended toward a guilty criminal protagonist as well. In *Paul Clifford* the trial scene takes a story initially about a criminal with redeeming qualities and shows how it is even more fundamentally about the possibility of a paradigm shift in the contemporary conventional distancing and censorious narrative perspective upon criminals.

Yet *Paul Clifford* had only just begun to broach this new literary perspective upon transgression. In its treatment of Clifford, as Bulwer himself recognized in the 1848 preface, the novel "rather deals with the ordinary surface of human life, than attempts, however humbly, to soar above it or to dive beneath." There was an even more *novelistic* version of the new perspective still to be explored. Specifically, the philosophical examination of the "solitary human heart" (as the 1848 preface calls it) that was crucially missing from *Paul Clifford* would explicitly and intentionally become part of the narrative technique in Bulwer's next and most influential Newgate novel, *Eugene Aram*. As the third-person narrator in this novel straightforwardly announces in a direct address to the reader, "it is not only the history of his life, but the character and tone of Aram's mind, that I wish to stamp upon my page" (II:iv). And Bulwer would commonly stipulate that such feeling attention to a character's inner perspective is a primary function of the novelistic narrator. "It is the notable convenience of us narrators to represent, by what is called *soliloquy*, the thoughts—the interior of the personages we describe. And this is almost the master-work of the tale-teller," he declares in his last Newgate novel, *Lucretia* (I:Epilogue). "The description of *feelings* is also the property of the novelist. The dramatist throws his feelings into dialogue,—the novelist goes at once to the human heart, and calmly scrutinises, assorts, and dissects them," he argues in "On Art in Fiction."[6]

The well-known tale Bulwer chose to rework for *Eugene Aram* is certainly conducive to excavating the psychology of its criminal protagonist. Aram is an educated and generally humane man who rationalizes participating in the murder of a despicable character. For years afterward he leads a scholarly, contemplative life, and finally (and famously) fabricates an ingenious court defense.

As in *Paul Clifford*, a sensational trial scene focused on the criminal's defense marks *Eugene Aram*'s denouement and reflects its formal structuring around a criminal's viewpoint. Asked "the thrilling and awful question—'What he had to say in his own behalf?'"—Aram claims innocence and delivers that "remarkable defence still extant, and still considered as wholly unequalled from the lips of one defending his own cause" (V:v). In Aram's multifaceted speech, we learn—as we do as well in its version in *The Newgate Calendar*—of the likelihood of finding any old skeleton in a hermitage where the murdered body was found; of how his poor health prevented his participation in the murder; of the fact that his law-abiding "life contradicts this indictment" (V:v); and so on. This courtroom defense is not a straightforward rendering of his views, as Paul Clifford's is. Readers know full well that Eugene Aram is equivocating. This novel's narrator follows Aram's struggle to live an ordinary, harmless life after his grim crime—a story more than half located in Aram's inner thoughts.

The trial scene represents something of an apogee for the self-enclosed, shared perspective of the omniscient narrator, the protagonist Aram, and the reader. Only we three understand Aram's position in the trial. Moreover, as we learn after Aram is convicted (despite his defense), he has fabricated his case for absolute innocence largely in order to protect those who would be crushed to discover him guilty in any degree. He has not merely defended himself in the trial; he has constructed—and maintained—himself through his defense as a virtuous character. It is a performance for others: "*Their* eyes were on me; *their* lives were set on my complete acquittal, less even of life than honour;—my struggle against truth was less for myself than for them" (V:vii). His "defence fulfilled its end;" his fiancée Madeline, whose health deteriorates during the suspenseful months of awaiting Aram's trial, dies shortly after his conviction "without distrusting the innocence of him she loved" (V:vii). (Her death, in turn, partly frees him to confess.) At his trial Aram has both protected Madeline and denied his guilt in the murder, in this too proving himself that potent literary mixture of hero and criminal whose existence Thackeray bewailed.

More important, Aram has performed for an audience within the novel that mirrors the critical audience outside the novel, who, like Madeline and the judge, hold a simple moral dualism whereby both in life and in literature a villain is a villain, and a hero, absolutely pure. The trial thus restages within the novel the literary pressures acting externally upon Bulwer. Bulwer's audience of actual readers—ourselves—of course know the full, more complex story of Aram's deadly deed and later travails. Aram's trial thereby captures the overarching tension animating the Newgate novel: Eugene Aram must conceal the crime to be accepted as a man, while the Newgate novel teaches that the man must be accepted even though he has committed a crime.

We might even see the trial—as illustrated by the frontispiece to the Standard Edition of *Eugene Aram* (and the frontispiece to this volume)—as itself a frontispiece to the form of the Newgate novel. In the engraving, a pure woman (Madeline, Aram's betrothed, in her wedding gown) is pictured in a conventional pose of concerned adoration for her noble hero in the dock. But this hero is guilty, not just technically but morally. Appropriately, then, he is triangulated (each is spotlighted) with the woman and the judge: to the woman he appears on a pedestal, while the judge who will condemn him looks down upon him. From our perspective, Eugene Aram occupies an intermediate space, a middle position between the condemning judge and the worshipping woman that in this context suggests his actual admixture of altruistic heroism and self-seeking criminality. Likewise, Aram's upright carriage and open stance signify neither self-possessed guiltlessness nor swashbuckling bravado. As we readers know, the situation is more complex—including in part the continuation of his proud attempt to transcend his past crime. And we alone understand this situation; notice that in contrast to the other figures (both in their appearance to us and in their views of Aram), we see Aram from head to toe: we know him whole, as it were. We look on this criminal protagonist from a third-person perspective, but in that perspective it is his story that dominates and matters to us.

At stake is a question of representing criminals, hinged upon the telling of the criminal's story, a performance metonymically connected back to the trial scene. (This is true even though in this instance, paradoxically, it is precisely Aram's inability to tell his tale in court that reveals his bigger story.) In the frontispiece, the court spectators transform what might merely be a picture of Aram into one that reflects upon his representation; we watch Aram being watched. Within the story, the representation of the criminal character is similarly at issue in the trial, but in a historic literary sense. Aram's defense speech runs for five pages (V:v), with barely any narratorial commentary, in essentially direct quotation of *The Newgate Calendar*.[7] A footnote, for instance, simply refers us for further information to "his published defence." Yet we are hardly back in *The Newgate Calendar*. Rather, this novel inverts the earlier *Newgate Calendar* representation of Aram. The omniscient perspective of Bulwer's novel has aligned us with Aram's perspective, in stark opposition to the *Calendar*'s, which at best sanctions only a reader's horrified fascination. In the novel, readers must attend to Aram's defense not merely—as in *The Newgate Calendar*—for its renowned ingenuity, the cleverest of attempts to evade the gallows, but as an extension of Aram's inner struggle, an unfolding psychosocial conflict.

No wonder in the anti-Newgate novel *Catherine*, Thackeray is obsessed with the Newgate novel's ability to make an audience "expend [their] sympathies on cutthroats, and other such prodigies of evil!"—*Catherine* itself is his "endeavour to cause the public . . . to hate them."[8] This focus on the reader arises in part from the special effect of the Newgate novel's omniscient third-person narration: relating a story from an overseeing point of view that not only follows a criminal character closely over time and through changing circumstances but also enters into the criminal's inward viewpoint, the Newgate novels were inevitably beginning to construct their readers' perspective on the outlaw from within the narrative, much as scenes painted with perspective construct a controlling viewpoint from which to look at them. By contrast, the narrative of first-person crime fiction, such as *Moll Flanders* (1722), represents to readers the relation of the storytelling criminal to his or her self, and—though readers may certainly be cued by the narrative in all sorts of ways as to how to evaluate the depicted criminal character—they must fashion any omniscient, third-person perspective themselves. Newgate fiction threatened readers because it began to blend the psychological immediacy and alignment of a first-person narrative into its own omniscient view of a leading, criminal character. At the heart of the controversy surrounding Bulwer's Newgate novels was their capacity to provide readers with an authoritative distance on the depicted criminal character and move them explicitly across that distance into communion with these most liminal members of society.

This is in part why Bulwer could not really answer his Newgate critics through his many defensive prefaces or even with the stand-alone pamphlet published specifically for this purpose, titled *A Word to the Public* (1847). The shock of the Newgate novels was always as much about the narrator's perspective as the story's content. In fact, Bulwer's subsequent defensive appendages—in constructing a supervising, expository third-person narratorial perspective—could never satisfy the perceived shortfall in the original narrator's perspective on its central criminal character. That was inbuilt. We might even say that the follow-up moralizings Bulwer produced for his Newgate novels reveal just what his narrator had needed to lay aside in the first place to enter into a sympathetic exploration of his criminal protagonists: a distancing, judgmental narratorial perspective and tone, still being broadcasted by the various *Newgate Calendars*.[9] In a post-Austen era, the novelistic narrator could no longer be attached to a narrative after-the-fact, like a verbal splint. Especially by the 1830s, the narrator of a realistic novel was not expected to stand at the side of the story and direct, but to weave together the third- and first-person perspectives, building up the reader's perspective from within. That was what Bulwer's narrator and the Newgate novels in general were pioneering in their omniscient treatment of criminal characters; there also lay the source of dissatisfaction.

In sum, the linchpin of this particular moment in literary history was this depiction of leading criminal characters' perspectives through a novel's omniscient third-person perspective, and this narrative perspective was at heart shaped by and reflected through climactic courtroom scenes. Ultimately, the Newgate novel succeeded in refiguring the censorious and distancing omniscient perspective on criminal characters still being promulgated by *The Newgate Calendar*. The related magisterial tone of such eighteenth-century omniscient narrators as Henry Fielding's in *Tom Jones* would from now on resonate as intonations of a past age. Developing an approach begun in William Godwin's *Caleb Williams* (1794), the Newgate novels of the 1830s and '40s again retried the characters of *The Newgate Calendar*, but this time they imagined for them—in literary terms—the sort of third-person form of defense that the lawyers had actually begun to provide in court (especially since the 1836 Prisoners' Counsel Act granted defense lawyers the right to address the jury and make closing speeches). For readers, this double perspective, deeply linked to the bi-focalization of observing and attending to a criminal's defense in a trial, allied an authoritative viewpoint on society with the criminal's own.[10] What the crime scene would later be to Edgar Allan Poe and detective fiction, the trial scene was to Bulwer and the Newgate novel: an all-important site for sculpting a new narrative perspective.

## NOTES

A previous version of this essay appeared in Jonathan H. Grossman, *The Art of Alibi: English Law Courts and the Novel*. pp. 137–46. © 2002 [Copyright Holder]. Reprinted with permission of the Johns Hopkins University Press.

1. William Makepeace Thackeray, *Catherine: A Story*, ed. Sheldon F. Goldfarb (Ann Arbor: University of Michigan Press, 1999), pp. 116, 119.

2. See Keith Hollingsworth, *The Newgate Novel, 1830–1847: Bulwer, Ainsworth, Dickens, and Thackeray* (Detroit: Wayne State University Press, 1963). Besides Hollingsworth's authoritative study, there are—inexplicably—few illuminating discussions of the Newgate novel. I try to pick up where Hollingsworth ends; as he provocatively theorizes at the conclusion of his study: "At a time when Bulwer and Dickens . . . would have extended the author's prerogative of omniscience as a technique for psychological exploration, Thackeray's [successful denigration of Newgate novels] constituted in some degree a hindrance" (p. 228).

3. This advertisement appeared in an 1869 edition of *Catherine* and in a number of subsequent editions; it is reprinted in Goldfarb's edition (1999), p. 190. Modern advertising of "Newgate fiction" reflects the fact that the label has shed its pejorative connotations.

4. See Patrick Brantlinger, *The Spirit of Reform: British Literature and Politics, 1832–1867* (Cambridge: Harvard University Press, 1977), pp. 35–38, 44–45.

5. *Examiner*, 17 January 1841, 35. John Forster is commenting on the Newgate element in Bulwer's novel *Night and Morning* (1841).

6. Edward Bulwer, "On Art in Fiction," *The Monthly Chronicle* 1 (1838): 144.

7. Andrew Knapp and William Baldwin, *The Newgate Calendar; Comprising Interesting Memoirs of the Most Notorious Characters . . . .* , 4 vols. (London: J. Robins, 1824–28), 2:246–57.

8. Thackeray, *Catherine*, p. 133.

9. The contrasting narratorial perspectives at issue in the Newgate controversy were neatly captured when a contemporary *Newgate Calendar*, Charles Whitehead's *Lives and Exploits of English Highwaymen, Pirates, and Robbers, Drawn from the Earliest and Most Authentic Sources, and Brought Down to the Present Time*, 2 vols. (London: Bull and Churton, 1834), struck back at Bulwer's *Eugene Aram* after its own summary of Aram's life, protesting that "Aram has been deemed a fit hero for a popular novel; and the execration with which he should have been consigned to posterity has been attempted to be converted into a sentimental commiseration" (2:313).

10. Sightlines, like acoustics, within the courtroom are obviously carefully constructed, not least so that the jury may view the witnesses and the prisoner. In England, separate overhanging, galleries were often provided for the public, unlike in France, where they typically had a place on the floor (see Katherine Fischer Taylor, *In the Theater of Criminal Justice: The Palais de Justice in Second Empire Paris* [Princeton: Princeton University Press, 1993], pp. 10–14).

# Bulwer's Godwinian Myth

Lawrence Poston

THE CONNECTION BETWEEN WILLIAM GODWIN AND EDWARD BULWER is no new subject, but modern critics have tended to discuss it to Bulwer's disadvantage. Patrick Brantlinger has argued that Bulwer was a "rather shallow" Benthamite (and by implication we may assume a rather shallow Godwinian), while Bjørn Tysdahl suggests that despite the importance of Godwin as "perhaps the most important unifying influence in Lytton's rather shapeless career as a writer," Bulwer "is much too versatile to be a docile disciple," and the presence of Godwin in his novels is that of "one who has been dismembered and whose parts remain separate."[1] Whether Godwin's politics and novelistic practice are, like the bride of Frankenstein, dismembered or simply diluted in Bulwer's novels, the general thrust of such remarks involves a patronizing assumption that Bulwer was too conservative at his core or too concerned with anticipating the literary market to cabin himself within the Godwinian project. Bulwer, if we adopt Brantlinger's formulation, was an inconsistent and finally inconstant radical whose early novels are at best only halfhearted imitations of the social-problem novel, and whose innate political conservatism prevented him from realizing the full force of Godwin's rationalist and reformist agenda.

Of such critics, only Pamela Clemit has given consideration to Bulwer, not merely as a disciple of William Godwin but as a practitioner of the Godwinian novel, which links him to Mary Shelley as well as her father.[2] Again, however, that consideration is brief and rather dismissive, though Clemit could reasonably contend that Bulwer's career lies outside the boundaries of her study. Yet I would argue that Shelley's influence, though less explicit, is equally profound in Bulwer's earlier fiction. The triangulation I propose for understanding the interrelationship of these three authors takes the following form. In such novels as *Caleb Williams*, *St. Leon*, *Frankenstein*, and several of Bulwer's novels to

78

be discussed here, Godwin, Shelley, and Bulwer engage issues of power and control at least in part by internalizing them in psychic dramas that sometimes take on occult or supernatural overtones. Even in that most statedly reformist of Godwin's novels, Caleb Williams fears Falkland as a quasi-divine (or quasi-demoniac) figure, someone who can see preternaturally into his soul and trace his every step. I have traced elsewhere the convergence of Godwinian occultism with Bulwer's fear of the consequences of the French Revolution, a convergence most powerfully registered in *Zanoni*.[3] Here I will dwell chiefly on the persistence of the theme of the doppelgänger, as expressed in the pursuit and the manipulation of one character by another—a manipulation that in novels like *Caleb Williams* and *Frankenstein* takes the form of a desire to make a Creature of someone else.[4] Such a pattern recurs particularly in Bulwer's earlier novels, in which political justice is not so much displaced as sublimated in individual contests for power over both the past (the repository of secrets that must remain buried) and the future (the zone of prospective liberation from injustice).

If one is to attack Bulwer for falling away from a reformist agenda, then it needs to be said that much the same process occurs in the novels of Godwin and Mary Shelley during the 1830s, as Gary Kelly and Mary Poovey respectively have pointed out.[5] In these novels it is the family, not the state, that is subject to discord and fracture; political themes tend to be domesticated and the theme of societal injustice subordinated to the injustice of individual human beings to each other. Bulwer taps into a particular mythic dimension in these writers in which political conflict is resolved by some sort of personal conversion whereby one authenticates a new and better self. Another way of saying this is that if *Paul Clifford* and *Eugene Aram* represent a turn away from the earliest Godwinian political fictions, they also capitalize on a tendency already present in Godwin's and Shelley's novels: to shift the focus from legislatively enacted political reform to personal self-redefinition. Yet, as I will also argue at the end, such novels point back to an outer world that will presumably be the beneficiary of personal reform and the reparation of personal (especially familial) relationships.

Bulwer's own comments on Godwin suggest both attraction and reserve. So far as I know he left no extended criticism of Mary Shelley's fiction, though their personal relationship is traceable through Shelley's correspondence. In the dedicatory epistle to the first edition of *Paul Clifford* Bulwer praised "the fine creator of

'St. Leon' and 'Mandeville' to whose style may be applied the sim-
ile applied somewhat too flatteringly to that of Tertullian—that
it is like ebony, at once dark and splendid."[6] Yet he also saw his
own efforts in that novel as blending the comic and dramatic with
Godwin's reflective and analyzing tendencies; that is, he seems
to have regarded his own work as an opening-up of a form too
constricted in Godwin's fictional practice. Much of Bulwer's early
fiction in particular seems to blend Godwin with the eighteenth-
century picaresque tradition and Goethe's *Wilhelm Meister*,
made available to the English public by Carlyle's 1824 translation. In an article on "Prose Fictions" in 1835, five years after
*Paul Clifford*, Bulwer admired Godwin's long meditation and
brooding over a subject and his "great knowledge of the darker
metaphysics" of character. But he felt that Godwin's method
often led him into too minute an inquiry into the human psyche
that verged on morbidity.[7] What Bulwer admired in Godwin, and
had early expressed in a column, was not "the premises of [God-
win's] philosophical opinions and the conclusions of his political
speculations" but rather "something dimly prophetic" in the earlier novels, with "their profound and immovable calmness, unruf-
fled as they are by party, or personality, or reflection of fleeting
interests." In short, it might be said, Bulwer seems to be intent
on defanging Godwin's radicalism.[8]

In 1830 Bulwer published a fable in the *New Monthly Magazine*, "Monos and Daimonos," which enacts in the starkest terms
the underlying narrative curve of much of his fiction.[9] Bulwer's
narrator is a rough, adventurous, solitary man, an un-Words-
worthian child of a harsh nature, who, after years of wandering,
decides to return to England. On shipboard he meets another
man, a loathsome being who will not abandon him and who is unable to fend for himself without the narrator. After a shipwreck,
this unwanted acquaintance pursues the narrator to a desert island where he still clings to him. The narrator murders him but
finds his companion restored to life and lying beside him in his
own bed. In every respect the "daimon" is the narrator's contrast: "an idle and curious being, full of the frivolities, and ego-
tisms, and importance of them to whom towns are homes, and
talk has become a mental aliment," yet he is also the narrator's
moral equivalent, for the narrator, selfish and uncouth, is so self-
absorbed that he refuses to extend aid to his fellow sufferers in
the shipwreck. At the end of the tale, we do not know whether to
trust in the physical reality of this other self until a third person

arriving on the scene discerns the footprints of what, circumstantially, can only be the alter ego.

Though we find here a footprint, as it were, of *Robinson Crusoe* in Bulwer's fable, the alter ego theme is mythologized in the story of the pursuer and the pursued, the unwanted visitant who persists in demanding an affection the narrator cannot give. Read as a personal parable, it may also reflect the foppish young author's sense of his own two selves, the man of society yet the instinctive recluse torn between the delights of companionship and the consolations of solitary retreat. But "Monos and Daimonos" is also a parable about politics, if by politics we understand not just the dust of party debate and legislative activity into which Bulwer was to enter, but also the uses and abuses of power in a social context. There is no such state as true aloneness, for if nothing else we are haunted by a being whom we cannot disclaim, a projection of our alternative self, as Edgar Allan Poe, emulating Bulwer's fable in "William Wilson," recognized. Otto Rank has argued that one's past clings to oneself and becomes one's fate when one tries to get rid of it.[10] Hell is both to be alone and, in Sartre's famous formulation, never to be alone.

The sources of "Monos and Daimonos" no doubt lie widely dispersed in Bulwer's reading in German fairy tales and the German romantics, but the fable has a Godwinian spine to it. The ignoble savage of a narrator bears a striking resemblance to the youthful Fleetwood of Godwin's novel by that name and the early Lionel Verney in Mary Shelley's *The Last Man*. The motif of the pursuer and pursued, who on some level are one and the same, tap the darker metaphysical implications of both *Caleb Williams* and *Frankenstein*. The Godwinian fascination with this deadly symbiosis is also linked in the fable to the theme of the fragility of human relationships, and the paralyzing (and even quite literally maddening) effects of isolation from other human beings in such novels as Godwin's *Mandeville*, where, as in *The Last Man*, the idea of utter aloneness is played out to its chilling conclusion.

"Monos and Daimonos" also condenses in its purest form a pervasive theme in Bulwer's fiction of the 1820s. In *Falkland*, Bulwer draws on Godwin for the name of his protagonist as well as that of Emily Mandeville, whose name seems to be a conflation of Godwin's protagonist in the 1817 novel by that name and Emily Melville in *Caleb Williams*. Falkland is perpetually in a state of solipsistic self-absorption, a pursuer whose successful seduction of Emily ends with her destruction. His soured idealism is unable to recover from an early love affair, and his misanthropy is reinforced by a Faustian disillusionment with the pursuit of knowledge, an Olympian disdain for the manners of society, and an obsession like that of Victor Frankenstein with the secret of death itself. What *Falkland* shares with the signature novels *Caleb Williams* and *Frankenstein* is a concern with the imbalances of power, a preoccupation with the way in which people make others into mere instruments of their own egoistic delusions.

*Pelham*, a rebuke both to the Werterism of *Falkland* and the dandiacal politics of Disraeli's *Vivian Grey*, revives Godwinian elements in the Tyrrel-Glanville plot, in which Glanville's experiments with his creature, Thornton, end with Thornton's turning against him. Glanville is a Falkland complicated by an urge toward serious political commitment. Perhaps too often and too facilely termed "Byronic," though indeed in his capacity for leadership he recalls the Byron figure Lord Raymond in Mary Shelley's *The Last Man*, he offers a dark, distorting mirror in which Pelham sees something of himself.[11] That Lacanian moment of self-discovery recalls the scene in which Mary Shelley's Creature for the first time confronts his own hideousness in the pond, as well as the subtextual level at which the Creature embodies Victor's own dark side. Thus Pelham's descent into the London underworld to clear Glanville's reputation is simultaneously a journey in self-discovery, just as his reading of James Mill on government marks a stage in his evolution as a political thinker.

In *Devereux*, the alter ego theme is intensified through an almost incestuous narrative of fraternal misunderstandings and divisions—between the protagonist Morton Devereux and his biological twin Gerald, and between Morton and his spiritual obverse, Aubrey. Morton Devereux is one of Bulwer's initially haughty, idle, quarrelsome, and sullen protagonists (deriving from such figures as Godwin's Fleetwood and Shelley's Lionel Verney). Because he makes no particular effort to win over others, even those who might be bound to him by fraternal love, the handsome but somewhat irresolute Gerald and the otherworldly, affectionate, effeminate Aubrey are both easily manipulated against him by the scheming Abbé Montreuil. Circumstantial evidence suggests that Gerald is Morton's rival for the affections of the heroine Isora, but in fact it is the unhealthily world-denying Aubrey who has been not only the unsuccessful rival but finally her murderer as well.

The early love of Aubrey and Morton for each other is described with a homoerotic intensity in which Aubrey's morbid piety and

Morton's headstrong temper bespeak a psychic kinship that Aubrey identifies in his letter of confession: "Brother, did you ever,
when you thought yourself quite alone—at night—not a breath
stirring—did you ever raise your eyes, and see exactly opposite
you a devil;—a dread thing, that moves not, speaks not, but glares
upon you with a fixed, dead, unrelenting eye?—that thing is before me now, and witnesses every word I write" (VI:iv). Aubrey,
seeing himself in a mirror, confesses to have fancied beholding a
demon, but he is also Morton's mirror, in which the latter sees a
visage distorted by his murderous thoughts of Gerald, thoughts
Gerald has likewise had of him. Aubrey's vow to Isora that the
bridal couch she shared with Morton would be "stained with
blood" likewise echoes the Creature's vow to Frankenstein, "I
shall be with you on your wedding night." Though in their reconciliation scene the brothers reach an understanding and a shared
knowledge, reconciliation stops short of full healing. Aubrey's ultimate punishment is the nightmare in which his eyelids have
been cut off so that he cannot shut out the image of his own damnation. Morton survives, but as a permanently wounded spirit.

   In two works of the 1830s, Bulwer explores this theme with
more richness and depth. In *Eugene Aram*, it is centrally stated
through the relationship between Houseman and Aram.[12] Aram's
agonized question to Houseman, "Is not the world wide enough
for us both?" (III:ii) is answered in the negative. Aram lives in
fear that Houseman, captured as a highwayman, will reveal the
criminal secrets that implicate them both, yet he is restrained
both by conscience and by fear of discovery from doing away with
Houseman. Houseman has no reason to attempt Aram's life,
every reason to prolong it both for financial gain and for sadistic
enjoyment of Aram's mental torments, much as the Creature has
no reason to destroy Victor. Both Houseman and Frankenstein's
monster, that is, derive their power from a knowledge of shared
responsibility. In both cases, the alter ego is the Other who knows
the Self. Only in entire candor and mutual trust can the relationship of these two suspicious men be to their mutual advantage,
but Aram's survival is to be purchased at the expense not only of
an advance on Madeline's dowry for bribing his pursuer, but also
of the deception of those who love him. Commercial exchange
here functions as an analogue to moral corruption. In the uneasy
equilibrium of the two men lies the hint of an elusive stability
beyond purchase. Aram's hell, like that of Victor Frankenstein, is
the recognition of unwanted kinship. As he says to Houseman,
"It is not easy for either of us to deceive the other. We are men,

whose perception a life of danger has sharpened upon all points; I speak to you frankly, for disguise is unavailing" (III:vii).

By turns Bulwer apotheosizes Aram and judges him. Like Victor, and like those other stern retributive overseers and hapless victims of Godwinian fiction, Aram neither turns his scholarship to the service of society nor accepts the Earl's offer of engagement in the public arena. No stranger to acts of individual charity, he nonetheless despises humanity in the mass and has turned away from schemes of social amelioration. He shelters his disdain for the world, as he explains to Madeline, behind "a stern and solitary independence of thought, which allows no watch, and forbids account of itself to anyone" (III:i).

The independence Aram desires is also from the determining aspects of his past deeds, and not until the end of the story will he accept the fact that his own past cannot be rewritten.[13] When he declares at the sound of the marriage bell that he will defy memory, he is attempting to cut the ties that link him to past horrors—but also to the innocent self that existed prior to his crime. To abolish memory is to block the sources of potential renewal that lie in "remembrances of early childhood" in which, at the touch of a something outside oneself, "a host of shadowy and sweet recollections steal upon us" (III:vi). But he cannot cancel out the now reproachful memory of boyish happiness among the mountains, and his thirst for new knowledge has similarly failed to liberate him from a retrospective vision, in this case a view of desolation. In a self-rebuke evocative of Mary Shelley's inventor, he asks, "When we rifle nature, and collect wisdom, are we not like the hags of old, culling samples from the rank grave, and extracting sorceries from the rotting bones of the dead?" (III:vi). The remark is morally obtuse but ironically apt, since (literal) bones from Aram's own past are responsible for his exposure.

In *Ernest Maltravers*, Bulwer seems in a manner of speaking to expel the Frankenstein motif by relegating it to the half-comical, half-threatening figure of Castruccio Cesarini, the mad poet, who is manipulated by Lumley Ferrers, later Lord Vargrave. Yet the theme of manipulation does relate to the career of the protagonist too. Ernest's danger is to succumb to the delusions of the altruist, whereby his patronage of a young woman comes to mask a sexual involvement. At his early age he "never damped the ardour of an experiment by the anticipation of consequences" (I:iv). The ardor of an experiment unmatched by such anticipation recalls Mary Shelley's overreacher. When he meets the young girl Alice, he vows inwardly to "educate this charming girl—he would write fair and heavenly characters upon this blank page—he would act the Saint Preux to this Julie of Nature" (I:iv). Like Browning's Jules in *Pippa Passes*, Ernest thinks here in terms of the plastic powers of art (not, like Victor Frankenstein, the dissecting properties of science); he will in a manner of speaking sculpt this girl to his own liking. But though he is not then haunted by his own creations, his path through life is haunted by both Cesarini and Ferrers who embody visions of alternative possibilities that he might have enacted himself.

If Ernest's name suggests both moral seriousness and a capacity for misadventure, the name of the Italian poet implies his desire to rule the world as a Caesar of letters. But it also dramatizes the impotence of that ambition, since in the words of de Montaigne, Ernest's wise French counselor, "Castruccio is not as farsighted as his namesake, the Prince of Lucca" (V:v). Bulwer's ironic reference to Mary Shelley's fictional rendering of the historical Castruccio in *Valperga* frames his description of Cesarini's self-centered and morbid fantasies, his vain and vainglorious pursuit of an art that eludes him. For Ernest, Cesarini is a somber warning of his own incapacities as a poet, and after reading Cesarini's poetry he consigns his own early work to the flames, as dejected as "a beauty who has seen a caricature of herself" (III:ii). That same ability to see himself objectively, a gift Cesarini conspicuously lacks, enables Ernest to urge Cesarini to rise above the desire to take revenge on Lumley Ferrers, who has tricked them both. Just as Ernest the mad poet that might have been is displaced onto the figure of Cesarini, so Ernest the Frankenstein-Creator is displaced onto Lumley Ferrers, an arch-manipulator who attempts to control both men, or, to use another analogy, a Falkland dwindled to the rank of parliamentary politician.[14]

By the time of *Alice*, the sequel to *Ernest Maltravers*, Cesarini has become incurably mad and is institutionalized, seeking delight in "desultory and unprofitable studies" (VI:i) and trying to pass off his madness as poetic agony. His involvement with Ferrers in a plot to deprive Ernest of the love of Florence has led indirectly to her death, and Cesarini turns on Ferrers as the nearest cause of his misfortunes. The poet's mad fits are accompanied by sudden bursts of physical strength, and his monstrous reappearances at odd times and place, like the Creature's, are sudden, demonic intrusions into the mundane order of things. With that perverse sense of timing characteristic of Frankenstein's Creature, Cesarini emerges from his hiding place to interrupt a tender scene between Ernest and Evelyn, a terrible and ominous opposition—a form connected with dreary associations of fate and woe. The figure had raised itself upon a pile of firewood on the other side of the fence, and hence it seemed almost gigantic in its stature. It gazed upon the pair with eyes that burned with a preternatural blaze, and a voice which Maltravers too well remembered, shrieked out—"Love—love! What! *thou* love again?" (VIII:vii).[15]

This latter-day monster, a victim of Ferrers's own metaphorical experiments on living tissue, flees into the woods when approached, reappearing at intervals to make desperate attempts on Ferrers's life, which finally succeed. His appearance on the pile of firewood—though Cesarini never finds the desolate peace of Victor's creation—seems clearly designed to evoke the funeral pyre of his Shelleyan predecessor.

*Ernest Maltravers* is perhaps the most consciously Goethean of Bulwer's fictions up to the end of the decade, and its agenda as bildungsroman distinguishes it from the previous works of Bulwer that I have discussed. The plight of Cesarini (who never gets, so to speak, beyond the firewood into the fire) is not central to the resolution of the novel. Rather, that resolution involves the assimilation of the mature hero into his society, successfully accomplished in a way that points ultimately in the direction of the domestic fiction of the Caxton trilogy at midcentury. Of the novels of the succeeding decade, *Lucretia* evidences Bulwer's most vivid reworking of the Monos and Daimonos theme. While Lucretia is taken off to the madhouse, Gabriel Varney, her fellow archschemer, is subjected to a far worse fate by being chained in prison forever to Grabman, the brutish "Grave stealer," the "Oulos Oneiros—the Evil Dream of the Greeks" (II:vi) from whom he will never be separated in this life. The "self-guided seeker after knowledge," in Bulwer's words, "has gained the fiend for the familiar" (I:ix). To live only for oneself, as Gabriel has done with remarkable persistence in this strangely compelling novel, is to create the doppelgänger from whom one can never be divorced and in whose brutish lineaments one detects the debased features of the self.

There is much to support the view that Bulwer is a failed radical, and to see him, in novels such as *Paul Clifford* and *Eugene Aram*, as abandoning the Godwinian agenda of political reform. It is certainly true that a novel like *Paul Clifford*, as Bulwer puts it in his 1840 preface, explicitly portrays perverted social institutions, in this case "a vicious Prison-discipline, and a sanguinary

Criminal Code" that corrupts a boy by the very process meant to redeem him. The novel's focus, however, is really on individual miscarriages of justice, personal deception, and concealment rather than on the law as a systematically corrupt engine of class warfare. One might also profitably and not irrelevantly compare the handling of the trial scenes in *Caleb Williams* and *Eugene Aram* to see how Bulwer softens the edges of the earlier novel and is (as already noted) unable finally to commit himself to a belief in Aram's guilt.[16] Although the novel touches obliquely on political and legal reform, the approach is almost entirely inward. To distinguish it from the Newgate fiction of his day, Bulwer declared in his 1840 preface that "the guilt of Eugene Aram is not that of a vulgar ruffian." For Godwin's single-minded patrician avenger, he substitutes a philosopher and natural scientist of distinctly attenuated Frankensteinian ambitions. Though, as with Godwin's Falkland, Aram's alleged crime is directed against a villain whose abuse of a younger woman has inflamed his sense of justice, he does not commit Falkland's further atrocity of allowing the blame to fall on someone else.

Yet Godwin had survived his own Jacobin period and, by the time of the 1830s, was writing novels not unlike Bulwer's. If the Godwinian edge is missing from *Paul Clifford* and *Eugene Aram*, it is equally absent from *Cloudesley*, which, despite some obligatory reforming asides on the evil of capital punishment, seems more indebted to a curious blend of Beaumont and Fletcher and the *Beggar's Opera* than to the *Enquiry concerning Political Justice*. In the decade marked by the endpoints 1827–1837, Godwin, Bulwer, and Mary Shelley are all presences on the fictional scene, but if Bulwer was never more than the halfhearted radical, Godwin's own radical voice was considerably muted. As Gary Kelly noted a quarter of a century ago, Godwin's substitution of what was originally the subtitle, *Caleb Williams*, for the main title *Things As They Are*, on the occasion of Bentley's 1831 reprint, reflects his movement from rationalist political reform toward a greater intent in the burdens of individual consciousness.[17] Mary Shelley's novels of the 1830s, *Lodore* and *Falkner*, tend (like her father's *Cloudesley* and *Deloraine*) toward psychological inwardness at the expense of the details of the external world. They trace the limits of Byronism and the expiation of past wrongs in the domestic polity, in an affirmation of family ties. Like her father's, her execution is perhaps more centered and stark, less eclectic and free-ranging than Bulwer's. Godwin's isolated heroes tend to become gradually disengaged from the web of circumstantiality that would otherwise display them as socially obligated creatures, and much of Shelley's fiction after *Frankenstein* reenacts the central loss of her own life, a loss that deepened an already acute sense of the tenuousness of human relationships.

Bulwer's appropriation of an underlying Godwinian mythos, the internalization of politics in the theme of the double or the alter ego, suggests a profound level of engagement both with the 1790s as a historical shadow cast over the 1830s, and with the romantic mythmaking that Godwin and Shelley had transmitted to his own imagination. But why, in the decade of reform, did these three closely associated writers take the direction they did? Why, in their privatization of the public sphere, did they recast the issue of power in the terms of familial, gendered, and psychological combat?

In the case of Bulwer, the debt to Godwin aside, his intentions were never fully Godwinian. He remains very much in tune with the political currents of his own day. In extracting one theme from a larger complex of interests, I do not provide here the necessary comprehensive reading of the novels under examination.

Still, these novels do not entirely privatize the Godwinian myth. Whether couched in the more or less contemporaneous world of *Falkland*, *Pelham*, and *Ernest Maltravers*, or the late Stuart world of *Devereux* seen from the relatively peaceful retrospect of the Hanoverian supremacy, that myth is finally restored to the context of public life. And it is on the verge of public life that Pelham and Ernest stand at the end of their respective stories. Just as Godwin remained a reformer but could no longer be construed as a Jacobin, so Bulwer's radicalism was assimilated during the 1830s into a moderate Whig view of the need for reform. These novels are invested by a sense that the new realities of politics require new leadership, and that the reparation of shattered domestic relationships is only a preface to a more effective reintegration of private and public lives. A much darker vision of political and social possibilities informs the trilogy of the 1840s—*Night and Morning*, *Zanoni*, and *Lucretia*—which trace the aftershocks of the French Revolution. But that is another story for another time.

## NOTES

1. Patrick Brantlinger, *The Spirit of Reform: British Literature and Politics, 1832–1867* (Cambridge: Harvard University Press, 1977), p. 44; B. J. Tysdahl, *William Godwin as a Novelist* (London: Athlone Press, 1981), pp. 163–64.

2. Pamela Clemit, *The Godwinian Novel: The Rational Fictions of Godwin, Brockden Brown, Mary Shelley* (Oxford: Clarendon, 1993): "The formal experimentation of Mary Shelley and Bulwer in the 1820s already suggests the need for a richer and more diverse treatment of contemporary society than is found in Godwin's novels of the 1790s, anticipating the more capacious, though widely diverging, modes of Dickens and George Eliot" (p. 218).

3. Lawrence Poston, "Beyond the Occult: The Godwinian Nexus of Bulwer's *Zanoni*," *Studies in Romanticism* 37 (1998): 131–61.

4. The approach I map out here has to some extent been anticipated by Allan Conrad Christensen, *Edward Bulwer-Lytton: The Fiction of New Regions* (Athens: University of Georgia Press, 1976) and Edwin M. Eigner, *The Metaphysical Novel in England and America: Dickens, Bulwer, Melville, and Hawthorne* (Berkeley: University of California Press, 1978). Their treatment of the subject is entirely compatible with my own, albeit with a different focus. Christensen's approach is archetypal, and he says relatively little about Godwin—although, particularly in commenting on how *"My Novel"* engages the theme of "enslavement of individuals to each other," he draws very near to Godwinian ground (p. 148). Eigner positions the theme of the doppelgänger in its origins in German romantic psychology (pp. 74–75) and notes its variations in Godwin and Mary Shelley (p. 83), but he does not extend the consideration to Bulwer as I do here. He does note, in book 2 of *Night and Morning*, the persistence of the "pursuit tradition established by Godwin in *Caleb Williams*" (p. 221).

5. Gary Kelly, *The English Jacobin Novel, 1780–1805* (Oxford: Clarendon, 1976), pp. 222ff., discerns this trend as early as Godwin's *St. Leon*. Robert Kiely, *The Romantic Novel in England* (Cambridge: Harvard University Press, 1972), p. 89, suggests that even in *Caleb Williams* there is a kind of privatization of the political landscape. Poovey's focus is less on Mary Shelley's retreat from Percy's political radicalism, though she sees that as implicit in *The Last Man*, than on her growing repression of the "unladylike" in favor of the "conventional ideology of proper feminine behavior," particularly in Shelley's last novel *Falkner*. See Mary Poovey, *The Proper Lady and the Woman Writer: Ideology as Style in the Works of Mary Wollstonecraft, Mary Shelley, and Jane Austen* (Chicago: University of Chicago Press, 1984), pp. 149, 161, and passim.

6. Edward Bulwer, "Dedicatory Epistle," *Paul Clifford*, 3 vols. (London: Henry Colburn and Richard Bentley, 1830), 1:xii. The epistle also singles out Godwin's *History of the Commonwealth* as "one of the most manly and impartial records ever written" (p. ix). Although the prefatory matter for Bulwer's novels sometimes consists of several successive prefaces, this particular epistle was eliminated in later editions; the novel in 1840 was inscribed to Albany Fonblanque. The eliding of Godwin's name, however, does not seem to rank as a significant gesture of effacement, since the 1840 preface to *Eugene Aram* not only discusses Godwin's own relinquishment of the subject for that novel but pays tribute to "the dark and inquiring genius of the author of *Caleb Williams*."

7. Edward Bulwer, "Prose Fictions and Their Varieties," *London Review* 1 (1835): 478.

8. Edward Bulwer, "The Lounger, No. 1," *New Monthly Magazine* 28 (1830): 366. Robert Kiely, *Romantic Novel in England*, pp. 81–82, has commented on the two-pronged tradition in Godwinian criticism in which readers "have either preferred the radical idealist (and shrugged off the fiction as imperfect popularizations of his thought) or . . . have admired the innovative psychological novelist (and dismissed the philosophy as eccentric abstractions."

Bulwer, I suspect, is one of the earliest of Godwin's critics to pose the issue just this way, placing himself unequivocally in the second camp.

9. Edward Bulwer, "Monos and Daimonos. A Legend," *New Monthly Magazine* 28 (1830): 387–92; quoted here from Knebworth, 35 (*The Student and Asmodeus at Large*).

10. Otto Rank, *The Double: A Psychoanalytic Study*, trans. and ed. Harry Tucker (Chapel Hill: University of North Carolina Press, 1971), p. 7.

11. On this point see Christensen, *Edward Bulwer-Lytton*, pp. 51, 238 n.11.

12. Christensen, *Edward Bulwer-Lytton*, p. 64, sees Houseman as Eugene's evil demon.

13. That license, one can hardly forbear adding in light of his acquittal of the actual murder in Bulwer's 1851 revision, appears to be reserved to the novelist's Second Thoughts department. The result robs the novel of its dramatic edge as well as its uncompromising morality.

14. Christensen, *Edward Bulwer-Lytton*, p. 93, notes the symbiotic nature of the Cesarini-Ferrers relationship.

15. Some editions other than Knebworth read "apparition" for "opposition."

16. See Jonathan H. Grossman's article in this volume offering a comparison of the trial scenes in *Paul Clifford* and *Eugene Aram*.

17. Kelly, *The English Jacobin Novel*, p. 180.

# England and the English:
# Perceiving Self and Other

Joachim Mathieu

IF A BOOK WRITTEN BY AN ENGLISHMAN IS ENTITLED *ENGLAND AND the English*, nobody will be surprised to find perceptions of Self in it; that it should also contain perceptions of the capitalized Other is somewhat more surprising. But only at first sight. For almost always when we define ourselves we do this against some Other. In short, the idiosyncrasies of one color are the more perceptible if contrasted with another. The same holds true for definitions of national identity. As I shall argue, such a contrastive approach is an essential characteristic of Bulwer's *England and the English*.

A first indication of this kind of approach can be found in the very first of the five books into which Bulwer's *England and the English* is subdivided. It is entitled "A View of English Character," and one might assume that this is simply an Englishman writing about the English. However, that Bulwer's view of English character is not only meant as an inward-looking exercise of self-examination becomes evident even before reading the first page of his analysis. For this first book is dedicated to Prince Talleyrand, the same Frenchman who had led the negotiations for France during the Congress of Vienna, and who, in 1833, the year of the publication of *England and the English*, was French ambassador to London. Evidently, *England and the English* is addressed to both an international and an English readership.[1]

Thus it is with regard to his international readership that Bulwer explicitly discusses questions of self-perception and foreign perception. For this reason it is important to have a look at the way Bulwer himself deals with perceptions of England by foreigners. In the context of this essay, this means turning to foreign views of England as the Other.

In two reviews of published accounts of foreign travel, written in 1831 and 1833, Bulwer had shown himself acutely aware of foreign perceptions of England—perceptions he often thought in need of correction. This is also a subject on which the reviewer of *England and the English* in the *New Monthly Magazine* comments:

> It was high time, we think, for a work like the present to make its appearance; at least, that an Englishman, thoroughly acquainted with the character and condition of his countrymen, should undertake to exhibit them to the world at large; and, in the spirit of enlightened patriotism, to supply them with the means of forming a just estimate of themselves with a view to the further improvement of their personal and domestic manners, as well as of their social and political institutions.
>
> To say nothing of the trash and twaddle which scribblers of inferior note are in the habit of pouring fourth on the Continent, the palpable deficiencies, the ludicrous misstatements, and the strangely erroneous opinions to which even foreigners of rank and consideration have given currency in that portion of their literature relating to 'England and the English' have long demanded correction and rebuke.[2]

The books Bulwer had reviewed in the *New Monthly*, which may thus have provoked him to "correct and rebuke" false foreign opinions in his own *England and the English*, are the *Tour in England, Ireland, and France in the years 1828 and 1829* by the German Prince Pückler-Muskau, and the *Semi-serious Observations of an Italian Exile* written by the Italian Count Pecchio.[3] Such accounts contain long-winded observations about such things as the English landscape without much reference to the inhabitants. Pückler is so fascinated by gardens and parks that his translator at one point remarks in a footnote: "The description is abridged. It is feared that the English reader has already been sated with parks and houses."[4] The oddity of Count Pecchio's perspective is instanced in his explanation of why the English are not the best of dancers:

> Why are not the English good dancers? Because they do not practise. The houses are so small and so weak, that he who would cut a caper in the third story must run the risk of thundering like a bombshell down into the kitchen, which is placed underground.[5]

Evidently fearing that such bizarre or not very informative foreign perceptions of the English Other may be commonplace, Bulwer counteracts them with more reliable information provided by an insider. An especially interesting example of Bulwer's approach is his treatment of the alleged English propensity to suicide. Again the international context of *England and the English* cannot be overlooked, for Bulwer introduces the subject as follows: "Another absurd and ancient accusation against us ought, by this time, to be known by our accusers, the French, to be unfounded on fact, viz., our *unequalled* propensity to suicide."[6]

Thus, right from the start Bulwer identifies this stereotype as a (wrong) hetero-stereotype, and he considers the French as its originators. Moreover, the question of the alleged suicidal tendencies of the English, which may seem a rather outlandish topic, does involve perceptions of Self (the stereotype refers to the English), perceptions of Other (the French) *and*—to make things somewhat more complicated—perceptions of the Other perceiving Self (the Englishman discussing what the French think about the English).

How then does Bulwer deal with this, in his eyes, faulty perception of England? At first it seems as if he simply rebukes the French "accusation" by stating laconically: "That offence is far more frequent among the French themselves than it is with us."[7] Bulwer is able, however, to substantiate this claim; and, after all, empirical proof is always useful when it comes to refuting false ideas.

As Bulwer points out, there were in 1816 seventy-two cases of suicide in London, whereas in Paris there were one hundred and eighty-eight, and the population of Paris was, moreover, "some 400,000 less than that of London!"[8] Although early-nineteenth-century statistics must be taken with a grain of salt, Bulwer's overall figures appear to be correct.[9] Bulwer is thus in a position to reverse the stereotype and to apply to the *French* a propensity to suicide. Yet in the spirit of *enlightened* patriotism Bulwer does nothing of the sort. Instead, he analyzes the real reasons for suicides among the English and the French: "With the French it is mostly the hazard of dice, with the English, the chances of trade, that are the causes of this melancholy crime."[10]

The next step in the argument involves, as is characteristic of the work, a fictional anecdote. The sheer absurdity of the prejudice is illustrated by the author's inability to find among the numerous English clubs any "club of suicides, all sworn to be the happiest dogs possible, and not to outlive the year!" Instead it appears to be among the French that suicide is committed with, as Bulwer states, "mirthful gusto." He relates the following imaginary conversation:

"Will you dine with me to-morrow, my dear Dubois?"

"With the greatest pleasure;—yet, now I think of it, I am particularly engaged to shoot myself; I am really *au désespoir!*—but one
can't get off such an engagement, you know."

"I would not ask such a thing, my dear fellow. Adieu!—By the way,
if you should ever come back to Paris again, I have changed my lodgings, *au plaisir!*"

*Exeunt* the two friends; the one twirling his mustachios, the other
humming an opera tune.[11]

Bulwer soon returns, however, to a more serious treatment of
the hetero-stereotype, a widely held misunderstanding, propa-
gated originally by Montesquieu:

In a word, when we shoot ourselves, we consider it no joke; we come
to the resolution in sober sadness; we have no inherent predilection
for the act; no "hereditary imperfection in the nervous juices" (as
Montesquieu, with all the impudence of a philosopher has gravely asserted).[12]

One of the reasons, if not the *main* reason, for the French mis-
conception that there must be an hereditary imperfection to account for the vast number of English suicides was the greater
freedom of the press in England. Whereas in other European
countries, due to social stigmatization or legal restrictions that
could affect a suicide's family, suicides were kept secret, the English press reported more freely about them.[13] Consequently,
travelers who read about suicides in English newspapers were led
to believe that the English, indeed, tended to kill themselves
more frequently than others. (Some eighty years after Bulwer,
C. F. G. Masterman in *The Condition of England* would continue
to complain about the "violence and madness" of the Sunday
press in England, in which "suicides sprinkle every page.")[14]

Bulwer's treatment of the faulty foreign perception of the English suicidal tendencies can be summed up as follows:

- The stereotype is identified.
- Facts are provided to disprove it.
- A fictional anecdote helps to illustrate the absurdity of the stereo-
type.
- A more serious discussion suggests possible reasons for the stereo-
type.

Once more directly addressing Prince Talleyrand, Bulwer
claims—with a not altogether untypical lack of modesty—to have

achieved his aim and gives the reason why it is so important to get an insider's view: "Your Excellency, may perceive, by their theories, which I think I have now for ever demolished, how necessary it is for an Englishman sometimes to write about England."[15]

Having become obsolete, the stereotype of England as a nation of suicides now possesses chiefly an anecdotal interest.[16] But in other passages Bulwer's perceptions of Self and Other demonstrate an enlightened patriotism that may seem of more profoundly enduring importance. For *England and the English* is by no means a chauvinist book praising England while degrading other countries. On the contrary, in fact, Bulwer's intercultural comparisons are often in favor of other countries. The bias may be considered quite unusual, since—according to Dean Peabody, who discusses national characteristics from the point of view of a social psychologist—it is more common that "ingroup judgments will be relatively favorable in comparison to those by outgroups."[17] In general auto-stereotypes concerning the ingroup will be more positive than hetero-stereotypes concerning the outgroup.

It is thus interesting that Bulwer, who is well aware of writing *England and the English* in the postwar era, after the victory over France at Waterloo, makes a conscious effort to avoid defining English national identity against a hostile foreign Other.[18] After all, he states explicitly, the English *"no longer hate the French."*[19] As in the treatment of suicide, wherein he has resisted any temptation to reverse the stereotype by seriously assigning to the French a suicidal propensity, he continues to strive for fairness. His correction of a wrong perception never entails the creation of a new prejudice.

While not wanting to do away with distinctions of a foreign Other and an English Self, Bulwer desires therefore to present the opposition as a non-hostile one. But since an element of hostility still remains useful for the purposes of self-definition, he finds a new hostile Other within a certain component of English society itself. Turning away in many passages from France, he discovers that versions of the Self and the Other now confront one another at home.

The hostile Other, which had over centuries been provided by the French,[20] is in Bulwer's *England and the English* found, namely, in the English aristocracy. As Gerald Newman has pointed out in his account, *The Rise of English Nationalism*, the English aristocracy of the late eighteenth and early nineteenth century had been perceived as particularly Frenchified.[21] So Bulwer quite easily transfers the role of the hostile Other to the English aristocracy. As even a cursory reading of *England and the English* will show, Bulwer's invective against the "aristocratic spirit" is the dominant theme of the book. It was immediately apparent, as R. H. Horne discerned in 1844, that the book "might have been entitled 'An Exposition of the Influences of Aristocracy.'"[22]

Bulwer's view of England as dominated by the "aristocratic spirit" is, then, far from positive. Other aspects of contemporary England too, such as the quality of the English as a "commercial people" (with whom wealth is more important than virtue), are negative. Such negative perceptions of England must be seen in the context of the need for social reforms, which is another recurrent theme of Bulwer's work in the year after the Reform Bill. So much needs to be reformed in England that one may even begin to wonder whether there is any positive English Self left to confront the aristocratic Other. And at this point, curiously, one becomes aware that the positive element is less associated with any English Self than with the foreign Other that has now become more friendly than hostile. It is abroad that Bulwer now finds many models to be imitated. As he also observes in *The Student*, the English should begin to take lessons from the French:

> It is unfortunate for you English that you do not pay more attention to foreign literature and foreign politics. You ought to hear what the rest of the world say of you;—you ought to see how grand, how true the views, which, from a just distance, Frenchmen in particular, form of your present situation. You are like a man who can only talk of himself, and to himself; one great National Soliloquist, wrapt in a Monologue![23]

Of the numerous comparisons with other countries found in *England and the English*, most are in favor of the Other. Scotland and especially Prussia are recommended as models in matters of education; in particular, France, the rival of old, emerges in a very positive light. According to Bulwer there is far less class-conscious snobbery in France, and the French Order of Merit is unreservedly recommended as an institution to be imitated.[24] The message here is one of hope. Even if the English system of education is not as good as the Prussian one, it may, once reformed, become superior to that of Prussia. The positive models from abroad should cause the English not to despair but to reform themselves.

The dialectic process of self-perception and foreign perception is thus one of the most intriguing aspects of Bulwer's analysis. England and the English are discussed not at all in "splendid isolation" but constantly in an international context. Whereas France had for a long time served as the negative foil against which "English character" could be defined, Bulwer has here chosen a different approach. Instead of making use of an international rivalry, he urges the English people to reject the spirit of their own aristocracy and to learn from other nations. One of the five books has indeed been dedicated, as I have mentioned, to the English people, whose national identity Bulwer hopes, as a Radical politician, to reconstruct.

Bulwer clearly belongs to a non-chauvinist tradition. Almost all cases of intercultural comparisons in *England and the English* are in favor of other countries that are commended to the English as examples. Yet Bulwer's position is a patriotic one, like that of other Radicals of his day. By no means always connected with conservatism, English patriotism in the eighteenth century and early nineteenth century tended to be progressive. Often enough patriots were not the supporters of the government but rather its opponents.[25] Such patriotism tended as in Bulwer's case to define itself in opposition to the Other constituted not by foreign nations but by the English aristocracy.

Bulwer's true patriot is the man that sees what is bad at home (the aristocratic spirit and the exaggerated commercial spirit) and what is good abroad. Viewing foreigners in an enlightened and non-hostile spirit, this English Self can carry on a dialogue with that friendly Other. And by definition this dialogue would make the "National Soliloquist" an outdated figure. In Bulwer's very modern and ever topical conclusion (especially in view of the menace of "cultural clashes" between East and West today) it is important to see oneself through foreign eyes in order to understand oneself and to observe models from abroad in order to reform oneself.

## NOTES

1. The second book is dedicated to the cryptic figure of an anonymous "_____ _____, ESQ." (There are, however, good reasons to believe that this might be Benjamin Disraeli.) The third book is dedicated to the Scottish theologian Dr. Thomas Chalmers, and the fourth to Isaac D'Israeli, Benjamin's father. The fifth and last book is dedicated to the English people.

2. Anonymous review of *England and the English*, *New Monthly Magazine* 39 (1833): 206–12, 206.

3. "A Foreigner in England," *New Monthly Magazine* 32 (1831): 500–506; "Count Pecchio's Notions of England," *New Monthly Magazine* 37 (1833): 13–16.

4. Ludwig Heinrich Hermann von Pückler-Muskau, *Tour in England, Ireland and France, in the years 1826, 1827, 1828 & 1829; with Remarks on the Manners and Customs of the Inhabitants, and Anecdotes of Distinguished Public Characters. In a Series of Letters by a German Prince* [1830–31 (German), 1832 (English)] (Zurich: Massie, 1940), p. 100.

5. Giuseppe Count Pecchio, *Semi-Serious Observations of an Italian Exile, During his Residence in England* (London: Wilson, 1833), p. 34.

6. Edward Lytton Bulwer, *England and the English* [1833], ed. with an introduction by Standish Meacham (Chicago and London: University of Chicago Press, 1970), p. 54.

7. Ibid.

8. Ibid.

9. As Günther Blaicher points out, caution is naturally recommended with any such statistics from the early nineteenth century; nevertheless, Bulwer's figures seem plausible, and Blaicher is able to quote from a French source from the late eighteenth century that confirms the figures (Günther Blaicher, "Zum Problem des Vorurteils in der Geschichte der englischen Landesbeschreibung," *Anglistik & Englischunterricht* 4 [1978]: 85–101, 95).

10. *England and the English*, p. 55.

11. Ibid.

12. Ibid. Cf. Günther Blaicher, "England als das 'klassische' Land des Selbstmords im 18. Jahrhundert," *Archiv für Kulturgeschichte* 50/2 (1968): 276–88. In an article on national stereotypes, Blaicher writes: "der Glaube des europäischen 18. Jahrhunderts an eine besondere Selbstmordneigung der Engländer erweist sich als Mißverständnis" ("Zur Entstehung und Verbreitung nationaler Stereotypen in und über England," *DVJs* [*Deutsche Vierteljahrsschrift für Literaturwissenschaft und Geistesgeschichte*] 1 [1977]: 549–74, 572f.).

13. With regard to such legal restrictions and "milder" English legislation in this respect, Blaicher is able to quote an English law of 1823 according to which suicides could be buried between 9 P.M. and midnight in a churchyard, "naturally" without any religious ceremony ("'Klassisches' Land des Selbstmords," p. 281). Famous cases of English upper-class suicides in the early nineteenth century were those of Viscount Castlereagh and Sir Samuel Romilly, both of which are alluded to in Byron's *Don Juan* (Romilly in *Don Juan*, 11:78, and Castlereagh in an especially unfriendly way as "carotid-artery-cutting Castlereagh," 10:59).

14. Charles Frederick Gurney Masterman, *The Condition of England* [1909], ed. with an introduction by J. T. Boulton (London: Methuen, 1960), p. 7.

15. Bulwer, *England and the English*, p. 56.

16. Interestingly enough, in his recent book *The English: A Portrait of a People* (Harmondsworth: Penguin, 1999), Jeremy Paxton reports that England "has one of the lower rates for suicide in Europe, only a small fraction of the rate in Hungary or even Switzerland" (p. 14).

17. Dean Peabody, *National Characteristics,* in *European Monographs in Social Psychology* (Cambridge: Cambridge University Press, 1985), p. 36.

18. For a more detailed discussion of the mostly positive perception of foreign countries, see especially the chapter "Looking Outside: 'The Important Comparison,'" in my *Edward Bulwer-Lytton's* England and the English:. *A Description of England in the "Age of Reform"* (Hamburg: Verlag Dr. Kovač, 2001), pp. 170ff.

19. Bulwer, *England and the English*, p. 38.

20. Cf. the thesis of Linda Colley in *Britons: Forging the Nation 1707–1837* (New Haven and London: Yale University Press, 1992), e.g., p. 6, which underlies her discussion of English/British nationalism.

21. "Contemporary moralists chronically complained of 'how enamoured of France' their highborn countrymen were" (Gerald Newman, *The Rise of English Nationalism: A Cultural History 1740–1830* [New York: St. Martin's Press, 1987], p. 36), and what certainly made the moralists' task easier was "the contrary tradition of xenophobic and anti-French feeling, particularly strong at the bottom of society" (p. 37). Moreover, Newman points out that "this 'French' symbolism was polemically tied to the English Quality [i.e., the aristocracy] like a can to a dog's tail" (p. 232).

22. R. H. Horne, *A New Spirit of the Age*, 2 vols. (London: Smith, Elder, 1844 [reprint, Farnborough, Hants.: Gregg, 1971]) 2:193.

23. Bulwer Lytton, *The Student, and Asmodeus at Large* (London: Routledge, 1875), p. 302. As attention has been drawn to Bulwer's use of the personal pronoun "we" before, it is interesting that Bulwer addresses the English here as "you." His rhetorical intention is sometimes to be seen as a member of the ingroup and at other times to appear as someone giving advice more or less from the outside.

24. Bulwer, *England and the English*, p. 326.

25. Raphael Samuel observes in his introduction to *Patriotism: The Making and Unmaking of British National Identity*, ed. Raphael Samuel, 3 vols. (London/New York: Routledge, 1989), 1:xvi: "In one venerable tradition it is radicalism which is the 'true' patriotism (in the eighteenth century 'patriots' were those who *opposed* the government of the day)."

# "At Home" with the Romans: Domestic Archaeology in *The Last Days of Pompeii*

Angus Easson

AMONG THE SURVIVALS OF THE ROMAN WORLD, PUBLIC MAGNIFI-cence bulks large. Only in the later eighteenth century, as Pompeii began to yield up its wonders, could a shift to Roman domesticity take place.[1] Bulwer seized on this archaeological recovery, fascinated by the buildings and artifacts of Pompeii. He owed much to Sir William Gell, the first publisher in English of the Pompeian excavations; yet in exploring the site and the art and objects preserved in the Naples museums, Bulwer showed a notable independence from Gell in selecting the material fabric of *The Last Days of Pompeii*. Like others, Bulwer acknowledged that if Pompeii revealed how the Romans lived, that revelation came through the city's sudden extinction. Not only does Bulwer oscillate between imagining how the past was different and yet how people then were recognizably us, he also shifts between satire and an elegiac plangency, prompted by archaeology's apocalyptic record of the "last day."

This essay explores Bulwer's excitement in the uncovering of Roman life and considers his representation of three domestic sites. Glaucus, a dandy whose house reflects his cold aesthetic, is challenged by the ideologies incorporated in the houses of the "Gothic" Arbaces and of the Christian Olinthus. If Bulwer eventually turns Pompeian life into a version of Biedermeier, that squares with his belief, however constricting, that at home the Romans were much like us.

Bulwer traveled abroad in 1833 with his wife Rosina, after a breakdown in health, for the sake of rest and change. The couple found neither,[2] which was scarcely surprising as the Bulwer marriage was close to breakdown as well; when Rosina was attracted to a Neapolitan prince, Bulwer became intensely jealous. Rosina

100

herself hated Italy (she made an exception of Naples), not least
for the filth of its streets—an inconvenience of that day noted by
other travelers, who at times felt that no place, no object, however venerable or steeped in classical associations, was safe from
pollution.

The Bulwers arrived in Naples late in 1833. Bulwer himself
spent much time visiting the sights, including the royal museums, though by November 23 he had still not visited Pompeii,[3]
the city overwhelmed by Vesuvius on 24 August 79 A.D. and an
object of fascination since excavations began in 1748. Once he did
so, it took possession of his imagination, struck as he was, as others before him and since, by how the Roman world and above all
the everyday and domestic world survived here unsullied by modern Italy. Here the "departing genius" of the classical world was
not subject to that slow change "which converted the gods into
the saints, and the temples into the churches of Rome; . . . here
in its native dwelling-place, with no time for escape, it was sealed
up by the sudden act of a single catastrophe, and here it remains
for ever undisturbed."[4] Even while still at Naples, Bulwer began
to write *The Last Days of Pompeii*, and it was published in late
September 1834, its success boosted by a major eruption of Vesuvius in August.[5]

Even before arriving in Naples, though, Pompeii's destruction
had seized upon Bulwer. At the Brera gallery in Milan, he had
been struck among modern pictures by a representation of Pompeii overwhelmed, full (as he noted in his diary) "of genius, imagination, and nature," but finding

> the most natural touch in an infant in its mother's arms:—her face
> impressed with a dismay and terror which partake of the sublime; the
> child wholly unconscious of the dread event—stretching its arms
> towards a bird of gay plumage . . . struggling in death, and all the
> child's gay delighted wonder is pictured in its face. This exception to
> the general horror . . . is full of pathos, and in the true contrast of fine
> thought.[6]

Excavations at Pompeii, actively in progress, had disclosed in
November 1824 one of its greatest treasures, the House of the
Tragic Poet, notable not for magnitude, but rather for richness
and quality of decoration.[7] Its owner was conjectured to be "a
jeweler, or rich goldsmith."[8] He and his family were dispossessed
by Bulwer in favor of his hero Glaucus, while the house's decora-
tions, probably based on Greek originals, became an extension of

the exquisite sensibility and taste of Glaucus, who not only possesses but has commissioned them.[9]

All around, the mundane and domestic reality of Pompeii was there in its streets and buildings, in its artworks and its artifacts, some still in situ, some removed to Naples. In describing the Forum, for example, Bulwer draws on a picture in Naples, showing business activities and a school, with (an empathetic scene to any nineteenth-century public school boy) one boy hoisted on the back of another, to receive a beating (III:i). Preparations for Diomed's banquet bring in, not most relevantly but fascinating for an age of developing technical convenience, "a portable kitchen . . . containing stoves for four dishes, and an apparatus for heating water" (IV:ii). In the museums Bulwer saw those pictures removed from the House of the Tragic Poet, including the great Achilles and Briseis,[10] while at Pompeii itself he saw the paintings and mosaics that remained in situ, in Glaucus's house and others.

It was at Naples too that Bulwer met Sir William Gell (1778–1836), to whom *The Last Days of Pompeii* is dedicated, a recognition of Gell's kindness and of his importance as an active disseminator of archaeological knowledge. Gell's career has some political interest: as one of Queen Caroline's chamberlains, he gave evidence on her behalf at the divorce trial. Now settled permanently in Naples, he acted as cicerone to English visitors, among them Walter Scott, who had visited Naples from December 1831 to May 1832.[11] Gell was full of knowledge and enthusiasm about the excavations. He attempted to sketch the finds before they faded or decayed, despite government-enforced interdictions on such recording, and conducted visitors round the excavations, though so crippled by gout and rheumatism that he had to be carried about in a chair.

William Gell's permanent importance lies in his pioneering publication of the Pompeian excavations in the first two significant works to appear in English: *Pompeiana*, dated 1817–1819 (though only in one volume), and, in 1832, another *Pompeiana*, in two volumes, covering excavations since 1819 and including the House of the Tragic Poet.[12] Bulwer, as well as dedicating his novel to Gell, draws the reader's attention to these publications, referring, for example, to the 1832 publication for an engraving of the Leda in the House of the Tragic Poet (I:iii).[13] It has been not unnaturally assumed therefore that Bulwer drew heavily in the novel on Gell's publications. Michael Grant, noting the impulse of the Milan painting, adds that Bulwer "obtained much of his information" from Gell's *Pompeiana*.[14]

Certainly Gell's work gives details of everyday life and of domestic recoveries that might appeal to anyone imagining the intimate details of Roman life through Pompeii's remains. As Gell noted, "the houses of Pompeii remain preserved to us in a state that leaves little to be desired upon the subject of many of those minor details, with which, until the discovery of that city, we were almost wholly unacquainted."[15] And indeed, Bulwer, himself fascinated, gives such detail, though not usually taken directly from Gell. It is perhaps easy to see why Bulwer would avoid some detail, such as Gell's reference to obscene pictures,[16] though Bulwer's Fulvius, the poet, has pictures in his collection he will not show to ladies (IV:iii). There are also Gell's references to the common Roman motif of "a species of triple Phallus in terra cotta of singular invention" and (a reminder of the filth of the nineteenth century) to the proximity of kitchen and latrine, where it "would appear, that in ancient, as in modern Italy and Greece, a proximity between the ultimate receptacle of the aliments and their place of preparation was considered desirable."[17]

However, other details might innocently have added authenticity, whether the graffiti ("Lucrio et Salus hic fuerunt"—"Lucrio and Salus were here") or the names painted on houses, indicating not owners but patrons in that peculiarly Roman social network of patrons and clients.[18] It might be from Gell that Bulwer took the hint of the great shade cover for the amphitheater (so crucial to a climactic moment on the last day itself): a wall announcement, along with a troop of gladiators and a chase of wild beasts, adds the inducement of "shades to keep off the heat of the sun . . . extended over the spectators."[19] And again Gell mentions the sprinkling of the crowd in the amphitheater with perfumed waters, the *sparsiones*—though these comforts of shade and perfume Bulwer might equally have taken from literary or historical sources, and he in no way matches the evocative technicality of Gell, who notes that since the *sparsiones* produced "a nimbus, a cloud or a shower, the perfumed waters were probably dispersed in drops by means of pipes or spouts over the audience."[20]

And while both Gell and Bulwer are fascinated by the ordinary objects found, retrievals of domesticity for which Pompeii is famous, what is equally striking in reading Gell alongside Bulwer is the absence of direct borrowing by Bulwer, whatever might seem the obvious temptations, even when similar objects (clearly seen therefore by Bulwer in the museums) crop up in the novel. Gell's description of culinary equipment, for example, is matched by but not identical with that in Diomed's kitchen. Gell lists "gridirons, colanders, saucepans, some lined with silver, kettles, ladles, moulds for jelly or pastry, urns for keeping water hot," all at the Portici museum.[21] Over a naturally extended narrative Bulwer includes, no doubt also from observation at Portici, stewpans and saucepans, cutters and moulds, egg-pans and sweetmeat shapes (IV:ii). Nor was Bulwer tempted to take over directly Gell's lists of what we might now call *objets* (literally) *trouvés*: "two hundred and fifty little bottles of common glass, forty-one bottles nine inches high, four decanters and many fluted tumblers, six tumblers eight inches high . . . with thirty cups of green glass, and four plates six inches in diameter."[22]

Again, in the novel's catastrophe Bulwer neatly elides a number of his characters (Julia, Calenus, and Burbo among them) into those real bodies found in the excavations, his narrative thus "explaining" why the bodies at Pompeii were found in particular places and with particular material objects: gold, a key, an axe. This desire for authentication is part of the novel's teasing play with the whole business of reality—the House of the Tragic Poet exists, so why not, as claimed, the House of Ione or the House of Arbaces?—and if the houses, why not their inhabitants, Glaucus or Ione or Arbaces? Yet this desire makes it the more surprising, perhaps, when we look at Gell, that Bulwer seems almost conspicuously to ignore the everyday artifacts found in the House of the Tragic Poet, any or some of which might, their fictional history and explanation woven into the narrative texture, have further authenticated that narrative: "A ring of onyx with the head of a youth . . . a vase for oil; a bucket; a lamp for two lights, with the head and feet of a bull . . . a broken key; two hooks; two heels for boots, with holes for the nails; locks, latches, and hinges."[23]

Yet however Bulwer declines to go to Gell directly, Gell provided another impulse in the creation of the novel, as surely as did those objects retrieved and taken to the museums of Naples, which Gell describes and which Bulwer saw. The absence of direct borrowing from Gell's published work indicates, indeed, Bulwer's avidity, prompted by Gell's enthusiasm, in studying the displays for himself, as it does his own engagement with the imaginative world opening before him. The two men were equally engaged in recalling Pompeii and its citizens to life, in laying open the Roman way of life in its domestic fabric and texture (literally, in the physical remains that might be touched).

Here at Pompeii the "departing genius" of Rome had been sealed up, preserved to future generations, and excavation gave it back as a peculiarly domestic "genius," in all its particularity of the everyday. Yet paradoxically that preservation had been possible only by the death of the city and of many of its inhabitants. The apocalyptic sense of violent ending, as well as the representation anew of the ordinary and everyday, lies in Bulwer's very title, *The Last Days of Pompeii,* and the tension between life and cataclysmic ending is an infusive mood of the novel. When Walter Scott was taken round Pompeii, in William Gell's chair, he exclaimed "frequently—'The city of the Dead' "[24]—a phrase Bulwer himself cites in the novel (II:viii). Pompeii allows us to see, through what was overwhelmed and buried, a city of the living, its buildings, its works of art, even through the very signs of the dead. The found objects speak to us, give us the city, even while they remind us, in their abandoned state or their physical condition—the fish and eggs in the dining room of the Temple of Isis, the calcined clothing of the slaves in the Villa of Diomedes (IV:iii)—of flight, panic, death and silence. Less gloomy than Scott, Bulwer clearly delights in describing destruction, while he insists—not least in his novel's title—upon the promised end.

It is indeed one of the paradoxes of the excavations that while Pompeii reveals in detail how people lived, yet all their activity ceased within the same few hours. For us to know them living, they had to die. It is a city preserved, yet extinct. The sense is strong not only of the past coming to life, but also of the past coming to us through the dead. In a novel called *The Last Days of Pompeii* we have that sense of time running out and come inevitably (in block capitals) to THE LAST DAY OF POMPEII. An earlier observer, John Chetwood Eustace, gives a good sense of both the excitement of discovery of the domestic, of ordinary life, and how that excitement must be conditioned by the very way in which that life was preserved for us, was sealed up:

> While you are wandering through the abandoned rooms you may, without any great effort of imagination, expect to meet some of the former inhabitants, or perhaps the master of the house himself, and almost feel like intruders, who dread the appearance of any of the family. . . .
> This sense of a city raised from the grave, where it had lain forgotten during the long night of eighteen centuries, when once beheld must remain for ever pictured on the imagination; and . . . to the fancy, it comes, like the recollection of an awful apparition, accompanied by thoughts and emotions solemn and melancholy.[25]

In developing his materials, as already noted, Bulwer could fit the dramatic finds at Pompeii to his narrative, shaping his story to the grand climax of eruption and destruction, and in doing so his characters (many of them quite literally) fall into place in the city's archaeological history. Julia and Calenus and Burbo end as archaeological finds, preserved as skeletons or impressions in the sand, on show in museums, in Bulwer's teasing mingling of fiction and reality. The priest found by the excavators near the Temple of Isis, with gold upon him, and the man who had futilely hewn his way through two walls with an axe, are resolved into the priest Calenus and his cousin the tavernkeeper Burbo (V:x). In 1771, the impressed forms of people who had taken refuge in the cellars of the Villa of Diomedes were discovered in the compacted sand. Gell described a skeleton in the villa's garden with a purse and a key, while in the vaults

> twenty-three of the family had betaken themselves for shelter and refuge. Various ornaments, as ear-rings, bracelets, were found . . . together with some few coins of gold, silver, and brass. . . . [T]he volcanic matter here penetrated in so fine a powder, that the forms of their persons and apparel remained impressed in the indurated matter. The mould of the bosom of one is yet shown in the Museum of Portici.[26]

The bosom so movingly preserved proves, in Bulwer's novel, to be that of the foolish Julia, daughter of the rich Diomed, while the man in the garden with a key (almost certainly a wine merchant, who owned the villa) becomes the novel's Diomed. So Julia, an object of satire earlier in the novel—luxuriating at her dressing table and reading the "soft" poetry of Tibullus as a "modern" girl might read Byron or Thomas Moore—becomes the compacted sand that echoes a long-lost bosom.

Three houses provide a focus for Bulwer's uses of this material and his own domestic conclusion from it: those of Glaucus (the House of the Tragic Poet); of Arbaces; and of the Christian conventicle. Glaucus, like other heroes of toga novels, is dazzling: of slender and beautiful symmetry, with a perfect harmony of features (I:i). He is also a Greek: not just of Greek origins, as was common enough in Magna Graecia. He was brought up in Athens and his father played host to St. Paul when the Apostle was on his way to Rome, a glance towards Glaucus's conversion. Bulwer foregrounds the house by presenting it first not as Glaucus sees it, but as "when first given once more to the day" (I:iii), an object of wonder to the modern diggers. That had been in 1824, but since visitors were prevented from sketching or taking notes for three to four years after excavations, and since Gell did not publish his description until 1832, there was real novelty for the novel's readers in the House of the Tragic Poet. First and foremost, Glaucus has taste and culture; Glaucus's house, identified by Bulwer as its owner's creation, is full of masterpieces, with Raphael invoked to measure the greatness of the Achilles and Briseis. At the entrance there is the mosaic of *Cave Canem*: the revelers go out into the night, "walking unbitten over the fierce dog . . . on the threshold" (I:iii), while paintings and mosaics cover walls and floor. Besides Achilles and Briseis, the works of art, transferred to Naples or left in situ, included the Rape of Europa, the Battle of the Amazons, and (giving Bulwer his name for the house) the mosaic of a dramatic poet directing preparations for a satyr play (I:iii). Some paintings were irrecoverably lost during excavation and in Bulwer's time others were already fading and perishing; at least five are now lost, though known through accounts and sketches.[27] Glaucus's house would, in its adornment and finish, be "a model at this day" for the house of "a single man in Mayfair" (I:iii): not perhaps the truest commendation of taste and culture. Here Glaucus gives his dinner party, the food exquisite rather than grossly elaborate—a starter of figs and herbs sprinkled with snow, the conversation echoing other dinner parties down the centuries.

Bulwer implies the decoration is Glaucus's choice, imported direct from Greece: historically this fine decoration (and of course it does exist, even though much has been removed from its original context) represents a general desire in Pompeii for Greek work and Greek culture.[28] Perhaps it is because these works are real that Bulwer makes nothing further of them, once he has played cicerone to the house-viewing reader. Other nineteenth-century novelists would have done more with them, as George Eliot does, for example, in juxtaposing Dorothea with the Vatican's Sleeping Ariadne, otherwise the Cleopatra, mythic women invoked to play against Dorothea's frustration and disappointment. Even the pictures in the Room of Leda (I:v)—Cupid and Venus, Ariadne—are not significantly drawn upon, but lie inert as the walls and floors upon which they are depicted. The readers may set to on the loves of the gods and heroes, on the power of love, on Ariadne abandoned and claimed by Bacchus—but neither Bulwer nor Glaucus hints at this.

The art establishes Glaucus's taste, and his Greekness. When introduced, Glaucus is an "Alcibiades without ambition" (I:iii), constantly conscious that Greece is no longer free, Athens only a

**Mosaic of a dramatic poet directing preparations for a play, from House of the Tragic Poet, Pompeii. Courtesy of Museo Archeologico Nazionale, Napoli, n. inv. 9986. With permission from the Soprintendenza per i Beni Archeologici delle province di Napoli e Caserta.**

slave beneath Roman tyranny, as though he (or Bulwer) elides some 250 years of history between Alcibiades and the Roman conquest of Greece.[29] However fully he explains Glaucus's dilemma, and Bulwer is aware of a narrative problem, aware of the reader's likely objections, he can find nothing for Glaucus to do, splendid though he is supposed to be. A dandy has to be made interesting, as Bulwer made Pelham, for all the faults and falsities of that eponymous hero; and as a lover Glaucus might be called, in a useful if scarcely critical Victorian term, a spooney. This is a man deeply sensitive yet incapable of sensing Nydia's pain and jealousy, incapable too of civic action or of study or of poetic endeavor to any professional purpose. He shows no interest in the culture or philosophy of Athens or Greece, not in Homer, despite the Achilles

**Interior of House of the Tragic Poet, Pompeii, as reconstructed by Bettina Bergmann and Victoria I. View from through the tablinum to the atrium. Courtesy of Bettina Bergmann and Victoria I.**

and Briseis on his wall, nor in the Pantheon, nor in Plato. If he did not wish to go into politics or actively participate in public life, his money would allow him to be a benefactor or at least a builder. At the end of the novel he is briefly given a new freedom in Christianity, achieved not under the compulsion of imminent death in the amphitheater, but through free choice, a freedom that includes a very modern freedom of dissent from his fellow Christians. Even this conversion, though, seems a dwindling into the merely domestic, despite his genial challenge to Sallust, the man instrumental in his salvation from the arena, to come from Rome and dispute on Christian truth.

More significant actions occur in the other two houses under consideration, which relate to the two forces struggling to master Glaucus: the dark destructive power of Arbaces, veiled under the rites of Isis, but in reality a will to power that must destroy what it cannot bend; and the visionary fervor of Olinthus and his fellow Christians, whom Glaucus duly joins, on his own terms. Arbaces the Egyptian is a fuller, darker figure than Glaucus. His fictional power is linked to the freer rein Bulwer gave himself in inventing his house: as invent he does, despite claiming that the reader may still see the house (V:xi). First presented with the moon shining full on the mysterious habitation, its mystery enforced in twin sphinxes that flank the entrance, Arbaces' house is in a secluded and remote part of the city (I:viii), unexcavated when Bulwer wrote, if indeed he had a fixed place in mind at all. The site offers four main interconnected spaces: the house proper; the astrological watchtower, a "lofty and pyramidal tower" (II:viii);[30] the Temple of the Fates; and the vaults, these last generated as much by Gothic fiction as the archaeologist's spade. These spaces are variously associated with Arbaces' belief in the divine power of Necessity, with his dark power over the lives of others, and above all with his juggling theatrical skills.

On this site, Arbaces devotes himself to Nature and Necessity as well as to power and also—partly for his own pleasure, partly as a trap—to sensuality. The secret passage and the entrances that open by passwords ("practical" features of the stage set, to admit women to the revels) declare the manipulative stage director and shade over into the arcane theater that Arbaces had devised. The uninitiated audience may accept the illusion, but those who have been behind the scenes know where the stage door is and how to enter "stage right."

The blind Nydia, admitted to the theater as a musician to the orgies, knows the garden gate and its password. She can lead Glaucus and Apaecides to rescue Ione from the Temple of the Fates; while imprisoned, she uses her knowledge of the garden in her comically frustrated attempt to fool her jailer and to free herself. The vault below the house is modeled in part on actual underground levels, like those excavated below the Villa of Diomedes, yet also reflects the Gothic world of power that lies below the upper world of veils and stage-managed revelations.

Arbaces is a villain who thinks. His very weakness, though, lies in that thought, since it leads him to credit his own knowledge. Bulwer mocks Arbaces, deconstructing his beliefs in a dream-vision that terrifyingly throws down the very basis upon which his belief is founded. In sleep, he sees Nature send the souls to their destinies in the world, while the lightning that breaks through the vision's carceral gloom is sufficient only to reveal the vast knowledge that Arbaces has not yet begun to comprehend. Necessity proves but to be the breath of God. He is allowed a vision, but only of exclusion and damnation. Arbaces, whose house is constructed as a series of manipulative theatrical levels—stage and scenery, wings and traps—is plunged by sleep into a darker and truer theater of the imagination.

To this house Arbaces lures Apaecides and Ione, siblings whose common nature intensifies respectively into fanatical belief and moral strength. As Arbaces struggles to control them, he necessarily enters into conflict with Glaucus, whom the Egyptian nearly destroys. Apaecides is led, in a house darkened, to Arbaces' half-lighted chamber, in an initiation that smacks of Freemasonry and trade unionism: Arbaces the Egyptian is an obvious Masonic figure. Apaecides is offered the truth, yet Arbaces "palters in a double sense." Arbaces proposes to reveal "the enigma of life itself" (I:viii) and (metaphorically) to lift the veil that conceals truth. Isis, he declares, "is nothing. Nature, which she represents, is the mother of all things" (I:vi), so that we have to lift the veil and stand face to face with the solemn loveliness of Nature.

Yet having revealed Nature and Necessity to Apaecides, Arbaces uses the images of day and night to switch from the metaphorical to the literal: from the dawn of enlightenment to a nocturnal orgy only too really and readily at hand: "And the day which thou givest to men shall be followed by the sweet night which thou surrenderest to thyself" (I:viii). The familiar (familiar from the Gothic tradition) black veil is drawn aside, indeed in a blasphemous parody of the veil of the Temple, is rent in twain, to reveal fully the beauteous forms, in the banquet of the senses, to which Arbaces conducts Apaecides: female beauty, perfume, music, food, even the skeleton (a common Pompeian, indeed Roman, motif), which is but another urging to the enjoyment of life.

While, in the Gothic tradition, some veils are true concealers of horror and some prove eventually to be contrivances, the reader here (however overwhelmed by the mise-en-scène with detail drawn from Suetonius and Petronius) is not deceived as Apaecides initially is deceived. At one level, it is a paradise of delights. At another level, as with the orgiastic suggestions of Reynolds's *Mysteries of London* or the salacious entertainments of "Chief Baron" Nicholson, Arbaces is exposed despite his expert stage management as panderer and procurer. Here Apaecides is initiated sexually and then, plunging from one extreme to another, revolts and turns to Christian austerity. Here, too, Arbaces tempts Ione in the Temple of the Fates, offering her visions of power through transparencies and phatasmagorias, devices, like the goddess's statue, not supernatural but theatrical.

Against this theater of false religion and inadequate reason, Bulwer places a site of revolution, the Christian house to which Olinthus takes Apaecides.[31] Bulwer seems not very informed about early Christianity, possibly is not very interested in Christianity at all. In the novel's closing upheaval, the Christians become apocalyptic fanatics, crying "woe to the harlot of the sea" (V:vii). Olinthus himself provokes popular fury by overturning the goddess's statue. He is of those men "who were formed to convert, because formed to endure" (I:viii), whose intolerance is his strength (Bulwer himself counters with talk of modern tolerance) and whose austere garb is dissenting if not puritanical. Yet these men have the influence, rooted in the domestic, of those modern dissenters characterized by Bulwer, who, "vehement in the pulpit . . . address the passions of their flock;—familiar at their hearths, they secure their sympathies. Thus the poor choose some dissenting, instead of the established sect."[32] The domestic Christians of Pompeii are largely undoctrinal, referring vaguely to the Scriptures, and placing great stress on immortality. There is no doctrine of grace or atonement; no sign of sacraments beyond baptism (given to Apaecides in record time); no priesthood. Olinthus speaks of the scriptural promise and Medon, the old slave, reads from Scripture and comments upon it (III:iii). But Bulwer does not pause, for example, on what might be the scriptural canon in 79 A.D.—Acts, presumably, and the Epistles—but what gospels, unless the proto-Mark? The Scriptures are there for Bulwer, but what the Scriptures consist of is quite another— and avoided—matter.

The Christians meet in a house in the suburbs, then and still unexcavated, amongst small and mean houses—symptomatic (not necessarily symbolic) of their occupiers' low social status: Clodius, the flash young Roman, remarks that not one of the Nazarenes is a gentleman—and modeled, one assumes, as much upon the squalor of nineteenth-century Naples as upon archaeological evidence. They meet in a closed house where the door opens at a knock and they are (mysteriously) admitted, in a way that parallels, almost certainly unconsciously on Bulwer's part, admission to Arbaces' stronghold. Conscious or not, the parallel stresses the ideological struggle between Arbaces and Olinthus, between Reason and Faith, while Bulwer's handling suggests his essential uninterest in what Christianity might mean to the Roman Empire. This Sunday meeting is conducted as a cross between a Quaker and a Dissenting fellowship. The congregation sits in silence, contemplating a crucifix. There is no altar, no ritual, no liturgy, no priest, no commemorative supper or *agape*. Medon, the slave, reads and expounds the Scriptures.

More notable are human presences. First, there is the elderly man who is a living witness to Jesus, since he is the son of the widow of Nain brought back to life (Luke 7:11 ff.). Why this man?

It may be Bulwer did not want a key player like Lazarus at this point, but this witness highlights the domesticity of the gathering. The widow's son represents the claim upon Jesus of family affections, of the domestic tie between mother and son, and of the widow's dependence in this world upon her son's support. Bulwer, his marriage shaky, might well recall his stern but loving mother and ignore Jesus's refusal (one of the Gospel's "hard sayings") to know his mother or brethren (Matthew 12:48; Mark 3:33). Second, the domestic motif is reinforced when the children come in, rather like the nineteenth-century nursery brought down to dessert, except that there has been no supper: the old slave, Medon, opening his arms, "they fled to the shelter—they crept to his breast" (III: iii).

It is scripturally justified, in "Suffer little children," and Medon teaches them the Lord's prayer. Yet the balance of feeling proves on the side of the domestic rather than the religious. While "in truth, it is difficult to conceive a ceremony more appropriate to the religion of benevolence," the emphasis of the sentence, even while picking up the word "ceremony," proves to be "a ceremony . . . more appealing to the household and everyday affections, striking a more sensitive chord in the human breast" (III:iii). We may pause to ask again whether Bulwer was really interested in Christianity. Largely, he offers generalized detail of an unoffending Protestantism, a religion of humanity, echoed too in the Brera's picture of Pompeii's destruction, as undoctrinal as it is merely emotional.

The novel's final domestic scene, the tranquil epilogue, suggests indeed the triumph of a harmless Christianity. In the fullness of time, in Athens, Glaucus is a Christian and his wife Ione is a Christian as well. This Christianity is a domestic and fugitive virtue. Glaucus may still lament the old cause of Athenian freedom, but he does nothing to achieve it. Instead, he embodies a domesticity, one reminiscent of the actuality of Pompeii and the familiar life preserved by the volcano, though now transplanted to an imaginary Greece. Nydia is commemorated in a garden cenotaph: Glaucus looks out from his study to it and the garden and the summer bees. He seizes on the story of Cupid and Psyche, accepting it as an allegory of love and the soul, but as freedom no longer calls, all is swallowed up in love, even Christianity. For Glaucus sees the myth not as shadowing Divine Love, but as the soul *asleep* in the arms of love, the smothering of religion, freedom, and life's activity by uxorious domesticity—all deeply ironic if we recall Bulwer's domestic circumstances in Italy as he wrote about the Romans (and Greeks and Egyptians) amidst their archaeological domesticity, "At Home" in *The Last Days of Pompeii*.

## NOTES

1. For this repeopling of Roman antiquity and consequent sympathy with the past, see Catharine Edwards, "The Road to Rome," in *Imagining Rome: British Artists and Rome in the Nineteenth Century*, ed. Michael Liversidge and Catharine Edwards (London: Merrell Holberton, 1996).

2. Second Earl of Lytton, *The Life of Edward Bulwer, First Lord Lytton*, 2 vols. (London: Macmillan, 1913), 1:260; the details below are at 1:271, 266.

3. Ibid., 1:270.

4. Ibid., 1:442.

5. See James C. Simmons, "Bulwer and Vesuvius: The Topicality of *The Last Days of Pompeii*," *Nineteenth-Century Fiction* 24 (June 1969): 103–5.

6. Lytton, *Life of Edward Bulwer*, 1:440.

7. The standard Pompeian reference for the house is Regio VI 8.3. See *Pompeii: Pitture e Mosaici* (Rome: Enciclopedia Italiana, 1993), 4:527–603; Nicholas Wood, *The House of the Tragic Poet: A Reconstruction* (London: Nicholas Wood, 1996); Bettina Bergmann (with Victoria I), "The Roman House as Memory Theater: The House of the Tragic Poet in Pompeii," *Art Bulletin* 76, no. 2 (1994): 225–56; Paul Zanker, *Pompeii: Public and Private Life*, trans. Deborah Lucas Schneider (Cambridge: Harvard University Press, 1998); and Ray Laurence, *Roman Pompeii: Space and Society* (London and New York: Routledge, 1994).

8. William Gell, *Pompeiana: The Topography, Edifices and Ornaments of Pompeii: The Result of Excavations since 1819*, 2 vols. (London: Jennings and Chaplin, 1832), 1:149.

9. The name, House of the Tragic Poet, established soon after its discovery, derives from its pictures, several of which represent scenes from Homer's *Iliad*. Bulwer always calls it the House of the Dramatic Poet, taking its name from the famous mosaic representing the rehearsal of a satyr play. For illustrations see Gell, *Pompeiana* (1832), plate XLV; Wood, *House of the Tragic Poet*, p. 16. For simplicity the house is here referred to, throughout, by its accepted name, the House of the Tragic Poet.

10. Wood, *House of the Tragic Poet*, p. 56; Gell, *Pompeiana* (1832), plate XXXIX: "perhaps, the most beautiful specimen of ancient painting . . . preserved to our times" (1:155).

11. *Sir William Gell in Italy: Letters to the Society of Dilettanti, 1831–1835*, ed. Edith Clay (London: Hamish Hamilton, 1976), p. 5; Gell's reminiscences of Scott in J. G. Lockhart, *Memoirs of the Life of Sir Walter Scott, Bart.*, 2nd ed., 10 vols. (Edinburgh: Robert Cadell/London: John Murray and Whittaker, 1839), 10:153–69.

12. William Gell and John P. Gandy, *Pompeiana: The Topography, Edifices, and Ornaments of Pompeii* (London: Rodwell and Martin, 1817–1819). For Gell's 1832 volumes, see note 8.

13. Gell, *Pompeiana* (1832), plate XLVIII. Bulwer also refers to the museums at Naples and (V:ii) to [George Clarke], *Pompeii*, 2 vols., Library of Entertaining Knowledge (London: Charles Knight, 1831–32).

14. Michael Grant, *Cities of Vesuvius: Pompeii and Herculaneum* (Harmondsworth: Penguin, 1976), p. 217.

15. Gell and Gandy, *Pompeiana* (1819), p. 139.

16. E.g., Gell, *Pompeiana* (1832), 1:11.

17. Ibid. and Gell and Gandy, *Pompeiana* (1819), pp. 173–74.

18. Gell, *Pompeiana* (1832), l:31; 1:7–8.

19. Ibid., 1:24.

20. Ibid., 1:93.

21. Gell and Gandy, *Pompeiana* (1819), p. 165.

22. Gell, *Pompeiana* (1832), 1:42.

23. Ibid., 1:177. The figure of Bacchus at Glaucus's dinner (I:iii) may derive from Gell's "head of Bacchus" (*Pompeiana* [1832], 1:149) or from a museum.

24. *Memoirs of . . . Sir Walter Scott*, Lockhart, 10:158.

25. John Chetwood Eustace, *A Classical Tour through Italy: AD MDCCCII*, 4th ed., 4 vols. (London: J. Mawman, 1817), 3:54–56.

26. Gell and Gandy, *Pompeiana* (1819), pp. 96–98. The retrieval of the dead by pouring plaster into the natural mould of the human form was only devised in 1864 (Grant, *Cities of Vesuvius*, p. 34).

27. See *Pompeii: Pitture e Mosaici* (note 7 above). Gell describes sixteen paintings and mosaics, plus unspecified fragments (*Pompeiana* [1832], 1:154–76); Bulwer refines his account to ten.

28. See Zanker, *Pompeii*, particularly pp. 17–19, 136–42.

29. Compare Macaulay's objection to this treatment of the Greeks (George Otto Trevelyan, *The Life and Letters of Lord Macaulay* [1876], popular ed. [London: Longmans, Green, 1889], p. 370).

30. The tower is possibly related to Gell's vignette of a strange tower, like a Persian "fire-temple," from a painting in the House of the Little Fountain (*Pompeiana* [1832], 2:134).

31. No evidence of Christianity at Pompeii has yet been found.

32. Edward Lytton Bulwer, *England and the English* [1833], ed. with an introduction by Standish Meacham (Chicago and London: University of Chicago Press, 1970), pp. 192–93.

# Lions of Basalt:
# Bulwer, Italy, and the Crucible of Reform

## Esther Schor

> Neither of us are in love with Italy. . . . The travelling here
> may be divided into three classes—plague, pestilence and fam-
> ine. Plague—the mosquitoes. Pestilence—the smells, and
> Famine—the dinners. . . . Poets ought to be strangled for all
> the lies they have told of this country.
> Rosina Wheeler Bulwer to Miss Greene, 1833

PERHAPS BECAUSE THERE WERE NO POETS AT HAND TO STRANGLE,
the Bulwers' Italian sojourn saw the collapse of their already
strained marriage. In truth, Italy's trio of "plague, pestilence and
famine" probably played a small role in ruining one of the century's worst and longest marriages; more likely, the couple came to
grief on the shoals of mutual vanity, antagonism, and vengeance.
But although the Italian journey of 1833–34 witnessed the de-
mise of Bulwer's marriage, it also brought forth two remarkable
novels: *The Last Days of Pompeii* (1834) and *Rienzi, the Last of
the Tribunes* (1835).[1] These novels are conceptually interleaved,
for each figures, rather differently, certain liabilities of the populism Bulwer had been espousing both as a Member of Parliament
and in his fiction and journalism. Bulwer's sojourn in Italy allowed him to contemplate "the people,"[2] as it were, from the bottom up: not as a downtrodden cause to be vindicated in pamphlets
and on the floor of Parliament, but as the motive, rationale, and
foundation stone for a possible sovereign state. Bulwer's stay in
Italy brought him in proximity to a Mazzinian popular politics
that the nationalist leader's exile in 1831 had only placed in
sharper relief; his brief residence in Italy brought home to Bulwer
the possible consequences of the positions he had been taking,
publicly, vociferously, and effectively.

    In this essay I will frame a discussion of Bulwer's Italian fiction
with a brief treatment of two of his writings about English poli-

116

tics: *England and the English*, composed in 1832–33 before his departure for Italy; and his pamphlet *A Letter to a Late Cabinet Minister on the Present Crisis*,[3] composed shortly after he returned in 1834. As dissimilar as they are in scope, narrative mode, and ambition, Bulwer's novels of Italy reveal both the dangers and the disappointments of an appeal to the people on the grounds of nationhood. In these quizzical, alarmed, and sometimes despairing fictions, Bulwer registers both the English crucible of Reform and the Italian struggle for nationhood.

## PEOPLE AND PUBLIC: *England and the English*

In *England and the English*, Bulwer addresses himself to the "disease" of Englishness and, secondly, to the "remedy" of Reform. As Bulwer notes: "The best way to find remedies for a disease is to begin by ascertaining its origin,"[4] which he construes as an unhealthy relationship between "the people" and the aristocracy. For Bulwer, the problem lies in the fact that "people have no exact and fixed position—that by acquaintance alone they may rise to look down on their superiors." Hence, because identity depends less on birth than on social status, there are an infinite number of class gradations in the "shot-silk colours of [English] society";[5] as a corollary, enormous pressure comes to bear on individual acts of affiliation. Bulwer, an apologist for both the monarchy and the established church, points out that the English aristocracy should check both king and commons; but now the "checking power is not content to be a check alone; it is like the sea, and gains in every place where it does not recede: as we have seen, it has entered, penetrated, suffused every part of the very influences which ought to have opposed it."[6] The result of all this jockeying for position are the vices of conformity: the promotion of a hollow respectability in lieu of moral principles, lack of independent-mindedness, materialism, contempt for the poor, and a dangerous reverence for wealth.

What, then, is the remedy for this "disease" of timid, materialist conformity? Simply put, the aristocracy is too deeply ingrained in English society to be overthrown, and its immense holdings of property and links to commerce endow it with an immense degree of power:

You may sweep away the House of Lords if you like; you may destroy titles; you may make a bonfire of orb and ermine, and after all your pains, the aristocracy would be exactly as strong as ever. For its power is not in a tapestried chamber, or in a crimson woolsack, or in ribands and stars, in coronets and titles; its power, my friends, is in yourselves; its power is in the aristocratic spirit and sympathy which pervade you all![7]

Bulwer's point is that the aristocracy and the middle class—even middle-class reformers—inhabit a common cultural sphere; hence, the contagion of reverence and respectability are pervasive, perhaps irremediable.

For at the other end of the social scale from the aristocracy there is also contagion, one that spreads from low to high: *"Their* crimes," he notes, "are our punishments."[8] In this powerful recognition, Bulwer acknowledges that the middle classes, though they might prefer to think otherwise, indeed occupy the same cultural sphere as the lower classes. Moreover, the middle classes are *culpable* for crimes committed by those in desperate poverty. Bulwer's view of the franchise is pragmatic and, at base, progressive: "While social habits descend from the upper to the lowest class, *political* principles, on the contrary, are reverberations of opinion travelling from the base to the apex of society. The Aristocracy form the Manners of Life, and the People produce the Revolutions of Thought."[9] And such revolutions derive from the fact that the working class do not live in fear of "concussions" with those less fortunate: "Who are they that feel the most deeply for the negro slave.—The people or the nobles? The people. Who attend the meetings in behalf of Poland? The aristocracy?," he sneers.[10] Thus, Bulwer perceives in the "agitated moment" of Reform a profound shift in the flux of influence; the aristocratic tide that had formerly inundated English society has been turned back. But precisely what undertow will issue from the working classes leaves Bulwer markedly uneasy.

No wonder Bulwer sees no easy remedy for the "disease" of Englishness, for it is more than the anemia of aristocratic values and more than the gangrene of poverty; it is the contagion of culture itself, the continuities that connect the middle class with both the aristocracy and the working classes. In *England and the English*, Bulwer's solution to the crucible of reform is to call for a new party to advocate a strong, centralized nation-state. Parrying a call in the radical press for a working-class political union, Bulwer calls for the transformation of a mingled society into a profoundly unified one:

To merge the names of People and of Government, to unite them both in the word STATE. Wherever you see a good and a salutary constitution, *there* you see the great masses of the population wedded to and mingled with the state. . . . In a well-ordered constitution, a constitution in harmony with its subject, each citizen confounds himself with the state; he is proud that he belongs to it, the genius of the whole people enters into his soul; he is not one man only, he is inspired by the mighty force of the community; he feels the dignity of the nation in himself—he beholds himself in the dignity of the nation. To unite, then, the people and the Government, to prevent that jealousy and antagonism of power which we behold at present, each resisting each to their common weakness, . . . we must first advance the popular principle to satisfy the people, and then prevent a conceding government by creating a directive one.[11]

Bulwer's enlightened dream of a merged state and nation casts a dark shadow: it climaxes on a call for the mystic marriage of a classless people and state, but cadences on the need for "directive" government, one that "procures the blessings of a free constitution by the vigour of a despotic one."[12] Behind Bulwer's brash confidence in "the people" lurks a fear of "the public":

The people are calm and reasoning, and have a profound sense of the universal interest. But you have a false likeness, my dear friends, a vile, hypocritical, noisy, swaggering fellow, that is usually taken for you, and whom the journalists invariably swear by,—a creature that is called "THE PUBLIC."

That Bulwer's new party was never formed may in part be laid to the oxymoronic state he imagined: a spouse to "the people"; a chastener of "the public"; and to the energies of the mob, a despot. In *The Last Days of Pompeii*, Bulwer takes a dark, topsy-turvy view of the energies that had made England a formidable industrial power.

## IMPERIAL RELIGION: *The Last Days of Pompeii*

Bulwer's presence in Italy (and, briefly, France) in the early 1830s brought him into a world in which revolution, nation-making, and imperial power were affairs of daily life. Let me briefly sketch the Italian situation as Bulwer encountered it in the mid-1830s. In 1816, the Congress of Vienna had reduced Napoleon's Italy to an assortment of small duchies and principalities under the repressive control of the Austrian empire, with a large swath of territory under the thumb of the papacy. Naples, where the

Bulwers sojourned during the winter of 1833–34, was under the sway of the Bourbons, who had declared Sicily part of the Kingdom of Naples in 1816. (Over a mutual flirtation—perhaps more—between the neglected Rosina and a Bourbon prince, the marriage came to grief and the Italian journey to a premature end.) The largest, most prosperous, and most progressive of these post-Napoleonic kingdoms was Piedmont, ruled by the house of Savoy: first by Vittorio Emanuele I, who abdicated to his brother Carlo Felice during the Piedmontese revolution of 1821; then by Carlo Felice from 1821 to 1831; and then by Vittorio Emanuele's son Carlo Alberto, who led the Piedmontese army against Austria in 1848 but fled to Portugal the following March after the debacle of Novara. Since the fall of Napoleon, nationalist and constitutional currents had been flowing intermittently in Italy, sometimes carried on within small, conspiratorial sects, sometimes coordinated with Italian exiles in Switzerland and France. About once a decade between 1820 and the first stage of unification in 1860, these currents sparked into revolutionary insurrections. Typically, revolutionary activity elsewhere on the Continent served as a conductor, and the July 1830 revolution in Paris was no exception. Because of deep divisions between radical and conservative factions among the nationalists, revolutionary activity in central Italy in 1831 was ineffectual in loosing Austria's grip.[13]

But perhaps the most important result of the failed 1831 revolutions was Giuseppe Mazzini's realization that a new revolutionary platform was necessary, one that would unite a variety of nationalist factions in a populism defined not by class but by ethnicity—or in his terms, peoplehood. As the historian Stuart Woolf has argued, Mazzini undertook to transform both a previous generation's Jacobin internationalism and the indigenous habits of carbonarism, a loose system of secret sects replete with passwords, strict hierarchies, and elaborate initiations.[14] Mazzini's original draft of the "General Instructions for the Brotherhood of Young Italy," written during the revolutions of 1831, was an awkward amalgam of Jacobinism and carbonarism. Mazzini considered it the task of "Young Italy" (or "Giovine Italia") "to present a single front to enemy and Friend,"[15] by directing the revolutionary activity executed within smaller carbonarist sects. Within a very brief span, perhaps less than a month, Mazzini redrafted the plan entirely, replacing his enlightenment rhetoric of natural rights (that called for the abolition of aristocracy) with an Hegelian vision of a progressively emerging democracy, providentially destined to issue in nationhood.[16] The emphasis on sect dissolves into one on sovereignty; this sovereignty he called the nation's "mission" and maintained that the "duty and belief" of each Italian man was to contribute toward fulfilling this mission. This second draft makes an explicit appeal to all social ranks, in fact, to the submergence of rank in favor of an ideal of sovereign peoplehood.

There are multiple, striking points of convergence between Mazzini's program and Bulwer's vision of the state in *England and the English*: the emphasis on peoplehood; the sense of duty; the quasi-mystical insistence on spirituality, not just ethics; the notion of nationhood transcending class difference; and, above all, the dialectical transformation between the sovereign State and a sovereign people. But where Bulwer had been free to imagine a *new* party, a *new* state, Mazzini and his cohorts had been arrested and exiled for their attempt to overthrow the ducal powers sustained by Austria. In Italy, after the defeat of Mazzini and his "Giovine Italia," Bulwer felt the ideal state of his imaginings wither under the fierce glare of Imperial power.

In *The Last Days of Pompeii*, imperial Rome is a brooding, leveling force that reduces individuality, homogenizes nationality and even obliterates autonomy altogether. But by setting his novel in the "heated and feverish civilisation" of Pompeii (III:i) rather than in the city of Rome, Bulwer examines the encroachment of imperialism on Pompeiian cosmopolitanism. Indeed, Pompeiian cosmopolitanism is paradoxical. On the one hand, Bulwer's meticulous descriptions of costume, architecture, food, and leisure suggests a polity variegated by ethnicity, class, religion and gender. On the other hand, the residents of Pompeii, whether "lords of Pleasure" or "minions and victims," share a variety of bestial pastimes. The elegant upper class divides its time among slave-holding, slave-trading, and flogging slaves; buying and selling prostitutes; gambling on gladiators and ogling them. Pompeii's comely mosaics depict the rapes of Leda and Europa; a telling sign declares, "'Beware the dog'" (I:iii). In a world that ceremonially pits men against lions in the arena, it should come as no surprise that men are described as wolves; even the ensnared female characters are figured as mice and wasps.

In the cosmpolis of Pompeii, a strain of bloodlust, greed, and perversity flows through the veins of aristocrat and commoner, Athenian and Neapolitan, human and beast, female and male. Rather than construe this as animation, however, Bulwer emphasizes their decadent passivity as subjects of empire:

> The world was one vast prison, to which the Sovereign of Rome was the Imperial gaoler; and the very virtues, which in the free days of Athens would have made him ambitious, in the slavery of earth made him inactive and supine. For in that unnatural and bloated civilisation, all that was noble in emulation was forbidden. . . . It is in small states that glory is most active and pure,—the more confined the limits of the circle, the more ardent the patriotism. (II:iv)

Despite the consonance of Bulwer's vision of the state with Mazzinian nationalism, this passage reverts to a Burkean theory of local, concentric loyalties.[17] Hence, he entreats his Italian contemporaries to aim for regional autonomy, not nationalism: "Italy, Italy. . . . [Y]our only hope of regeneration is in division. Florence, Milan, Venice, Genoa, may be free once more, if each is free. But dream not of freedom for the whole while you enslave the parts; the heart must be the centre of the system, the blood must circulate freely everywhere" (II:iv). As I will show, Bulwer's vision of Italy's prospects changes over time—though as late as 1850, he would write to Walpole, "in all Europe I have seen nothing so heroic and with so good a cause; but, alas! so hopeless."[18]

In *The Last Days of Pompeii,* Bulwer allegorizes empire in the person of the Egyptian priest, Arbaces, who voices a grim truth: that empires live and die by power. "The time shall come," prophesies Arbaces, "when Egypt shall be avenged! when the barbarian's steed shall make his manger in the Golden House of Nero! and thou that hast sown the wind with conquest shall reap the harvest in the whirlwind of desolation!" (II:viii). The consolation for one empire lies, perversely, in the relentless conquest of another. In a series of stiff monologues, Arbaces explains that religion is but "sublime allegories" (I:iv), fables developed by the priests of Egypt to solidify their power: "that which in reality was Government they named Religion" (I: vi). In the figure of Arbaces, Bulwer suggests that if religion can be facade for imperial government, then imperialism derives its power by making a religion of itself: "Think you it is the man, the [Emperor of Rome], that thus sways [the vast and various tribes of earth]?—no, it is the pomp, the awe, the majesty that surround him—*these* are his impostures, his delusions; our oracles and our divination, our rites and our ceremonies, are the means of *our* sovereignty and the engines of *our* power" (I:vi).

But given that Arbaces is a priest, not a ruler, his imperial ambitions are articulated in his grim demystifying philosophy of Necessity: "Of that which created the world, we know, we can know, nothing, save these attributes—power and unvarying regularity;—stern, crushing, relentless regularity—heeding no individual cases—rolling—sweeping—burning on;—no matter what scattered hearts, severed from the general mass, fall ground and scorched beneath its wheels" (I:viii). Though Arbaces disdains the allegory of religion, it is telling that his own philosophy of Necessity is rendered as a high romantic dream vision, a projection of his own domineering will. While Arbaces prides himself on his powers of prophecy, Bulwer shows us that he has merely made an idol of his own desires. In Arbaces, Bulwer ironizes the ironist.

In fact, the only figure who correctly prophesies the disaster is the old witch who lives on the mountain. Whereas Arbaces has been brooding over Necessity, and the Nazarenes over Christ, the witch has been studying carefully the signs of nature: "I have of late marked a red and dull stream creep slowly, slowly on. . . . So, when I rose this morning . . . the stream itself was broader, fiercer, redder than the night before" (V: i). Not only is the witch, who dwells in a lair among animals, closely identified with nature, but she refuses to abstract a fatal force motivating nature. In the hostile relations between Arbaces and the witch, Bulwer suggests a psychological, gendered dimension to the imperial fantasy of control: that ultimately, political absolutism displaces a masculine desire to control Nature itself. Arbaces' sexual boast that "woman is the main object, the great appetite, of my soul" (I:iv) has ramifications in the political as well as the psychological and metaphysical spheres.

Hence, while Bulwer tropes imperial conquest in the framing and imprisonment of the Athenian, the novel's denouement makes clear that the real enemy of empire is not freedom but instinct. Within the Pompeiian amphitheater, Bulwer develops his erstwhile identification of humans and beasts—"the gladiators were objects of interest as well as the beasts—they were animals of the same species" (IV:xvii)—in new and harrowing directions. Though the audience is articulated both by class and by gender, it is united in a passion for pain and bloodshed: maidens exult in a fatal slash, widows lament that a gladiator's death throes are so brief, a young girl relishes news of not one, but two victims: "I always said we should have a man for the lion; and now we have one for the tiger too!" (IV:xvii). All the while the "tender hearted" upper classes gloat over bets won, lamenting bets lost. The gladiators, Bulwer observes bitterly, are entirely disposable: "His body was dragged at once from the arena through the gate of death, and thrown into the gloomy den termed technically the

spoliarum" (V:ii); fresh sand is strewn while the audience receives a refreshing shower from hidden pipes.

Although *The Last Days of Pompeii* has often been reduced to
its sensational catastrophe, Bulwer's achievement is to evoke instinctive energies so convulsive as to render the eruption of Vesuvius a fiery redundancy:

> *"To the lion with the Egyptian!"*
> With that cry up sprang—on moved—thousands upon thousands!
> They rushed from the heights—they poured down in the direction of
> the Egyptian. In vain did the aedile command—in vain did the prae-
> tor lift his voice and proclaim the law. The people had been already
> rendered savage by the exhibition of blood—they thirsted for more.
> . . . Aroused—inflamed by the spectacle of their victims, they forgot
> the authority of their rulers. It was one of those dread popular convul-
> sions common to crowds wholly ignorant, half free and half servile;
> and which the peculiar constitution of the Roman Provinces so fre-
> quently exhibited. (V:iv)

Just as the heedless, lawless, savage mob falls upon Arbaces, Vesuvius erupts high above in streams of "ghastly red," unloosing
the authority of Roman law, and with it, the grip of empire: "The
sudden catastrophe . . . had, as it were, riven the very bonds of
society, and left prisoner and gaoler alike free . . ." (V:vi). Rome,
the "Sovereign Jailer," is finally undone by its own merciless se-
verity; Arbaces dies beneath an "Imperial Statue" of Augustus.
Perhaps the best emblem of empire is the Roman sentry who remains "erect and motionless at his post. That hour itself had not
animated the machine of the ruthless majesty of Rome into the
reasoning and self-acting man" (V:vi). Between the animal mob
and the inanimate sentry lies the dream of an awakened, enlightened people—the dream of *Rienzi, the Last of the Tribunes*.


## THE LIONS OF BASALT: *Rienzi*

If *The Last Days of Pompeii* probes the convulsive energies of a
people under the sway of empire, *Rienzi, the Last of the Tribunes*
broaches a corollary danger: the failure of a people to become animated by a nationalist vision. The ferocious, feverish Pompeiians
meet their opposite numbers in the immobilized populace of four-
teenth-century Rome, so unwilling to take responsibility for the
reform of their state that they forfeit statehood entirely. *Rienzi*
explores in magnificent detail two preoccupations of *England and*

*the English*: the degraded state of the aristocracy, and the notion of a state "wedded" to its people.

That Bulwer's Rienzi took shape in the shadow of the exiled Mazzini was as plain to the Italians who swiftly translated it as it was to the English reviewers who read it as radical propaganda for Young Italy.[19] In *Rienzi*, Bulwer imagines the sustained, complex, and ultimately doomed process by which a leader uses his gifts and his passion to arouse a nation into a sense of its own potency. But while Bulwer's ostensible argument is to vindicate Rienzi and indict the people for their failure at Reform, the figure of Rienzi is deeply unstable—haunted on the one hand by his own theatricality and on the other by the specters of demagoguery and absolutism. Ironically, as we shall see, the inner life of Rienzi is as opaque as the "lions of Basalt" brought to Rome from the land of the Pharoahs.

Rienzi approaches the people—"without arms, without rank, without sword or ermine" (I:iii)—as an electrifying orator. From the perspective of the aristocratic Adrian di Colonna, he seems a spiritual presence: "Every cheek was flushed—every tongue spoke: the animation of the orator had passed, like a living spirit, into the breasts of the audience" (I:iii). With each subsequent address, however, Rienzi's oratory becomes increasingly theatrical and self-dramatizing. In the Church of the Lateran (for Rienzi has, at the outset, the confidence of the Pope and bishop) a rudimentary amphitheater has been erected, and Rienzi emerges dramatically from behind purple curtains clothed in a dazzlingly white Roman toga. To many, Rienzi seems oracular, "preternatural and inspired" (II:iii); to the urbane Bishop of Orvieto, a ciceronian orator; to the aristocratic Raselli (not realizing he is soon to be Rienzi's father-in-law), " 'Diavolo!' " (II:iii). By multiplying these responses to Rienzi, Bulwer accords us an ironic distance on Adrian's initial judgment. Rienzi is, above all, a performer, and he presides over "the most magnificent spectacle the Imperial City had witnessed since the fall of the Caesars" (IV:v).

Ironically, Rienzi's private moments only enhance his theatricality. In a chapter entitled "The Actor Unmasked," Bulwer oddly positions Rienzi as the object, not the subject, of his own meteoric rise. Rienzi's frequent soliloquies, often taken to be a pitfall of Bulwer's narrative style, are crucial in suggesting that even in private he is performing—to an audience of himself: "Rome is bound up with me—with a single life. The liberties of all time are fixed to a reed that a wind may uproot. But oh, Providence! hast thou not reserved and marked me for great deeds?"

(I:x). Increasingly, Bulwer disguises, rather than unmasks, the actor, casting him in a variety of roles, including Napoleon, Cromwell, Macbeth, and Saul. Clearly, Rienzi's ability to be many things to many people lies at the root of his popularity; moreover, it is responsible for his picaresque survival on the Continent between his excommunication by the Pope and his later return to Rome. But in the latter half of the novel, Bulwer connects Rienzi's role-playing to a progressive disintegration of his personality. In time, Rienzi's heroic composure gives way: the stoical hero weeps, the sober republican takes to drink. Ultimately, Rienzi's profound sense of a religious vocation, rather than his charismatic (if increasingly disordered) personality, becomes the primary instrument of his ambition.[20]

A comprehensive survey of these ambitions lies beyond the scope of this essay. Given that contemporary readers compared them to Mazzini's, however, it is worth pausing over how differently Rienzi and Mazzini relate to imperial prerogatives. Mazzini saw clearly that the Austrian empire was the chief impediment to Italian nationhood; furthermore, unlike many in the nationalist cause he recognized France, too, as an imperial danger. But Rienzi's relation to empire is more oblique. Redeeming Rome from the grip of the feuding noble families entails parrying the military companies from the north hired by the aristocrats. The German emperor has but a shadowy existence in this novel: Rienzi's time in his orbit in Prague is narrated only after the fact, and the various negotiations between mercenaries and this emperor are mentioned in a cursory fashion. As in *The Last Days of Pompeii*, Bulwer's emphasis lies not on representations of imperial powers, but rather on the imperial imagination and the historical process by which such imaginings are translated into domination.

Such imaginings are harbored by Rienzi's nemesis, the dashing Provençal condottiere Walter de Montreal, whose virile, "towering ambition" (I:xii) is mitigated by an almost effeminate chivalric grace. Like Rienzi, Montreal has had to be various things to various parties; he, too "had learned to sound a people—to know how far they would endure—to construe the signs of revolution—to be a reader of the times" (II:iv). Beneath the bitter rivalry between Rienzi and Montreal for "mastery" of Rome lie parallel readings of these times. First, both observe that the nobility is the root of all evil in Rome; and both hold independence of mind to be a paramount virtue in a leader. Just as Rienzi dreads to be leagued definitively with any faction—in fact, the novel puts him in a swiftly shifting series of negotiations with the nobles, the people, the Bishop of Orvieto, the Pope, and Montreal himself—Montreal disdains attempts to "fix" his rank. At their first meeting, Montreal asks Rienzi, "Is not ambition a common sentiment between us?" (II:iv), a ringing question that resonates when Montreal's arrest late in the novel brings the two face-to-face again:

> And, there, as these two men, each so celebrated, so proud, able, and ambitious, stood front to front—it was literally as if the rival Spirits of Force and Intellect, Order and Strife, of the Falchion and the Fasces—the Antagonist Principles by which empires are ruled and empires overthrown, had met together, incarnate and opposed. They stood, both silent,—as if fascinated by each other's gaze,—loftier in stature, and nobler in presence than all around. (X:iii)

Even as the antagonists face off for their final conflict, the exquisite mirroring between them suggests how impossible it is to prise apart the two antagonists. Both Montreal's falchion and the fasces comprise a weapon—the very weapon, wielded by Rienzi, by which Montreal will fall.

But there is another crucial premise that connects the two leaders: both Rienzi and Montreal understand that no matter who ruled, "the people were to be the victims" (II:iv). At the outset, however, there is a marked difference between their respective estimations of, in Montreal's phrase, "the garlic-chewing mob" (II:iv). While Rienzi believes the people to be capable of regenerating themselves, Montreal dismisses even the possibility of a civil government for Rome: "Rienzi! . . . In peaceful times, or with an honest people, he would have founded a great dynasty. But he dreamt of laws and liberty for men who despise the first and will not protect the last" (VII:vii).

Bulwer's treatment of the Italians echoes Montreal's, developing a distinction between two ethnic strains: the southern Italians, who are crafty, sly, effeminate, cowardly, lazy, deceitful, cheating and untrustworthy; and the northern Italians, who might have risen to Rienzi's vision: "with a brave, noble, intelligent, devoted people to back his projects, the accession of the Tribune would have been the close of the thraldom of Italy . . ." (IV:iii). Whereas the Pompeiians' answer to imperial absolutism is the unleashing of violent instinct, the sodden Romans flatly refuse to fund a defensive army; they balk at Rienzi's attempt to levy a new tax. Over the dearness of salt and wine, over the people's "listless" lack of passion for their state, Rienzi loses his hold on Rome. "[W]ith all the aims of the patriot, [Rienzi] felt all the curses of the tyrant" (IX:iv). *Rienzi* is the tragedy not only of Rienzi's fall, but also of Montreal's vindication, for Rienzi comes to acknowledge that his trust in the people was ill-placed.

It seems telling that Bulwer figures the imperial will in *Rienzi* as an Egyptian statue:

> Not far from the side of Rienzi, [the setting sun] brought into a strange and startling light the sculptured form of a colossal Lion of Basalt, which gave its name to a staircase leading to the Capitol. It was an old Egyptian relic,—vast, worn, and grim; some symbol of a vanished creed, to whose face the sculptor had imparted something of the aspect of the human countenance. . . . The awe which the colossal and frowning image was calculated to convey, was felt yet more deeply by the vulgar, because "the Staircase of the Lion" was the wonted place of the state executions, as of the state ceremonies. And seldom did the stoutest citizen forget to cross himself, or feel unchilled with a certain terror, whenever, passing by the place, he caught, suddenly fixed upon him, the stony gaze and ominous grin of that old monster from the cities of the Nile. (II:viii)

Here, on this site where state authority is represented by its terrifying, absolute power to take human life, Bulwer sets Rienzi's ascent to the position of tribune; here also occur the executions of both Martino Di Porto and Walter de Montreal. But it is not until the papal bull announcing Rienzi's excommunication is posted upon the same statue that he senses "some solemn and appointed connection between his fate and that old Lion of Basalt" (V:v). Indeed, when Rienzi fashions himself on the emperor Vespasian, he does not disclose that it was Vespasian who had built the Colosseum, the site where the imperial lions devoured the empire's dissidents. The imperial lion becomes Rienzi's fatal mascot: here he celebrates his return to Rome—and precisely here, beside the lion glowing "as if itself of fire" Rienzi meets his mortal fate before the "the serried throng" who shout for his death (X:ix). As the nobles—"Rome's true tyrants"—return, the novel ends with "the tramp of raging thousands" shouting "Viva 'l Popolo." Rienzi announces desperately, "That cry scares none but tyrants!" (X:ix), but within minutes, he is stabbed by Cecco and the avenging Angelo: *sic semper tyrannis*. Ironically, while *Rienzi* was read as propaganda for the Italian cause, the novel harbors a reactionary reading of the Italian scene: the populist tribune is unmasked as a tyrant, and the Romans are constructed neither as a nation nor as a class, but as an inferior, southern race desperately in need of northern governance. Indeed, this racializing of the Italians would persist into the new introduction Bulwer composed in 1848, where he notes, "[I]t is still a grave question whether Italy is ripe for self-government," and casts his hopes in the direction of Sardinia.

## BULWER'S "OCHLOCRACY": *Letter to a Late Cabinet Minister*

Yet the story of Bulwer's Italian sojourn has an English denouement as well. A few months after his return to England in 1834, William IV took the unlikely opportunity afforded by the death of Lord Spencer to dissolve the Whig government. Under the aegis of Wellington and Peel, the Tories made a few calculated overtures toward the Reformist camp—just enough to restore them to power, where they intended to set about undoing the Whig accomplishments of 1832.

Or so they thought. Published as a pamphlet on November 21, 1834, the *Letter to a Late Cabinet Minister on the Present Crisis* was perhaps Bulwer's most important intervention on behalf of Reform. While Bulwer's closest ties in Parliament lay with the Radicals rather than the Whigs, he took it upon himself to plead for the restoration of a Whig cabinet, and he was widely credited with playing a major role in salvaging Reform.[21] According to Bulwer's grandson, twenty-one editions (in both "cheap" and "dear" forms) of the pamphlet were sold in six weeks, about the number of copies of Burke's *Reflections* sold in its first year of publication. Ten pamphlets appeared in response, and most Whig candidates pilfered from it when on the hustings.[22]

But despite its resounding—and efficacious—endorsement of Reform, the pamphlet offers a far more damning view of the "people" than *England and the English*. Indeed, Bulwer locates the danger of a Tory government not in the contraction of the franchise, but in the danger of "ochlocracy"—mob rule:

> For this is the danger—not . . . that the Duke of Wellington will crush liberty, but that . . . the indignation for the aristocracy, if the Duke should head it against Reform—the contempt for the aristocracy if the Duke should countermarch it *to* reform—the release of all extremes of more free opinions, on the return which must take place, sooner or later, of a liberal administration;—the danger is, lest these and similar causes should in times, when all institutions have lost the venerable moss of custom, and are regarded solely for their utility—

induce a desire for stronger innovations than those merely of reform.[23]

With his characteristic contempt for the devious aristocracy, Bulwer deems "ochlochracy" as a Tory artifact, defining it in a footnote as "the plebeian partner of oligarchy, carrying out the business under another name. The extremes meet, or as the Eastern Proverb informs us, when the serpent wants to seem innocent, it puts its tail in its mouth!"[24] This criticism, of course, touches not only the Tory oligarchs but the working classes themselves, who submit to being instruments of a Tory party content to swallow them up when convenient. Identifying himself as "one known to embrace the cause of the people,"[25] Bulwer excoriates "the people" as inflammable (like the fiery Pompeiians) and as easily manipulated by the aristocracy (like the complacent Romans of *Rienzi*):

> You talk of public opinion—history tells us that public opinion can be kept down. It is the nature of slavery, that as it creeps on, it accustoms men to its yoke. They may feel, but they are not always willing to struggle. Where was the iron-hearted Public Opinion, that confronted the first Charles, threw its shield round the person of Hampden, abolished the star-chamber, and vindicated the rights of England, when, but a few years afterwards, a less accomplished and more unprincipled monarch, sent Sydney to the block—judges decided against law—Parliament itself was suspended—and the tyrant of England was the pensioner of France. The *power* of public opinion woke afterwards in the reign of James II but from how shameful a slumber.[26]

In *England and the English,* Bulwer imagined a mystic marriage of state and nation, in which the state's institutions are a direct expression of the national character. But by the time he writes *A Letter to a Late Cabinet Minister*, Bulwer has come to see the purpose of Reform as remaking the nation through the state's institutions. As he writes in the 1848 introduction to *Rienzi* : "It is as true as it is trite that political freedom is not the growth of a day—it is not a flower without a stalk, and it must gradually develop itself from amidst the unfolding leaves of kindred institutions." That Bulwer remained a Reformist as long as he did testifies to Allan Christensen's assessment of Bulwer on the centenary of his death as "the Victorian who held onto an especially pure version of Romantic idealism."[27] But when he returned to Parliament in 1852, Bulwer, like Burke, had crossed to the other side of the aisle, a Conservative reluctant to dismantle protectionist legislation. As Bulwer writes in the *Letter,* "we are standing on a present, surrounded by fearful warnings from the past."[28] Though Bulwer had in mind an English past, his Italian novels show that fearful warnings issued also from the annals of Italian history—from Roman antiquity as much as from an aborted Roman renaissance—and from the present, in the struggle of the Italian people to become a nation.

## NOTES

1. Commendatory letters on *Pompeii* from Disraeli, Hemans, Lady Blessington and others may be found in the second Earl of Lytton, *The Life of Edward Bulwer, First Lord Lytton,* 2 vols. (London: Macmillan, 1913), 1:443–47. In 1836, John Auldjo reported from Naples that over a hundred copies had been sold to Italians and more had purchased it in French translation (see Lytton, *Life,* 1:445). James L. Campbell, Sr., *Edward Bulwer-Lytton* (Boston: Twayne, 1986), p. 21, hazards that "during his lifetime Bulwer may have been the most widely read novelist next to Dickens." On the question of Bulwer's Carlylean rethinking of the historical novel, see Elliot Engel and Margaret F. King, *The Victorian Novel before Victoria: British Fiction During the Reign of William IV, 1830–37* (New York: St. Martin's Press, 1984), pp. 39–60. On *Rienzi* as an inspiration for George Eliot, see Hugh Witemeyer, "George Eliot's *Romola* and Bulwer Lytton's *Rienzi,*" *Studies in the Novel* 15 (1983): 62–73.

2. On configurations of "the people" in Bulwer's Caxton novels, see Allan Conrad Christensen, *Edward Bulwer-Lytton: The Fiction of New Regions* (Athens: University of Georgia Press, 1976), pp. 136–69.

3. The pamphlet, published in London by Saunders and Otley (1834), is reprinted as *The Present Crisis: A Letter to a Late Cabinet Minister* in the Knebworth Edition of *Pamphlets and Sketches* (London: Routledge, 1875), pp. 9–48. Citations refer to this edition.

4. Edward Lytton Bulwer, *England and the English* [1833], ed. with an introduction by Standish Meacham (Chicago and London: University of Chicago Press, 1970), p. 33.

5. Ibid., p. 31.

6. Ibid., p. 369

7. Ibid., p. 371.

8. Ibid., p. 52.

9. Ibid., p. 108.

10. Ibid., p. 42.

11. Ibid., pp. 397–98.

12. Ibid., p. 141.

13. For overviews of the period of Italian history between Waterloo (1815) and the Kingdom of Italy (1861), see Denis Mack Smith, *Italy: A Modern History* (Ann Arbor: University of Michigan Press, 1969), pp. 1–26; Stuart Woolf, *A History of Italy 1700–1860: The Social Constraints of Political Change* (1979; London: Routledge, 1991), pp. 227–468; Harry Hearder, *Italy: A Short History* (Cambridge: Cambridge University Press, 1990), pp. 153–97; Christopher Dug-

gan, *A Concise History of Italy* (Cambridge: Cambridge University Press, 1994), pp. 87–142.

14. Woolf, *History of Italy*, pp. 309–12; see also Denis Mack Smith, *Mazzini* (New Haven: Yale University Press, 1994), pp. 5–8.

15. Qtd. in Woolf, *History of Italy*, p. 305.

16. For a discussion of Mazzini's revisions, see Woolf, *History of Italy*, pp. 305–6.

17. Edmund Burke, *Reflections on the Revolution in France* (Garden City, NY: Doubleday, 1973), p. 59.

18. Lytton, *Life of Edward Bulwer*, 2:127.

19. Campbell, *Edward Bulwer-Lytton*, p. 78; Michael Sadleir, *Bulwer: A Panorama* (Boston: Little, Brown, 1931), p. 336.

20. For a treatment of how Bulwer shaped his historical sources in characterizing Rienzi, see Andrew Brown, "Metaphysics and Melodrama: Bulwer's *Rienzi*," *Nineteenth-Century Fiction* 36, no. 3 (December 1981): 261–276. Brown treats in detail Rienzi's metaphysical propensities, which I discuss in comparison to Arbaces' in a longer version of this essay. My focus here, however, is on how Bulwer diminishes Rienzi's claims to be a visionary, particularly in the latter half of the novel.

21. Campbell, *Edward Bulwer-Lytton*, pp. 11–12.

22. Lytton, *Life of Edward Bulwer*, 1:474.

23. Bulwer, *Letter to a Late Cabinet Minister*, p. 27.

24. Ibid., p. 41.

25. Ibid., p. 27.

26. Ibid., p. 45.

27. Allan C. Christensen, "Edward Bulwer, First Baron Lytton of Knebworth, 25 May 1803—18 January 1873," *Nineteenth-Century Fiction* 28, no. 1 (June 1973): 85–86.

28. Bulwer, *Letter to a Late Cabinet Minister*, p. 28.

# The Historical Context of
## *Athens: Its Rise and Fall*

### Catherine Phillips

IN AN ARTICLE ON "LIVING LITERARY CHARACTERS" WRITTEN IN MAY 1831, Letitia Landon advanced the thesis that each era gets the writers appropriate to it. The period of the 1830s she described as an age in which

> people only permit themselves to be entertained while laying the flattering unction to their souls that it is the vehicle of information. . . . We will not allow an author to display his talents merely . . . for honour: we expect that he should have a purpose in this display, and that purpose one of tangible benefit. It is this that makes the excellence of the writer before us. . . . Mr Bulwer is the first novelist who has placed his best reward, and his great aim, in the utility of his writings.[1]

The article appeared in the *New Monthly Magazine*, in which the useful Edward Bulwer was publishing a series of "Conversations with an Ambitious Student in Ill Health," later to be part of a collection of autobiographically influenced fiction entitled *The Student*. In the introduction to that volume, Bulwer alluded to "an historical work, in which I am now, and at different intervals, have, for years, been engaged." The historical work to which he was referring was *Athens: Its Rise and Fall*. When two out of a projected four volumes appeared in 1837, he said that he had not designed the work "for colleges and cloisters, but for the general and miscellaneous public." His plan as stated in the advertisement placed before the table of contents was:

> to combine an elaborate view of her [Athens'] literature, with a complete and impartial account of her political transactions. The two volumes now published bring the reader, in the one branch of my subject, to the supreme administration of Pericles; in the other, to a critical analysis of the tragedies of Sophocles. Two additional volumes

will, I trust, be sufficient to accomplish my task, and close the records of Athens at that period when the annals of the world are merged into the chronicle of the Roman Empire. In these latter volumes, it is my intention to complete the history of the Athenian Drama—to include a survey of the Athenian Philosophy—to describe the Manners, Habits, and Social Life of the People, and to conclude the whole with such a review of the facts and events narrated as may constitute, perhaps, an unprejudiced and intelligible explanation of the *causes* of the Rise and Fall of Athens.[2]

Unknown to Bulwer until 1835, two other men had also seen the need for a history of Greek life and literature accessible to those not classically educated. They were Connop Thirlwall, Bishop of St David's, and George Grote. In June 1835 Thirlwall wrote (in the advertisement to the first edition of his eight-volume history) that he thought it probable that his work

> might fall into the hands of two different classes of readers . . . one consisting of persons who wish to acquire something more than a superficial acquaintance with Greek history, but who have neither leisure nor means to study it for themselves in its original sources; the other of such as have access to the ancient authors, but often feel the need of a guide and an interpreter. The first of these classes is undoubtedly by far the largest [*sic*]; and it is for its satisfaction that the work is principally designed.[3]

Bulwer stated that he became aware of Thirlwall's eight-volume history only after he had submitted the first two of his volumes to the press. As a result of reading Thirlwall's work while his own was being prepared for publication, he decided to delay submitting his third volume; and, when in 1846 Grote's work began to appear, Bulwer gave up all idea of completing his own history.[4] Grote had been writing his volumes since 1822, but his work in Parliament, where he tried to establish the secret ballot, delayed their publication. The first two volumes did not appear until 1846 and the last not till ten years later.

Both Bulwer and Grote wrote with the awareness that their readers examined Greek political history with nineteenth-century political assumptions and sought in it arguments that they applied to contemporary politics. Their work was prompted by William Mitford's five-volume *History of Greece* published between 1794 and 1810, which had dominated British views of the relative merits of Spartan oligarchy and Athenian democracy.[5] Mitford had been encouraged to write his history by Edward Gibbon. He had profound doubts about the viability of democracy, partly because he was working in the midst and immediate aftermath of the French Revolution. His views are suggested by a sentence from his consideration of the reforms of Solon, of whom he remarked that, "having confirmed to the Assembly of the People a power more universally and uncontrolably [*sic*] absolute than any despot upon earth ever did or ever can possess, his great concern was to establish some balancing power, capable in some degree of obviating the evils which a sovereign multitude is ever ready to bring upon itself."[6]

George Grote used the term "democracy" in full recognition of the distinction between the Athenian system with its slaves and contemporary representative government but, as Julius Beloch later asserted, his stance was as partisan as Mitford's had been:

> The Greeks are for Grote no more than disguised Englishmen from the middle of the 19th century. And since the author belonged to the liberals, the Greek democrats are always right and the oligarchs always wrong; Grote's history becomes a glorification of the Athenian democracy. As a reaction against the underestimation of that democracy, which was common down to his time, this was completely justified and useful; but it is just as unhistorical as the opposite conception.[7]

Although Victorian attitudes were also clearly influenced by contemporary politics, the widespread adoption of Grote's history in public schools and universities meant that his preference for Athenian democracy over Spartan oligarchy came to characterize British attitudes to Greek history. Had Bulwer completed his history rather than allowing himself to be deterred, he might have become the writer seen as being important in the change, since he had independently taken much the same political stance as Grote but published his work nine years earlier.

The reforming opinions underlying many passages in *Athens* were expressions of Bulwer's own attitudes; this can be proven by comparing them with his other writings and activities. Bulwer was an aristocratic advocate of the first Reform Bill, entering Parliament in July 1831 with those colors nailed to the mast in his maiden speech. His views are evident in his articles in the *New Monthly Magazine* (where as editor in 1832–33 he has been accused of turning a "slightly Whiggish, literary journal" into a "vigorous radical organ shouting 'Reform' at the top of its lungs")[8] and in correspondence published by his son.[9] It is this practiced political commitment that informs much of Bulwer's history of Athens—where, for example, he remarks of Spartan government:

> The mode of election was curious. The candidates presented them-
> selves successively before the assembly, while certain judges were en-
> closed in an adjacent room where they could hear the clamour of the
> people without seeing the person of the candidate. On him whom they
> adjudged to have been most applauded the election fell. A mode of
> election open to every species of fraud, and justly condemned by Aris-
> totle as frivolous and puerile. Once elected, the senator retained his
> dignity for life: he was even removed from all responsibility to the
> people. . . . I can conceive no elective council less practically good than
> one to which election is for life, and in which power is irresponsible.
> (I:vi)

By way of contrast, in a purple passage, he praises Athens under Solon:

> we see at once the all-accomplished, all-versatile genius of the nation
> [Athens], and we behold in the same glance the effect and the
> cause:—every thing being referred to the people, the people learned
> of every thing to judge. . . . All that can inspire the thought or delight
> the leisure were for the people. Theirs were the portico and the
> school—theirs the theatre, the gardens, and the baths; they were not,
> as in Sparta, the tools of the state—they *were* the state! Lycurgus
> made machines and Solon men. (II:i)

Bulwer was aware, however, of the danger of degenerate democracy and so cautions his readers: "Even democracy had its il-
legal or corrupt form—in OCHLOCRACY or mob rule; for
democracy did not signify the rule of the lower orders alone, but
of all the people—the highest as the lowest." Characteristically,
he was trying to educate his readers as to the most useful comparisons he thought could be drawn from classical history:

> We should remove some very important prejudices from our minds, if
> we could once subscribe to a fact plain in itself, but which the contests
> of modern party have utterly obscured—that in the mere forms of
> their government, the Greek republics cannot fairly be pressed into
> the service of those who in existing times would attest the evils, or
> proclaim the benefits of constitutions purely democratic.

He goes on to point out that the Greek republics were not true
democracies, since they depended on an enslaved working population that freed citizens to spend time on politics. He also notes
that it is impossible for everyone to be involved in the steering of

a state unless that state is as small and compact as a city. These differences between ancient Greece and modern nations lead him to deduce that the ancient republics are

> properly models to us not in the form but the spirit of their legislation. They teach us that patriotism is most promoted by bringing all classes into public and constant intercourse—that intellect is most luxuriant wherever the competition is widest and most unfettered—and that legislators can create no rewards and invent no penalties equal to those which are silently engendered by society itself—while it maintains, elaborated into a system, the desire of glory and the dread of shame. (I:vii).

Bulwer's title, *Athens: Its Rise and Fall,* immediately provokes comparison with Gibbon's *Decline and Fall of the Roman Empire,* although the interruption of Bulwer's work leaves us with only the rise. Bulwer's view of Gibbon was not entirely positive. A remark in one of his "Conversations with an Ambitious Student" points towards improvements over his predecessor in the writing of history that he experimented with in *Athens*: "No man can give us history through a falser medium than Hume and Gibbon have done." Expanding on the point, he adds:

> And this not only from the occasional inaccuracy of their facts, but their general way of viewing facts. Hume tells the history of factions, and Gibbon the history of oligarchies—the People, the People, are altogether omitted by both. The fact is, neither of them had seen enough of the mass of men to feel that history should be something more than a chronicle of dynasties, however wisely chronicled it be: they are fastidious and graceful scholars; their natural leanings are towards the privileged elegances of life: eternally sketching human nature, they give us, perhaps, a skeleton tolerably accurate—it is the flesh and blood they are unable to accomplish: their sympathies are for the courtly—their minds were not robust enough to feel sympathies with the undiademed and unlaurelled tribes: each most pretends to what he most wants—Hume, with his smooth affectation of candour, is never candid—and Gibbon, perpetually philosophizing, is rarely philosophical.[10]

Bulwer's criticism of Gibbon for a lack of philosophy echoed that of Samuel Taylor Coleridge and was by 1831 something of a commonplace. The many passages on the theory and practice of government that he inserted into *Athens* would seem to be his attempt to improve upon this unphilosophical aspect of his predecessor. Of the laws of Solon, for instance, he writes:

> The first law that Solon enacted in his new capacity was bold and decisive. No revolution can ever satisfy a people if it does not lessen their burthens. Poverty disposes men to innovation only because innovation promises relief. Solon therefore applied himself resolutely, and at once, to the great source of dissension between the rich and the poor—namely, the enormous accumulation of debt which had been incurred by the latter, with slavery, the penalty of default.

After describing Solon's methods in canceling debts and repatriating those who had been sold abroad, Bulwer concludes:

> But though (from the necessity of the times) Solon went to this desperate extent of remedy, comparable in our age only to the formal sanction of a national bankruptcy, he rejected with firmness the wild desire of a division of lands. . . . At first, these measures fell short of the popular expectation, excited by the example of Sparta into the hope of an equality of fortunes; but the reaction soon came. . . . Solon was not one of those politicians who vibrate alternately between the popular and the aristocratic principles, imagining that the concession of to-day ought necessarily to father the denial of to-morrow. He knew mankind too deeply not to be aware that there is no statesman whom the populace suspect like the one who commences authority with a bold reform, only to continue it with hesitating expedients. (II:i)

It is an account that resonates with Bulwer's practical experience of British government of the day and that in its sympathies contrasts strikingly with Mitford's.

Bulwer's criticism of Gibbon for a lack of "flesh and blood," however, seems to be the comment of a writer of historical fiction, and his development of techniques by which he could attempt something that he felt was more satisfactory grew, I would suggest, out of his writing of fiction. In a perceptive article, "The Novelist as Historian," James Simmons remarks that "even as late as 1876 the prominent historian Edward A. Freeman noted that . . . the general reader derived his impressions of a past epoch from the historical romances rather than the histories. This readiness of readers to gain their history from romance was further stimulated by the fact that historical instruction [of periods after the classical] had not yet been allotted a place in the curricula of most English schools."[11] He maintains that

> the difference between a historical novel by a Bulwer or a Macfarlane and a more formal history by a Froude or a Macaulay was only one of degree rather than of kind. For all these historians the emphasis fell upon a concept of history as a narration rather than a dissertation.

They represented a reaction against the analytical, abstract, and stylistically "dead" histories of Sharon Turner, Henry Hallam, James Mill, and other professionals. The progression was away from a concept of history as abstract exposition toward an idea of history as fully developed narrative drama.[12]

Clearly true of the historical romances *The Last Days of Pompeii* and *Rienzi* with which Simmons deals, Bulwer's awareness of the importance of narrative in history to make it attractive to his chosen audience is also evident in his statement in the "Advertisement" to *Athens* that

in order . . . to interrupt as little as possible the recital of events, I have endeavoured to confine to the earlier portion of the work, such details of an antiquarian or speculative nature, as . . . may afford to the general reader . . . perhaps a sufficient notion, of the more important scholastic inquiries which have engaged the attention of some of the subtlest minds of Germany and England [and] may also prepare him the better to comprehend the peculiar character and circumstances of the people to whose history he is introduced; and it may be well to warn the more impatient, that it is not till the Second Book that disquisition is abandoned for narrative.

The manuscript of the unpublished third volume shows how fluently Bulwer wrote—there are hardly any revisions. With a cogent articulacy that must have been a considerable asset to a politician, Bulwer orders his material so that the reader is economically provided with those facts that are necessary to make the story most telling at each point.[13]

Simmons notes that "throughout the 1830s and 1840s many Victorian reviewers leveled considerable criticism at [Sir Walter] Scott and his followers (Wm. Harrison Ainsworth and G P R James), objecting both to the lack of any real intellectual substance in their fictions and to the innumerable liberties taken with historical fact." One reviewer in *Blackwood's* stressed that "the writer must take care not to falsify or misrepresent historical personages and events. His obligation is less to the story at hand than to his readers who will be attending to the historical portions of the narrative."[14] This is very much in keeping with Letitia Landon's emphasis on the usefulness expected of writing with which I started. Simmons goes so far as to suggest that the second generation of writers of historical romance, of which he sees Bulwer as the "innovator and foremost exponent," "were not content to go to history for an exciting backdrop nor to portray an age merely through a representation of its costumes, manners, and architecture. The historical novel in their hands became a vehicle for the exegesis of a historical period; an exegesis from the standpoint of a historian, not a romancer."

In his historical romances Bulwer would seem to have tried to be more historically accurate than Walter Scott and Shakespeare cared to be.[15] But there was also another experience that I would suggest helps to explain how Bulwer came to write such strongly historical novels. It was an innovation that, like some scientific inventions, had an element of serendipity to it. Bulwer had come across a biography of Rienzi by a Jesuit, Père de Cerceau, and he compared it with a number of other sources, including an edition by a Signor Zefirino Re, who pointed out in notes some of the inaccuracies in Cerceau's account. Gibbon had followed Cerceau in a number of particulars that give a peculiar shape to this part of the *Decline and Fall*. The early section of the account of Rienzi's ascent to power is predominantly positive, but the description of his descent leads to an incriminating devaluation of his personality that is puzzling, a weakness that would have struck a writer like Bulwer as inconsistent drawing of character.

In the 1835 preface to the first edition of *Rienzi*, Bulwer notes that "having had occasion to read the original authorities from which modern historians have drawn their accounts of the life of Rienzi, I was led to believe that a very remarkable man had been superficially judged, and a very important period crudely examined. And this belief was sufficiently strong to induce me at first to meditate a more serious work upon the life and times of Rienzi." Even after he abandoned the historical biography for a historical romance, he regarded the completion of the volumes, he said, as a kind of duty, a remark that shows his goal of achieving "historical" faithfulness rather than fanciful "romance."

Bulwer's appendices, devoted to analysis of the facts that he could glean about Rienzi, show the techniques that we find in *Athens*: a reasoning through of a sequence of incidents to the most likely explanations as to why they happened. He attributes, for example, the refusal of the people to support Rienzi against the impending oppression of the Count of Minorbino to the fact that Rienzi was excommunicated:

> This strange apathy the modern historians [Gibbon and Sismondi] have not accounted for, yet the principal cause was obvious—Rienzi was excommunicated! In stating the fact, these writers have seemed to think that excommunication in Rome, in the fourteenth century, produced no effect!—the effect it did produce I have endeavoured in these pages to convey.

The causes of the second fall and final murder of Rienzi are equally misstated by modern narrators. It was from no fault of his—no injustice, no cruelty, no extravagance [all charges that Gibbon makes of him] . . . *it was from a gabelle on wine and salt that he fell*. To preserve Rome from the tyrants it was necessary to maintain an armed force; to pay the force a tax was necessary; the tax was imposed—and the multitude joined with the tyrants, and their cry was, "Perish the traitor *who has made the gabelle!*" (Appendix I)

There does not seem to be anything in the manuscripts or extant letters that tells us explicitly the extent to which Bulwer's contemporary historical work on *Rienzi* assisted that on *Athens* and how that on *Athens* developed the techniques in *Rienzi* though they clearly share common features. In both it is easy to see the fruits of his own experience of Parliament, and in combining that political experience with the novelist's "warmer" interest in human beings, Bulwer believed that he had found, as the preface of 1848 to *Rienzi* suggests, the formula for his success:

From the time of its first appearance, "Rienzi" has had the good fortune to rank high amongst my most popular works—though its interest is rather drawn from a faithful narration of historical facts, than from the inventions of fancy. And the success of this experiment confirms me in my belief, that the true mode of employing history in the service of romance, is to study diligently the materials *as* history; conform to such views of the facts as the Author would adopt, if he related them in the dry character of historian; and obtain that warmer interest which fiction bestows, by tracing the causes of the facts in the characters and emotions of the personages of the time. The events of his work are thus already shaped to his hand—the characters already created—what remains for him, is the inner, not outer, history of man—the chronicle of the human heart; and it is by this that he introduces a new harmony between character and event, and adds the completer solution of what is actual and true, by those speculations of what is natural and probable, which are out of the province of history, but belong especially to the philosophy of romance.

Although Bulwer was convinced that this was the source of his success and the popularity of *Rienzi* led him to follow the same historical method in *The Last of the Barons* and *Harold*, Andrew Sanders points out that the approach, which deliberately restricts the imaginative fancy in his novels, limits his exploration of human psychology.[16] This would explain why Bulwer could be so popular to an epoch that sought from his books palatable history, and rather less attractive to a later one with a keen interest in the subconscious. The hybrid technique undoubtedly enlivens an avowedly historical piece like *Athens,* where it produces an imaginative contextualizing of facts (though for an era like ours, it causes the opposite problem by providing romanticized history when we expect from books, if not from television, more critical and factual scholarship).

When, for example, we compare Thirlwall's and Bulwer's accounts of the participation of Themistocles and the Athenians in the battle of Salamis, we can see the vividness of Bulwer's approach. Following Herodotus, Thirlwall attributes the abandoning of Athens by the majority of its people to Themistocles' interpretation of an oracle. The oracle declared that the Athenians would find safety from Xerxes in wooden walls, and Themistocles interpreted the walls to be those of the Athenian ships. Like Herodotus, Thirlwall reports the oracle in some detail and then summarizes the debate in which the other Greek states were persuaded to vote in favor of staying at Salamis and fighting at sea there:

> Adeimantus still vehemently opposed his [Themistocles'] proposition, and is said even to have thrown out an ungenerous taunt against Themistocles and Athens: *a man who had no country was not entitled to a vote.* Themistocles sternly repelled the insult, and then turning to Eurybiades, declared that the Athenians were resolved, if their allies persisted in their design, not to fall a useless sacrifice, but to take their families and fortunes on board and sail away to the rich land of Siris in the South of Italy, where a colony of Ionians had already founded a flourishing city. This threat determined Eurybiades, or, if he had been before convinced, furnished him with a decent plea for changing his plan. His authority or influence decided the resolution of the council.[17]

By way of contrast, Bulwer dramatizes the exchange between Adimantus [*sic*] and Themistocles and between Themistocles and Eurybiades, and he does not hesitate to invent dialogues revelatory of the relationship among the three men:

> "It becomes you," said Adimantus, scornfully, alluding to the capture of Athens, "it becomes you to be silent, and not to advise us to desert our country;—you, who no longer have a country to defend! Eurybiades can only be influenced by Themistocles when Themistocles has once more a city to represent."
>
> "Wretch!" replied Themistocles, sternly, "we have indeed left our walls and houses—preferring freedom to those inanimate posses-

sions—but know, that the Athenians still possess a country and a city, greater and more formidable than yours, well provided with stores and men, which none of the Greeks will be able to resist:—our ships are our country and our city."

"If," he added, once more addressing the Spartan chief [Eurybiades], "if you continue here you will demand our eternal gratitude:—fly, and you are the destroyers of Greece. In this war the last and sole resource of the Athenians is their fleet:—reject my remonstrances, and I warn you that at once we will take our families on board, and sail to that Siris, on the Italian shores, which of old is said to have belonged to us, and in which, if the oracle be trusted, we ought to found a city. Deprived of us, you will remember my words." (III:vii)

The writing of a history such as *Athens* required, in addition to the teasing out of known actions by famous historical figures, the vivifying of common attitudes and experience. Although he was to use the technique more in later historical romances, Bulwer made some use of it in *Athens*, often through anonymous observers. One example is the traveler who sees the mine at Sunion that so crucially enabled Themistocles and the Athenians to build up their navy:

Around the country by the ancient Thoricus, on the road from the modern Kerratia to the Cape of Sunium, heaps of scoriae indicate to the traveller that he is in the neighbourhood of the once celebrated silver mines of Laurion; he passes through pines and woodlands—he notices the indented tracks of wheels which two thousand years have not effaced from the soil—he discovers the ancient shafts of the mines, and pauses before the foundations of a large circular tower and the extensive remains of the castles which fortified the neighbouring town. A little farther, and still passing amongst mine-banks and hillocks of scoriae, he beholds upon Cape Colonna the fourteen existent columns of the Temple of Minerva Sunias. In this country, to which the old name is still attached, is to be found a principal cause of the renown and the reverses of Athens,—of the victory of Salamis,—of the expedition to Sicily. (III:iii)

This technique focuses factual description through a human consciousness that mediates it for the reader. Bulwer may have learnt the trick from writing *The Last Days of Pompeii*, for which he threw aside the writing of *Rienzi* when he moved from Rome to Naples in 1832. He explained that *The Last Days* "required more than *Rienzi* the advantage of residence within reach of the scenes described." "The city," he wrote, "whose fate supplied me with so superb and awful a catastrophe, supplied easily from the first survey of its remains, the characters most suited to the subject and the scene." Each element of the period prompted Bulwer, according to his preface, to invent an appropriate character to reveal it, from "the half-Grecian colony of Hercules, mingling with the manners of Italy," and the "early struggles of Christianity" to "the trade of Pompeii with Alexandria." An acquaintance's casual observation that the blind would be most favored in the "utter darkness which accompanied the first recorded eruption of Vesuvius" led him to make Nydia, one of the central characters, a blind girl. This was another way of approaching a historical subject—to take a period and invent characters to illustrate it—and in this case the combination produced a work whose success has endured.

Bulwer's *Athens,* in contrast, never became as popular as Grote's history. Abandoned as redundant by its author, less overtly scholarly than Thirlwall's and Grote's accounts with their multiple volumes, their notes in Greek, and their many maps, *Athens* nevertheless shows Bulwer's inventiveness in yet another field. He grasped the need for a counterbalance to Mitford's views and saw the opportunity of a readership eager for accessible education, one for whom his work in Parliament affirmed a genuine concern.

Bulwer abandoned his work at what were, in the eyes of the Victorians, the high points of Greek achievement. The history as he left it to that audience ends with an analysis of Sophocles' plays that includes a generous selection of passages translated from them, and he concludes astutely that this intellectual contribution is the lasting glory of Greece. But his discarding of *Athens* before he embarked on study of the more sociological aspects of its decline may suggest that ultimately it was narrative that he most liked constructing. The manuscript of the third volume contains mostly narrative and has only a few notes on social relations, including a rather uneasy account of Uranian conventions and the legal position of women. There is also less on Greek philosophy than Bulwer evidently originally intended to provide. History was clearly useful to him when it provided a large structure within which he could modulate the ebb and flow of tension, as in the opening chapter of *Rienzi* with its dramatic fight and promise of consequences to be explored later. But the constant fine distinctions of Thirlwall and Grote and the amount of research necessary for each paragraph may ultimately have decided him against trying to compete in the field of pure history.

For Bulwer, history was a constructed narrative and, as his preface to *Rienzi* makes clear, the difference between it and the historical romance lay only in more faithful attention to historical fact. That the innovative techniques used in *Rienzi* and *The Last Days of Pompeii* were simultaneously being developed in *Athens: Its Rise and Fall* suggests how important it is that we be aware of Bulwer's purely historical work in our assessments of his historical fiction. Along with useful information and accurate analysis, his aim in all was to convey, much as television does today, vivid ideas of the past to a wide audience.

## NOTES

1. [Letitia Landon], "Edward Lytton Bulwer," in the series "Living Literary Characters," *New Monthly Magazine* 31 (May 1831): 437.

2. As in the case of Bulwer's novels, all references to *Athens: Its Rise and Fall* are to the Knebworth edition. A new edition of *Athens: Its Rise and Fall*, ed. Oswyn Murray, is scheduled to be published by Routledge in 2004.

3. Connop Thirlwall, D.D., Bishop of St David's, *The History of Greece*, 8 vols. (London: Longman, Brown, Green and Longmans, and John Taylor, 1845), 1:v.

4. "When the manuscript of the present unfinished work was already in the hands of its publishers, the appearance of Mr. Thirlwall's 'History of Greece' induced the Author of 'Athens' to suspend his labours; and he finally abandoned them in consequence of Mr. Grote's great work upon the same subject" (Preface to Knebworth edition of *Athens: Its Rise and Fall*).

5. "In his Preface to that work [his History of Greece], Mr. Grote himself had frankly declared, 'If my early friend Dr. Thirlwall's "History of Greece," had appeared a few years sooner, I should probably never have conceived the design of the present work at all; I should certainly not have been prompted to the task by any deficiencies such as those which I felt and regretted in Mitford.' But it was from a strong sense of those deficiencies that Lord Lytton had commenced his narrative of Athenian history; and, therefore, he had no motive to continue it when the historical method he had employed was being exhaustively applied by Mr. Grote to the same field of historical research" (preface to Knebworth edition of *Athens: Its Rise and Fall*).

6. William Mitford, *The History of Greece*, 5 vols. (London: T. Wright, 1794–1810), 1: 257.

7. Quoted by Mortimer Chambers from his translation of Julius Beloch, *Griechische Geschichte* (Strasbourg, 1912), in his article, "George Grote's 'History of Greece,'" in *George Grote Reconsidered*, ed. William M. Calder III and Stephen Trzaskoma (Hildesheim: Weidmann, 1996), pp.19–20.

8. Mary Ruth Hillier, introduction to *New Monthly Magazine*, in *The Wellesley Index to Victorian Periodicals*, (London: Routledge and Kegan Paul, 1979), 3:166.

9. See, for example, letters to Lord John Russell on social reform and on the Reform Bill in *Speeches of Edward Lord Lytton, with Some of his Political*

*Writings and a Prefatory Memoir by his Son*, 2 vols. (Edinburgh and London: William Blackwood and Sons, 1874), 1:xxxi–xxxii, 1–6.

10. "Conversations with an Ambitious Student in Ill Health: Conversation the Fifth," *New Monthly Magazine* 31 (April 1831): 301.

11. James Simmons, "The Novelist as Historian: An Unexplored Tract of Victorian Historiography," *Victorian Studies* 19, no. 3 (March 1971): 295.

12. Ibid., p. 298.

13. The manuscript of most of the third volume is in the Hertford County Record Office, D/EK W12.

14. Simmons, "Novelist as Historian," p. 298.

15. See, for example, Andrew Sanders, introduction and "The New Seriousness: Edward Bulwer-Lytton's *Harold*," in *The Victorian Historical Novel, 1840–1880* (London: Macmillan, 1978), pp. 1–31, 47–67.

16. Ibid., pp. 49–51.

17. Thirlwall, *History of Greece*, 2:335.

# Rosina Bulwer Lytton: Irish Beauty, Satirist, Tormented Victorian Wife, 1802–1882

## Lord Cobbold

"THE FIRST MISTAKE I MADE," ROSINA WROTE IN HER UNFINISHED autobiography, "was being born at all." Certainly her tormented and controversial life has suggested to many that in this judgment at least she was correct. But that would be unfair. Rosina had great beauty, sparkling wit, and an independent spirit at a time when ladies were expected to know their place and when men ruled supreme in custom and in law. She deserved to live, and it is time for her life to be reviewed dispassionately from the perspective of a very different age.

Rosina Anne Doyle Wheeler was born on 2 November 1802 in a rambling Irish country house in County Tipperary. She had an elder sister, Henrietta, and the two girls were the only surviving children of Francis Massy Wheeler and Anna Doyle Wheeler. Anna Wheeler was a considerable beauty and very clever. She was also imbued with "democratic and levelling principles." Her husband was a hunting squire, happiest with a riding whip or whiskey bottle in his hand. When Rosina was 10, Anna Wheeler left her husband and set sail for Guernsey with her two daughters. On the way the ship foundered off the Welsh coast, but happily all managed to reach Milford Haven in an open boat. Later they continued to Guernsey and took up residence with Anna Wheeler's uncle, who was governor of the island. For four happy years the girls lived a life of luxury with their eccentric great-uncle.

French visitors, a French governess, and trips to Paris broadened the horizons of the two sisters. Rosina developed "to a high pitch of perfection" the art of mimicry. "I was endowed," she writes, "with a terribly keen sense of the ridiculous, and once knowing a person's peculiarities, I could not only imitate their face, voice, and gestures, but could extemporise whole scenes of adventures for them, and furnish dialogues of what they would have said had they been placed in such circumstances."[1]

The family left Guernsey when Rosina was fourteen. The next four years were divided between school in Kensington and visits to her mother at Caen in Normandy, where Anna Wheeler had become "Goddess of Reason" to a group of radical free thinkers. (In 1825 Anna Wheeler together with William Thompson published an important contribution to the early history of feminism, *Appeal of One Half of the Human Race, Women, Against the Pretensions of the Other Half, Men.*)

At eighteen, Rosina was living in London with her great-uncle, now retired from Guernsey, and beginning her entrée to London society. To her in her early twenties have been ascribed "most of the virtues and many of the amiable weaknesses peculiar to her nationality. She was, that is to say, warm hearted, sensitive, and generous to a fault, of an intensely passionate and highly strung organisation, proud, no doubt, possibly too apt to feel keenly neglect or coldness, but ever ready to forgive even the most unpardonable offences." At the time of her introduction into London society she was "one of the most, if not *the* most beautiful girl that was ever seen" in the words of Edmund Byng, a contemporary. Her biographer describes her as tall with an exquisite complexion, dark hair, and bright grey—or, as she called them, green—eyes, sparkling and changing color with every emotion. Her nose was finely chiseled, her eyebrows delicately penciled, her forehead broad and high, her mouth small, her teeth perfect, and her chin somewhat square and determined. She had a remarkably fine figure, bust, and arms, and small feet. Much later a friend describes her as "just past her prime, but gloriously beautiful still, and she retained her beauty to old age."[2]

This beautiful and vivacious girl was much in demand by society and literary hostesses. Among her early encounters was Lady Caroline Lamb, who befriended her. In 1825 at a literary gathering she first met Edward Bulwer in the company of his mother. Her description of this meeting, written much later and disputed by Edward in his account, is nevertheless amusing and perhaps gives clues to the troubles that lay ahead. Having described his mother's appearance in deprecating detail, Rosina writes,

> It is proverbial *que les extrêmes se touchent*; . . . for if this lady was the incarnation of the dowdy and the out-of-fashion, her son, upon whom she leant . . . was altogether as antipodical an impersonation

of modes and fashions and *chics* considerably in advance of their age.
. . . His cobweb cambric shirt-front was a triumph of lace and embroi-
dery, a combination never seen in this country till six or seven years
later, except on babies' frocks. Studs, too, except in racing stables,
were then non est; but a perfect galaxy glittered along the milky way
down the centre of this fairy-like *lingerie*. His hair, which was really
golden, glitteringly golden, and abundant, he wore literally in long
ringlets, that almost reached his shoulders.[3]

Bulwer, as a Cambridge undergraduate, had been captivated by
the predatory charms of Caroline Lamb, and it had amused her
to dally with his innocence. That Bulwer's love for Caroline had
been "nine-tenths a hunger for excitement, flattery and admiration," writes one of his biographers, "and only one-tenth the
emotion which men call love, could hardly have been evident to
ignorant but complacent youth. And it is not too much to say
that the young Bulwer came to Brocket ready dressed for sacrifice."[4] But Bulwer's sacrifice at Caroline's altar was nothing to
the torment that was to follow his meeting with her protegée,
Rosina. Encouraged by Caroline Lamb, their romance blossomed
amongst the bluebells and buttercups of Brocket in the summer
of 1826.

Edward's mother, Mrs. Bulwer-Lytton, charmed initially by
Rosina's beauty, turned against her when their engagement was
proposed. Influenced no doubt by the radical views of Rosina's
mother, Anna Wheeler, and by her limited inheritance, Mrs.
Bulwer-Lytton opposed the marriage in spite of repeated entreat-
ies from her son. After two postponements the couple were finally
married at St. James's Piccadilly on 29 August 1827. Rosina was
twenty-five and six months older than Edward.

So began one of history's most disastrous unions between man
and woman. They set up house in Oxfordshire. Edward, cut off
financially by his mother, determined to write for his living. And
it was not long before he was leaving the family home for London
for literary inspiration and, it seems, alternative distractions. It
is tempting from a modern perspective to suspect a physical problem. It is easy to see Rosina mocking this sensitive and egocentric
young man. Her sense of fun and her talent for mimicry can so
easily have been used at delicate moments, wounding pride instead of introducing laughter.

The first serious problem was Edward's insistence that their
first child, Emily, should be put out to foster parents. He did not
want his wife's time "to be taken up by any damned child." His

first successful novel, *Pelham*, had just been published, and he was in much demand in London salons. Rosina was not by nature maternal; but the wrench of a first-born child from a mother's breast is a traumatic event. While she accepted her fate at the time, it was a wound that never healed, the memory of which fired her rancor increasingly in the years to come.

Edward's absences from their Oxfordshire home increased, and in the summer of 1829 it was decided to move to London and a new home at 36 Hertford Street. Life at Hertford Street was a social whirl. "Entertaining was lavish and continuous." Disraeli, a regular visitor, describes one such evening in a letter: "Our host, whatever may be his situation, was more sumptuous and fantastic than ever. Mrs Bulwer was a blaze of jewels and looked like Juno; only instead of a peacock she had a dog in her lap called Fairy."[5] Rosina's dogs were to take the place of children in her affections.

To support life on this scale, Bulwer worked "with an almost savage industry." During the next "three tearing, raging years of social climbing, domestic squabbling, political wire-pulling, parliamentary work, editing and pamphleteering, he produced three more novels, a long satirical poem and, most impressive of all, that remarkable piece of constructive research *England and the English*."[6] He was also elected to the Reform Parliament as Liberal member for St. Ives. Ironically it was Rosina's small Irish property that Bulwer used as qualification for his first seat in Parliament.

A son, Robert, was born in November 1831. This time—according to Mary Greene, Rosina's Irish friend and early mentor, who was to play an important role in the battles to come—it was Rosina who did not wish to nurse the child; it

> was not an employment for a lady of fashion, besides . . . she did not even love her children. However, he was nursed in the top of the house, where he was very little seen or known, and poor little Emily had been long before sent off to a school where she was as miserable as a creature of her age (4) could be, and neither father nor mother knew anything about her; and many of their most intimate acquaintance did not know there was such a child in the world.[7]

To what extent these comments, written much later, were influenced by subsequent events is impossible to say, but it is clear that neither Rosina nor Edward was suited to parenthood, and for whatever remorse Rosina may later have suffered, she was

Rosina Bulwer Lytton with lapdog. Courtesy of Knebworth House.

herself in large part to blame. "The attitude of Bulwer and Rosina toward these helpless unfortunates," writes Michael Sadleir, "cannot by any sophistry be defended. But it can to some extent be understood, . . . by the rather vulgar flippancy toward child-bearing, parental responsibility and propagation generally which . . . was regarded as chic by the bright young people of the eighteen-twenties."[8]

In September 1833 Edward and Rosina decided to winter in Switzerland and Italy. Pressure in the household had reached bursting point. "To money troubles, to uneasy ambitions, and to the various other distractions of an increasingly distracted household, was now added a wife's jealousy of another woman."[9] Far from being an escape from Bulwer's ostentatious philandering, the journey was doomed by his decision (not shared with his wife) to meet the lady in question and her complacent husband on the Channel ferry and to spend their days in Paris à quatre. This episode went a long way to destroy Rosina's hitherto staunch affection for her husband and undoubtedly opened the door to an indiscretion of her own when they reached Naples. Here, while Bulwer busied himself with his new Pompeii project, Rosina found distraction in the gallant attentions of a Neapolitan prince. Some time after, Rosina wrote in her diary: "Played on the guitar for an hour, and sang many songs I had heard or dreamt. . . . Ah! Naples, dear Naples, you are the *only* place in which I ever *felt* young (for I did not do so as a child), and what was the result? did I commit more follies? No. Mais qui vit sans folie n'est pas si sage qu'il pense."

When Edward realized what was going on, he flew into a passion and subjected his wife to serious physical violence and an immediate return to England. Once at home, tempers remained severely strained. On one occasion Bulwer seized a carving knife and rushed upon his wife. As her maid, a witness, later wrote in a sworn affidavit, Rosina cried out and he "dropped the knife, and springing on her like a Tiger, made his teeth meet in her left cheek, until her screams brought the men servants back into the Dining Room."[10] After this incident Rosina left and stayed with Mary Greene, who was looking after Emily in Hounslow. Attempts at reconciliation were made, including an offer by Mrs. Bulwer-Lytton, who had become reconciled to the marriage, to visit her in the country—Rosina's only recorded visit to Knebworth after marriage. The visit was not a success. There were more quarrels, and Rosina, Mary Greene, Emily, Robert, his nurse, and a cook-maid moved to lodgings in Gloucester. Again there was a reconciliation. The family moved back to a house in Acton, while Bulwer moved into the Albany.

Then came the incident that caused the final break. Rosina's account, strongly disputed by her husband, is that Bulwer had promised to dine with her at Acton but had sent a late note to say that he was ill and could not come. Rosina, believing the truth of the excuse, decided to visit him in London with "medicines and other comforts." She arrived about 11 P.M. When Bulwer opened the door in his dressing gown, she saw two cups of tea on the table and a young lady "making a precipitate retreat into the bedroom."[11]

Bulwer demanded a formal separation. The deed of separation was signed on 19 April 1836 after less than nine years of marriage. Rosina was thirty-three. Under the deed, Rosina was to receive £400 a year for herself and £50 each for care of the children. Rosina and the children left for Ireland, where they lodged with Mary Greene's sister near Dublin.

From 1839 to 1847 Rosina lived abroad in Paris, Florence, and Geneva. She had no communication with her children. Emily meanwhile had been dispatched to Germany, where she was desperately unhappy. Robert was at boarding school. Bulwer saw little of them. He lived with another woman and had a second family. His career was flourishing. He had moved to Knebworth after his mother's death in 1844.

Exasperated by the pittance on which she was expected to live while he was now so prosperous, Rosina returned to England determined to obtain a more generous allowance. This Bulwer was prepared to agree to but only if she would agree to a divorce. And that was only possible if Rosina would admit to infidelity but refrain from producing evidence in public of his own indiscretions. Rosina refused.

In 1848 she learned that Emily was living in a seedy boarding house in Brompton. Weak and neglected, she had contracted typhoid. Mary Greene was out of favor with Bulwer, and Emily "was shut up with a strange old nurse for some days, and only when the doctor came did she see anyone else."[12] Rosina's and Mary Greene's account of Emily's last tragic hours differ sharply. Rosina took a room in the same lodging house and, advised by the doctor not to make herself known to the delirious child for fear of worsening her condition, sat on the stairs all night listening to her suffering but, she insists, never making herself known to the child. Next morning Bulwer, hearing of her presence, told the doctors to remove her from the house. Emily died later that day.

Rosina was of course accused of causing her daughter's death. She in turn accused Bulwer of neglect. The innocent victim was nineteen years old. Emily's tragic death further embittered the relationship.

In 1855 Rosina moved to Taunton, where she lived for many years in the Giles Castle Hotel in the friendly care of its owner, Mrs Clarke. Provocations on both sides continued, culminating in the most spectacular sequence of events in the whole sorry saga. Rosina was in debt and struggling to live on her meager allowance. Bulwer was now rich, and in 1858 he was appointed Colonial Secretary in Lord Derby's government. Acceptance of this office necessitated a vote of approval by the electors of Hertford, and Bulwer was to attend a public meeting to secure confirmation of his nomination. Rosina decided to travel to Hertford and expose her husband's conduct on the hustings. Together with Mrs. Clarke, she traveled overnight from Taunton and arrived at five in the morning in Hertford.

By seven she had arranged for placards she had had printed to be posted up all over town inviting the people of Hertford to meet her at noon. The nomination in fact took place at eleven, and Bulwer had made his speech and had been nominated by the time Rosina arrived. In her own words:

> The moment I drove into the field the mob began to cheer; . . . I instantly alighted, and walked over calmly and deliberately to the hustings, just putting the crowd aside with my fan, and saying, "My good people, make way for your member's wife." They then began to cheer and cry, "Silence for Lady Lytton!" Sir Liar's [Bulwer's] head fell literally as if he had been shot; . . . I then said, in a loud, calm, and stern voice, "Sir Edward Bulwer Lytton . . . it is to you, in the first instance, that I address myself. In the steps your cruelty and your meanness have driven me into taking this day, I wish you to hear every word I have to say; refute them if you can; deny them if you dare!" Then turning to the crowd, I said, "Men of Herts! if you have the hearts of men, hear me!" "We will. God bless you! Speak out!" Here Sir Liar, with his hands before his face, made a rush from the hustings.[13]

Rosina then made a long speech detailing all her complaints against her husband. "How can the people of England submit to have such a man at the head of the Colonies, who ought to have been in the Colonies as a transport long ago." At the end she was cheered and feted.

Four days later she received a visit in Taunton from Hale Thomson, a sixty-year-old medical practitioner, who had been sent by Bulwer to ascertain his wife's mental condition. Under the law at the time, all that was needed was two signatures from "qualified" medical men for a husband to have his wife certified as insane and locked up in an institution. Bulwer, exasperated by the Hertford affair, determined to have Rosina restrained. But Thomson, after a seven-hour interview, pronounced that he had "never found a clearer head, or a more logical mind, or sounder flesh and blood, than Lady Lytton's."[14] This he reported to her husband. But Bulwer's mind was made up.

Rosina offered in writing to end her campaign if he would agree to pay all her debts (about £2,500) and increase her allowance to £500 a year. Ten days after Thomson's visit, Rosina decided to go to London once again to press her case. Her grandson, Victor, describes what then occurred:

> When she arrived at Mr Hale Thomson's house by appointment in the afternoon of June 23, Lady Lytton was informed that arrangements had been made for her removal to Inverness Lodge as a person of unsound mind, on the medical certificate of Mr Thomson and Mr Ross. She naturally protested vehemently against such action, but, since the requirements of the law had been complied with, she was powerless to resist and therefore drove off quietly with Dr Gardiner Hill to his Home at Brentford. . . . Although there was nothing harsh, cruel, or tyrannical about Lady Lytton's treatment at Inverness Lodge, it was an act of supreme unwisdom on her husband's part to send her there.[15]

When news spread of her incarceration, there was a public outcry. The people of Taunton threatened to march to London. The *Daily Telegraph*, the *Somerset Gazette*, and the *Hertfordshire Gazette* demanded a public inquiry. It is said Queen Victoria intervened with the prime minister, Lord Derby. Under this pressure, Bulwer backed down. Rosina was released on 17 July after twenty-four days. Bulwer accepted her demands for settlement of her debts and raised her allowance to £500.

Robert, now a junior diplomat at the Hague, offered to take his mother to France for a break and a chance of reconciliation. Here it might be hoped that the story could have had a happy ending. Rosina was fifty-five, her son Robert twenty-six. He had witnessed the Hertford incident, the first time he had seen his mother for twenty years. This was an opportunity to bury the past. Mother and son and a friend of Rosina's traveled via Paris to Bordeaux. All started well, with Rosina expressing herself entirely happy and satisfied, assuring her son that "in the sunshine of his presence all the shadows of her life had melted away."[16] Sadly it was not to last. Robert's place "between Scylla and Charibdis" proved untenable. Daily letters from his father and the deluge of grievances from his mother kept the old wounds open. Tempers flared again, and Robert gave up the cause and left for Paris. Rosina called on him there on her way home. They never saw each other again. It was 1858.

Rosina returned to Taunton. In 1866 Bulwer was elevated to the peerage. Rosina's resentment still burnt within her. That year she put together a manuscript of various biographical writings and hysterical diatribes against her husband with a view to possible publication, calling it "My Blighted Life." But she decided wisely not to publish and withdrew the manuscript. Bulwer died in 1873, after which Robert increased her allowance by £200.

One final disaster was to occur. In 1880, when Robert returned from his four years as Viceroy of India, "A Blighted Life" was published, and the whole story was once again thrown into the public arena. Rosina insisted that publication had been without her consent from an illicit copy of the manuscript made fourteen years before. Robert froze her allowance, but then accepted her story and reinstated it.

Rosina's last years were spent at a small house, "Glenômera," in Upper Sydenham. Louisa Devey, her friend in later life, writes: "Although in her eightieth year, she possessed to the last the remains of a beauty that had been so noted in her youth. Neither her general tone nor manners had deteriorated through adversity . . . she was full of anecdote and wit."[17] She died on 12 March 1882 and was buried in the churchyard of St. John the Evangelist, Shirley, near Croydon, in an unmarked grave. No member of her family attended her funeral. In vain had she requested in her will for the following quotation from Isaiah to be placed on her tombstone:

> The Lord shall give thee rest from thy sorrow, and from thy fear, and from the hard bondage wherein thou wast made to serve. (Is. 14:3)

Looking back on this extraordinary story after more than a century, what is to be made of it? It is easy to see why Bulwer's son and grandchildren took his side and shunned the memory of a bitter and unreasonable woman. It is fair also to respect Bulwer for his outstanding success in literature and politics, in spite of the continuous provocation from an ever-present tormentor. But in this modern age, when the rights of women have long since been taken for granted, we can more easily find sympathy for the much wronged wife. That Edward and Rosina were incompatible; that the marriage in modern times would have ended rapidly in divorce; that Emily's life would now have been saved is obvious to us. But it is more difficult to imagine just how painful and degrading it must have been to be deceived, abused, and rejected in an age when all power was in the hands of man.

Rosina was a proud, beautiful, talented, determined, and independent soul. In adversity she published thirteen novels and countless articles and pamphlets. She played the guitar, she sang, and she stood on a platform and challenged the men of Herts. Cheated she was and obsessed she became. And as she grew older, her obsession lost its reason and all humor. But true she was to herself and to her principles. In the long struggle for women's rights, Rosina's mother, Anna Wheeler, was an early prophet— the "Goddess of Reason." Rosina was a victim, but by her resistance, by her cry for justice from the hustings, and by the outcry for her release from incarceration, she played her part. It was left to her granddaughter, Constance Lytton, to continue the fight and see it won.

## POSTSCRIPT

On Sunday 12 March 1995, the 113th anniversary of Rosina Bulwer Lytton's death, her family placed a stone on her grave at the Church of St. John the Evangelist, Shirley, bearing the quotation from Isaiah that she had requested in her will. She had written another poetic epitaph for herself too:

*My Epitaph*
*by Lady Lytton*

Long has been the way, and very dreary,
With heavy clouds of blackest wrongs o'ercast;
But the pilgrim, spent and weary,
Gladly sees the goal at last

When Death o'erthrows the glass of time,
He scatters all its sands of sorrow;
And the freed soul doth upward climb
To welcome God's eternal morrow

## NOTES

1. Rosina's autobiographical notes, printed in Louisa Devey, *Life of Rosina, Lady Lytton: A Vindication* (London: Sonnenschein, 1887), p. 29.

2. Devey, *Life of Rosina, Lady Lytton*, pp. 71, 398, 72, 399.

3. Ibid., p. 50.

4. Michael Sadleir, *Bulwer and His Wife: A Panorama 1803–1836* (London: Constable and Co., 1933), p. 55.

5. *Lord Beaconsfield's Correspondence with His Sister 1832–1852*, ed. Ralph Disraeli (London: John Murray, 1886), pp. 3–4.

6. Sadleir, *Bulwer and His Wife*, p. 152.

7. Mary Greene, manuscript recollections, Knebworth Archives typescript, p. 20.

8. Sadleir, *Bulwer and His Wife*, p. 163.

9. Ibid., p. 169.

10. Devey, *Life of Rosina, Lady Lytton*, p. 79.

11. Ibid., p. 111.

12. Greene MS, p. 193.

13. Rosina's account, printed in Devey, *Life of Rosina, Lady Lytton*, p. 283.

14. Ibid., p. 292.

15. Second Earl of Lytton, *The Life of Edward Bulwer, First Lord Lytton*, 2 vols. (London: Macmillan, 1913), 2:273.

16. Ibid., 2:278.

17. Devey, *Life of Rosina, Lady Lytton*, p. 389.

# Writing for Revenge:
# The Battle of the Books of Edward and Rosina Bulwer Lytton

## Marie Mulvey-Roberts

> Lady Craven then wrote books without the slightest allusion
> to her husband or his, if possible, more infamous family, but
> merely to make herself a little independent in circumstances,
> but this was precisely what his mean cruelty, and calculating
> persecution most objected to, most dreaded, because pecuni-
> ary independence is power. . . . So Sir August resorts to crush
> his wife's books.
>
> —Rosina Bulwer Lytton, *Memoirs of a Muscovite*

THE INTERACTION BETWEEN LIFE AND FICTION WAS A RECURRING
theme in the fraught marriage of the novelists Edward and Rosina Bulwer Lytton. Their troubled relationship erupted into a
conflict that was waged on many fronts: legal action, public decla-
mation, and private protest. Whenever the feud invaded their literary productions, it aggravated existing misrepresentations of
each warring party towards the other. The textual combat, which
stoked real-life dramas whilst displacing tensions between the estranged husband and wife, soon took on a life of its own.

This "battle of the books"[1] marks an important site in the
growing public dialogue of confrontation between the sexes that
would eventually lead to reforms granting greater autonomy for
married women.[2] Rosina's blatant fictionalization of the failure
of her marriage to a doyen of the highest literary circles was in
the vanguard of female resistance to the male-dominated writing
establishment. Frustratingly for her, Edward was honored and
eventually ennobled for his contribution to literature, while she
remained a relatively minor writer struggling to survive in the
literary marketplace. Rosina persistently blamed her failure to
gain both recognition and remuneration on her husband and his
literary coterie.

Was she a victim of a conspiracy orchestrated by him, or was she suffering from delusions?[3] With her Wildean wit and Swiftian satire, the Irish-born Rosina took women's writing into dangerous new territory, transgressing the prescribed boundaries of femininity, particularly in regard to the duty expected of a Victorian wife. Although Bulwer never succeeded in snatching the pen out of her hand, her punishment, like that of his eponymous heroine Lucretia, was incarceration in a lunatic asylum in 1858.

This move to silence Rosina was the culmination of the mutual antagonism between husband and wife. This had reached an impasse in 1834 during a trip to Naples, when their seven-year marriage irrevocably broke down. Conflict was inevitable from the outset of their trip to Italy, as Edward had tactlessly insisted that his mistress, Mrs. Stanhope, accompany them.[4] That her presence and his behavior soured Rosina's appreciation of Italy is evident from her diatribe in a letter to Mary Greene, who was looking after their two children, Emily and Robert:

> Neither of us are in love with Italy & therefore I devoutly hope that we may be back in dear England by the end of December—The Travelling here may be divided into 3 classes—plague—pestilence & famine. Plague—the mosquitos—Pestilence—the Smells and Famine—the [bad] Dinners. . . . Poets ought to be strangled for all the lies they have told of this Country . . . take away the Fine Arts from Italy—and it becomes a dirty Barbarous *Ugly* Country of which poor unappreciated England—Ireland—Scotland or Wales are worth fifty of it.[5]

In retaliation for being so publicly humiliated, Rosina flirted with a Neapolitan prince. Taking this as a personal affront, Edward, who had been working on what would be his most successful novel, *The Last Days of Pompeii* (1834), counterattacked with an appropriately seismic reaction that heralded the last days of their marriage. After returning to England, he was so violent towards his wife that a servant fled the scene in terror. Legal separation was the only recourse, as Edward, ever protective of his political career, wanted to avoid the publicity of a divorce.[6]

Rosina, however, was not prepared to submit to the conditions he set without a fight. She was dissatisfied with the financial settlement and later protested about losing her children with no rights of access. As a Victorian husband, Edward had a battalion of legal weaponry with which to subdue and silence his spouse. Unable to afford the legal costs to challenge his decisions, Rosina resorted instead to protest and proceeded to broadcast her grievances far and wide, using her novels as missiles. The wronged wife and the persecuted husband were stock figures in her fiction, staging the misery of their private lives for a wider audience in a unique conflation of fiction and real life. Their tempestuous marriage already had the ingredients of a best-seller. The plot may be read as follows: the husband, a well-known writer and leading politician, is besieged by the scandals of his domestic life, brought to public attention by his wronged wife, whose career as a novelist is fueled by her desire for vindication and revenge.

While numerous bibliographers have paid close consideration to Bulwer's literary output, little heed has been paid to Rosina's. The most definitive list of her publications has been collated by her biographer and loyal friend, Louisa Devey. Among the thirteen novels listed, Devey attributes to Rosina *Mauleverer's Divorce*,[7] written under the name of Hon. George Scott, an amalgamation of the names of two of her favorite writers, George Gordon, Lord Byron and Sir Walter Scott. Rosina had started to write the novel in 1858, but the events of that year proved so disruptive that she was unable to continue. The manuscript was eventually passed to the novelist Emma Robinson for completion.

There seems no reason to doubt that Rosina was the author of another novel ostensibly written by Hon. George Scott, which has also been ascribed to her by Devey. Entitled *Clumber Chase*, it betrays the hallmarks of Rosina's inimitable style, as well as drawing on biographical material such as the dispute between Edward and their son Robert over the latter's ambition to be a poet (under the name of Owen Meredith). In the novel, this dilemma is mirrored in Sir Allen's determination to thwart the literary ambitions of his son Gilbert, who has written a collection of poems. Sir Allen is "furious to think his son should meditate any such public method as authorship, of making his existence patent to the world, and so 'clashing,' as he phrased it, with his father."[8]

Far less characteristic of Rosina's writing is *Where There's a Will There's a Way*, as it has the moralizing tone of the biblical parable of the wise and foolish virgins, who appear in the guise of Victorian factory girls. Ascribed to her by Devey, it is dated 1871, though no novel of that title can be traced for that year. There is, however, a novella of a similar title that appeared in 1861, published by Joseph Masters.[9]

Rosina started writing to earn a living following her separation from her husband, who had given her an annuity of £400 a year, which she regarded as miserly and insufficient for her needs.[10]

She resolved to capitalize on the miseries of her marriage by making them literally the subject of her first novel, *Cheveley*, thereby turning it into a best-seller.[11] It was to be for Bulwer what Caroline Lamb's *Glenarvon* (1816) had already been for Byron.[12] Through the dedication to "No one, nobody, Esq, no hall, nowhere," Rosina projected her own feelings of being negated by her husband and his family by puncturing his pride in his ambition, family name, and home. Despite her detestation of his family, she had no compunction about using their name herself, knowing that it would help sell her books. When Edward was made a baronet for his services to literature (and Whig politics) in 1838, Rosina was congratulated on becoming a Lady, to which she famously replied that "she wished she could return the compliment and make a gentleman out of him."[13] She mocked his title by calling him Sir Liar or Sir Coward, which rhymes with Sir Howard, a name she had given to the Bulwer character in two of her novels, *The Budget of the Bubble Family* and *The Peer's Daughters*.

The roman à clef, within which identifiable persons from real life are thinly disguised fictional characters, proved to be the ideal vehicle for Rosina's talent for mimicry, caricature, and satire. This genre enabled her to blend Restoration caricature and wit with the move towards modernity as indicated by the subtitle, *A Photographic Novel*, supplied for *The World and his Wife, or a Person of Consequence*.

For her first novel, *Cheveley*, Rosina's villain is George Grimstone, Lord de Clifford, a composite of her husband and his brother William Bulwer. Members of Edward's set who are satirized include Albany Fonblanque, who becomes York Fonnoir—and whose "complexion," we are told, "is like a badly-embalmed mummy"[14]—and Dickens's biographer John Forster, who as Mr. Fuzboz is described as "a sort of lick-dust to Mr Fonnoir, and to Mr Anybody and everybody else of any celebrity to whom he could get access."[15] Edward's ancestral home, Knebworth House in Hertfordshire, is fictionalized as a gloomy Elizabethan pile called Grimstone, home of the Dowager Lady de Clifford, alias Mrs. Bulwer, who had inherited the Tudor building. The minor character of Lady Stepastray is based on two of Bulwer's friends, Lady Blessington and Lady Stepney, the author of *The New Road to Ruin* (1833). Lady Stepastray is portrayed as a "lion-hunter," having had several husbands and lovers. According to Rosina, "though she had not entirely left off love," she had written the "Old Road to Ruin" and "considering she had been going it for the last fifty years, she could not have possibly selected a subject with which she was more conversant."[16]

In her later novel, tantalizingly entitled *Behind the Scenes*, the Bulwer character, Henry Ponsonby Ferrars—who tries unsuccessfully to commit bigamy with the novel's heroine, Edith Panmuir—is significantly both an author and M.P. His German mistress is a ghostwriter, a barbed reference to the rumors that for the translations into German published under his name, Edward had secretly employed his daughter's German governess to do the translating for him.[17] The hero of *Behind the Scenes* has an illegitimate son whom he does not acknowledge, which alludes to the offspring of Edward's extramarital affairs. The rest of the cast includes Issachar Benaraby, who besides being a dandy was also a man of letters and ruthless politician. He ascends briefly to the position of chancellor of the exchequer just like Bulwer's friend, Benjamin Disraeli, on whom he is modeled.[18] Following the publication of the novel, Rosina wrote to her artist friend A. E. Chalon on Easter Monday 1854, predicting that the real-life portrayal of Edward and his clan would pale before her fictional equivalents: "when my Life is published and bare unvarnished *facts* stated—authenticated by the wretched animal's own letters—the world will then see what faint shadowy creations such water—or rather milk and water—colour sketches the Ponsonby Ferrars tribe are."[19]

With *Very Successful!*, Rosina overreached herself in her lampooning of Bulwer as Sir Janus Allpuff, Benjamin Disraeli as Jericho Jabber, and John Forster as Fudgester. Edward was so incensed by the ridicule that he threatened to bring an injunction in order to prevent its republication. Rosina was furious, as his threats and bribes had intimidated her publisher Frederick Clarke of the Caxton Head Taunton and his London agent, Whittaker.[20] Even provincial libraries had been discouraged from circulating the text on the grounds that it was unsuitable for ladies to read.[21] Rosina exposed Edward's attempts to suppress her books in some of the prefaces to her novels, which she turned into veritable declarations of war. Indeed the naming of her novel *Very Successful!* can be seen as a defensive maneuver since it ensured that at least the most negative of reviews would contain something positive, even if it was only in referring to the title of the book.[22]

Ironically, Bulwer had provided Rosina with metafictional ammunition from his own novels. If only he had heeded the warning of one of his own characters, Sir Reginald Glanville in the novel

*Pelham* (1828), who advises the eponymous hero never to be "tempted by any inducement into the pleasing errors of print; from that moment you are public property; and the last monster at Exeter 'Change has more liberty than you" (xlvi). In his first novel, *Falkland* (1827), the way in which Bulwer's title hero romanticizes adultery must have seemed to Rosina later on like a fictional apprenticeship for his real-life infidelities. Just as Don Juan is assumed to have been modeled on Byron, so was it widely held that Bulwer had based the dandified Pelham on himself. Tellingly, Lord Vincent, one of the characters in *Pelham*, defines a novel as "the actual representation of real life" (lii). By having his hero proffer such utterances as "If I was immoral, it was because I was never taught morality" (xxxvii), Bulwer ensured that *Pelham* would be highly controversial. Even though real life, particularly in regard to Edward, was a driving force in Rosina's fiction, she shifted the onus on certain readers for presuming that in the novel *Behind the Scenes*, she was vilifying her husband. She stated unequivocally in a letter to A. E. Chalon: "if [Edward's] *dear friends will* go on assuming that he and every villainy are synonymous (which far be it for me to deny) the cruelty is in *them* and not the scandal in me."[23] By way of contrast, in a letter to Wilkie Collins Rosina could not have been more explicit about Edward's villainy. She pointed out that "the great failure of your book [*The Woman in White*] is the villain; Count Fosco is a very poor one, and when next you want a character of that sort I trust you will not disdain to come to me. The man is alive and constantly under my gaze. In fact he is my own husband."[24] Collins, by passing the letter to Bulwer, made him fully aware of his wife's dubious approbation of his suitability as model for a villain.

In spite of having escaped the imprisonment of marriage for the freedom of the writer and its occupational hazards, Rosina's textual attacks upon Edward, fought under the shadow of his greater publishing success, held her in another form of subservience. Her obsession with him as a combatant, both in real life and as a literary subject, maintained their codependency. Instead of detaching her creative self from Bulwer, Rosina became a perverse sounding board for his life and work, even to the extent of using her novels as conduits for entering his texts. The tactics she used were those of a metafictional invasion of his novels by deploying the weapons of parody and pastiche. The marital was now truly conflated with the martial, as Rosina included in her novels digressive diatribes against her husband. She was fully aware that a woman's conduct was seen to reflect upon her male relatives, particularly if she dared enter the public arena as an author:

> Generally speaking, women have either fathers, brothers or husbands, who would shrink from having an authoress for a daughter, sister, or wife; and the reason is obvious, it arises from a fear that they might either disgrace or distinguish themselves, the two results equally distasteful to the pride of man.[25]

As an innovator of literary forms,[26] Edward was again imitated by his wife. For her novels, Rosina created a new fictional hybrid by combining Bulwer's silver-fork novel invented for *Pelham*, with the roman à clef and the scandalous memoir, a genre more commonly used by mistresses and courtesans than by wives.

Her own version of her husband's Newgate novels may be found in *Bianca Cappello*, the equivalent of Edward's controversial *Paul Clifford* (1830). Rosina's title heroine is not a female highwayman but a woman who falls on the moral wayside by becoming the mistress of Francesco de' Medici. The novel is dotted with the intrigues of that notorious family against a backdrop of the Inquisition. Rosina baited Bulwer for the success of his criminal heroes, the murderer *Eugene Aram* (1832) and the thief *Paul Clifford* (1830). In *Cheveley* she refers to him as Mr. Trevyllian, who wrote a novel called *The Unnatural Son*, "which being full of terrible things was naturally much admired."[27]

Rosina would have had no compunction in applying this description to Bulwer's most admired novel, *The Last Days of Pompeii* (1834). Her repost to his triumph is a short story called "Artaphernes the Platonist, or The Supper at Sallust's: A Roman Fragment" (1838). Published under the name of Mrs. Edward Lytton Bulwer, the story delineates, under fictional disguises, the "terrible things" done to the wife of the author of *The Last Days of Pompeii*.[28] Sallust's supper in Bulwer's novel is the setting for some unsavory comments about feeding slaves to fish in order to improve the quality of the cuisine (I:vii).

In a letter to Chalon, Rosina conjures up the image of a husband being eaten and notes the possible ways of serving this dish, "hot, cold, *roasted* or *devilled*."[29] Her gastronomic tips may also be seen as an oblique parody of her countryman Jonathan Swift's satire *A Modest Proposal* (1729), which includes cooking methods for the babies of the starving Irish in a savage proposition that they be sustenance for the rich. In a metaphorical sense, Rosina also went on to roast her husband in public by attacking him on the hustings where he was standing for re-election in Hertford in 1858. Here too he may have struck her as the appropriate butt for a Swiftian attack because both as a Whig and as a Tory he had supported the reactionary Corn Laws, believed in some quarters to have contributed to the Great Famine in Ireland and uprisings against the English.[30]

The French Revolution is the background to Bulwer's mystical *Zanoni* (1842), to which we may discern a response in Rosina's novel *The Peer's Daughters*. This book contains a female character called Zamora and the Transylvanian charlatan, Count Saint-Germain, who, it is thought, provided Bulwer with a model for his quasi-Rosicrucian and immortal hero Zanoni.[31] (A question has also been raised about whether Bulwer in 1860 met Saint-Germain, who was allegedly two thousand years old.)[32] In *The Peer's Daughters*, Saint-Germain is described as "the great unsepulchred orphan of the past, who must live on."[33] He reveals to Raphael Valasquez, a young Spanish nobleman, that he has taken the elixir of immortality, which enables him to change sex and class and live in various periods of time. Raphael persuades Saint-Germain to grant him eternal youth too, but after only ten years he is ready to give up his immortality and to age naturally. Saint-Germain wants in his turn to end his immortal existence by being reincarnated as Robespierre, knowing that he would be executed for the enormity of his crimes. This grim aspiration parodies the virtuous Zanoni's death by guillotine.

Rosina's attacks upon Edward, his circle, and family, naturally provoked counter-hostilities. She was obviously the target of an anonymous poem entitled *Lady Cheveley; or The Woman of Honour* (1839).[34] In keeping with the notion expressed in *Pelham* that a novel is "the actual representation of real life," Rosina was accused of committing mental adultery on the grounds that her heroine in *Cheveley* pays attention to a man other than her husband. The first suspect for authorship was Edward, but so vehement was his denial that it may lead us to look elsewhere. Perhaps the author was Mrs. Bulwer, who was still smarting from having been savaged in her daughter-in-law's novel. *Lady Cheveley* was followed by another anonymous poem called *Cheveley's Donkey; or, The Man in the Ass's Hide: a Roman Fable*.[35] Since this verse descended to the very depths of doggerel, it seems unlikely that Mrs. Bulwer was the author.

More likely is the possibility that Bulwer retaliated against Rosina in several of his novels. With respect to the theme of cannibalism between spouses, his futuristic *The Coming Race* (1871)

expresses male anxiety about monstrous man-eating females—
who, worst of all, might eat men on their wedding night. Called
"gys" (pronounced "guys"), these women are stronger and taller
than men, sometimes reaching a height of seven feet. Not surprisingly, they also embody Bulwer's particular fear of the liberated
and assertive American woman, the bête noire of the coming race.
Through his futuristic novel, Edward unwittingly demonstrated
how women could revenge themselves for the wrongs inflicted on
them in the past by monstrous husbands. What for him was a
nightmarish image can also be seen as a radical fictional reconstruction of his destructive and rebellious wife, for whom he felt
"dread at her presence and relief at her parting." Because of Rosina, he was forced to confess to his mother that "my career is
blighted; my temper soured; my nerves shattered; and if I am to
go on for ever in this way because she insists on continuing to
force herself upon me, God knows what I shall do at last."[36] As
Rosina wryly noted after his death: "Marriage, like every other
misfortune, when once it gets into a family, there's no knowing
where it may end!"[37] For her it could have ended in a lunatic asylum at Brentford had it not been for a public campaign waged on
her behalf that freed her in little over three weeks.

Not so fortunate is Bulwer's eponymous heroine in *Lucretia;
or, The Children of Night* (1846), where narrative closure leaves
her in the perpetual enclosure of a madhouse. Through his fascination with mad women characters in *Pelham*, *Godolphin* (1833),
and *Lucretia*, Bulwer may well have created a distorted mirroring
of the madness that he claimed was afflicting his wife.[38] In view
of this, his physical incarceration of Rosina later on is a corollary
to his previous virtual imprisonment of her within the text of *Lucretia*. (In figurative terms, she would eventually write herself out
into her own narrative reconstruction of her incarceration in her
autobiography, *A Blighted Life: A True Story* [1880].)

Just as Rosina had vilified Edward in so many of her novels,
was he now demonizing her through the character of Lucretia, a
raving lunatic, who insanely murders her husbands? Certainly it
is tempting to read into his novel the breakdown of their marriage. The time that the heroine spends alone with her husband,
Olivier Dalibard, is described as "that mute coma of horror,"
when at night "they lie down side by side in the marriage-bed—
brain plotting against brain, heart loathing heart. It is a duel of
life and death, between those sworn through life and beyond
death at the altar." And although in this case there is a superficial calm, "the monsters in the hell of the abyss war invisibly

below" (I:epilogue). In the war between the spouses in the novel, even intertextuality is deployed as a weapon. Lucretia has alighted upon a passage from *The Life of a Physician of Padua, in the Sixteenth Century*, which her soon-to-be-poisoned husband fails to recognize in time:

> It related to that singular epoch of terror in Italy, when some mysterious disease, varying in a thousand symptoms, baffled all remedy, and long defied all conjecture—a disease attacking chiefly the heads of families, father and husband—rarely women. In one city, seven hundred husbands perished, but not one wife! The disease was poison. (I: epilogue)

After the collapse of their marriage, Edward was indeed in continual fear of being harmed by Rosina, though she never lived out his fictional representation of the Lucretian madwoman.

In *Lucretia*, further similarities may be found between the title heroine and Bulwer's mother-in-law, the feminist and communitarian philosopher Anna Wheeler.[39] Lucretia's originally masculine intellect, which resembles that of Wheeler, is portrayed as a precursor to madness: "Lucretia had none of the charming babble of women—none of that tender interest in household details, in the minutiae of domestic life, which relaxes the intellect while softening the heart. Hard and vigorous, her sentences come forth in eternal appeal to the reason" (II:xviii). Known as the "Goddess of Reason," Anna Wheeler's sentences came forth in speeches and pamphlets as well as in the socialist feminist treatise she co-authored with William Thompson, entitled *Appeal of One Half of the Human Race, Women, Against the Pretensions of the Other Half, Men, to Retain them in Political, and Thence in Civil and Domestic Slavery* (1825). Her proselytizing for the rights of women may well have seemed "hard and vigorous" to some. She had alarmed Disraeli as she "poured forth all her systems upon [his] novitiate ear" when he met her while dining at the Bulwers. She seemed to him "not so pleasant" as his hosts and as "something between Jeremy Bentham and Meg Merrilies, very clever, but awfully revolutionary."[40]

In view of her reputation as an icon of female rationality, Edward performed a supreme disservice to his mother-in-law by alleging that she had lost her reason by the time of her death in 1848, ten years prior to Rosina's incarceration. This was part of his scheme to ensure that his wife remained confined in the asylum. By drawing up for the lunacy commissioners a false statement that Rosina's parents had died insane, Bulwer hoped to strengthen the case against her with the taint of congenital madness. Wheeler's only contact with lunacy, however, had been while visiting, in the company of fellow socialist Flora Tristan, Bethlehem Hospital. Here she was verbally assaulted by a lunatic calling himself the messiah, who accused her of causing his assassination.[41]

A less direct attack on Wheeler takes place in Bulwer's novel *Pelham,* where the hero's uncle, Lord Glenmorris, endeavors to broaden his nephew's education by introducing him to the work of the utilitarian James Mill. They both peruse "the whole of Mill's admirable articles in the Encyclopaedia" along with a pamphlet on government in which Glenmorris draws attention to "its close and mathematical reasoning, in which *no flaw could be detected, nor deduction controverted*"(xxxvii).[42] Through this lavish praise, Edward is ridiculing his mother-in-law. For Anna Wheeler, Mill's article on government in the 1824 *Encyclopaedia Britannica* was highly flawed, as it supported the government's exclusion of women from politics, which came to be encoded within the Reform Act of 1832. Mill's most contentious assertion is that women ought to be denied political rights on the grounds that the interests of most of them are involved either in "that of their fathers or in that of their husbands."[43] It was after reading this passage that Wheeler had proposed to Thompson that they write the *Appeal*. But since Rosina was so often out of sympathy with her mother, it is highly probable that she was responsible for the ironic contradiction of Wheeler's position in *Pelham*.

Was Rosina too, like the mother with whom she failed to sympathize, a collaborator in an important book for which she received scant recognition?[44] It was left to a later generation to make recompense, when her grandson Victor, the second Earl of Lytton, hints at the debt that Edward may have owed his wife in the composition of *Pelham*:

> This novel is the only one the composition of which the author and his young wife might have enjoyed together. The qualities esteemed are those which both could admire. The personalities laughed at were those which both would take pleasure in ridiculing. It was the product of the only happy period in their married life—the first two years spent at Woodcot.[45]

Certainly the novel bears the hallmarks of her wit and his discipline. What a wonderful writing partnership they might have relished if other incompatibilities had not forced them to oppose one another! Never again was Bulwer to write a novel that matched *Pelham* for its sparkling Regency wit and incomparable observations of fashionable society; nor was Rosina ever to rival it in any of her literary productions.[46]

While much of Rosina's writing is tedious, repetitive, and histrionic, her novels are redeemed by their biographical interest, their outspoken digressions on the rights of women, their colorful evocation of London society, and their biting wit. Where Edward was concerned, she was willing to sacrifice the interests of the novelist on the altar of self-vindication, which is a prime reason why her work has been overlooked. *A Vindication* is the subtitle of Louisa Devey's biography, and vindication is the substance of Rosina's address to posterity in 1864 in which she tacitly endorses Edward's familiar aphorism, "the pen is mightier than the sword":[47]

> I am also fully aware of literary posthumous chivalry, and its Bayard courage! upon the safe vantage ground of posterity! therefore, when I have been dead some hundred years,—how pens will start from their inkstands, like swords from their scabbards, to avenge me! While Electric Caligraphy will not have left sufficient ink in Christendom to blacken Sir EDWARD, the CAESAR BORGIA of the nineteenth century (with the beauty and courage left out) up to his natural hue. Gentleman of 1964, I cannot find words to thank you—for all I shall have to say then, is what I pray now—*Implora Pace!*[48]

Posterity may have been slow in avenging Rosina, but surely the time has come to appreciate her novels as insightful repositories for the wrongs suffered by married and separated women. Her battles with Bulwer waged through books as well as in real life never subsided into any rapprochement. Yet for their tragicomic effect on contemporary spectators and their undoubted significance in the unresolved nineteenth-century war between the sexes, her novels deserve greater recognition.

## NOTES

1. Rosina admired Swift, whose satire *The Battle of the Books* (1697) inspires the subtitle of this essay. Swift appears as a character in Rosina's novel *The Peer's Daughters, A Novel*, 3 vols. (London: Newby, 1849).

2. The most obvious of these are the Married Women's Property Acts of 1870 and 1882, which eventually enabled every married woman to keep all personal and real property acquired before and during marriage.

3. Rosina was diagnosed as suffering from dementia when she was confined at Inverness Lodge at Brentford, run by Dr. Hill.

4. Although they were joined by her husband Robert Stanhope, he appears to have been complicit with the couple's intentions. Michael Sadleir describes how their "ostentatious philandering" became more and more pronounced until it caused in Naples "much unnecessary scandal." See Michael Sadleir, *Bulwer and His Wife: A Panorama 1803–1836* (London: Constable and Co, 1933), pp.169–70.

5. Dated Tuesday, 14 October 1833, written from Hôtel des Quatres Nations in Florence, held at Hertford County Record Office, ref. D/EK C29/8.

6. The Matrimonial Causes Act had become law the year before in 1857, allowing secular divorce in England. Neither party could take advantage of it because they could not agree on grounds to present to a court. For a woman an admission of adultery was sufficient, while it was necessary for a man to confess to another charge, such as desertion, extreme cruelty, or incest, in addition to adultery in order to secure a divorce.

7. See Louisa Devey, *Life of Rosina, Lady Lytton: A Vindication* (London: Sonnenschein, 1887), p. 422. Rosina's novels include *Cheveley: or, The Man of Honour*, 3 vols. (London: Bull, 1839); *The Budget of the Bubble Family*, 3 vols. (London: Bull, 1840); *Bianca Cappello: An Historical Romance*, 3 vols. (London, Bull, 1843); *Memoirs of a Muscovite*, 3 vols. (London: Newby, 1844); *The Peer's Daughters* (op. cit. n. 1); *Miriam Sedley, or The Tares and the Wheat: a Tale of Real Life*, 3 vols. (London: Newby, 1850); *The School for Husbands: or Moliére's Life and Times*, 3 vols. (London: Charles J. Skeet, 1851); *Behind the Scenes: A Novel*, 3 vols. (London: Charles J. Skeet, 1854); *Very Successful!*, 3 vols. (London; Whittaker, 1856); *The World and his Wife or a Person of Consequence, a Photographic novel*, 3 vols. (London: Charles J. Skeet, 1858); *Clumber Chase, or Love's Riddle Solved by a Royal Sphinx: A Tale of the Restoration* by the Hon George Scott (London: T. Cautley Newby, 1871); Anon. [Rosina's authorship is uncertain], *Where There Is a Will There Is a Way* (London: Joseph Masters, 1861).

8. Bulwer Lytton, *Clumber Chase*, 1:177.

9. Rosina has been wrongly identified as having written the novel *The Prince-Duke and the Page: An Historical Novel*, 3 vols. (London: Boone, 1841). It does not appear in Devey's list, but it is ascribed to Rosina in, for example, the catalogue of the British Library. As she was only the editor, the real author, Charles Rosenberg, was understandably annoyed by this misattribution.

10. This was equivalent by today's standards to £20,000 per annum, which is not such a miserly amount.

11. The novel ran through many editions.

12. Lady Caroline Lamb, who had been a friend to both Edward and Rosina, provided the latter with a model for the roman à clef with this Gothic imbroglio. She portrays herself as the exciting Calantha and Byron as the fascinating but treacherous Glenarvon.

13. Devey, *Life of Rosina*, p. 403.

14. Bulwer Lytton, *Cheveley*, 2:117.

15. Ibid., 2:118.

16. Ibid., 2:143.

17. For Bulwer to seek the assistance of a native speaker would have been perfectly understandable, especially since his spoken command of the language was not particularly good.

18. Benjamin Disraeli held this position in the ephemeral Derby administration of late 1852.

19. *Unpublished Letters of Lady Bulwer Lytton to A.E. Chalon, RA,* ed. S. M. Ellis (London: Eveleigh Nash, 1914), p. 82.

20. Rosina's publisher Edward Bull remained loyal to her. After his death in 1843, she went to other publishers, who were less able to withstand pressure from her husband.

21. *Lady Bulwer Lytton's Appeal to the Justice and Charity of the English Public* (Taunton: privately printed, 1857), p. 4.

22. *Very Successful* turned out to be better received than most of her novels. But the praise by one critic for the *Plymouth Journal* is tempered by the knowledge of her reputation as a well-known personality: "if Lady Lytton really is the brain-turned termagant which we are told she is . . . , then she ha[s] achieved by far the most marvellous literary feat! ever accomplished, for she has written at least *one* book" exhibiting "an unusually noble well-cultivated intellect" (quoted in *Appeal to the Justice and Charity of the English Public,* p. 43).

23. *Unpublished Letters,* p. 82.

24. T. H. S. Escott, *Edward Bulwer; First Baron Lytton of Knebworth* (London: George Routledge & Sons, 1910 [reissued Port Washington, N.Y: Kennikat Press, 1970]), pp. 331–32. In a letter to her friend and physician Dr. Price, quoted in Devey, *Life of Rosina,* p. 364, Rosina writes: "If you can read novels do read 'The Woman in White' by Wilkie Collins. It will remind you slightly of my history. Sir Percival Glyde and Count Fosco are very pretty rascals as far as they go, but mere sucking doves compared to the fiends I have to deal with."

25. Bulwer Lytton, *Cheveley,* 1:215.

26. See John Sutherland, *Victorian Fiction: Writers, Publishers, Readers* (London: Macmillan, 1995), pp. 107–9.

27. Bulwer Lytton, *Cheveley,* 2:93.

28. Rosina Bulwer Lytton, "Artaphernes the Platonist, or The Supper at Sallust's: A Roman Fragment by Mrs Edward Lytton Bulwer," *Fraser's Magazine* 27, no. C (April 1838): 513–520.

29. *Unpublished Letters,* p. 84. Here Rosina is comparing Edward unfavorably to Charlotte Smith's profligate husband.

30. For a view that does not hold the Corn Laws responsible for the famine in Ireland, see Charles Snyder, *Liberty and Morality: A Political Biography of Bulwer-Lytton* (New York: Peter Lang, 1995), pp. 76–80, 99–110.

31. See E. M. Butler, *The Myth of the Magus* (Cambridge: Cambridge University Press, 1948), pp. 244ff. It is more likely that Zanoni was based on the saintly Saint-Martin, who crusaded against charlatanism and was a follower of Pasqualis, the founder of a number of secret societies associated with the Rosicrucians. See John Senior, *The Way Down and Out: The Occult in Symbolic Literature* (New York: Cornell University Press, 1959), p. 51.

32. See Andrew Lang, *Historical Mysteries* (London: Smith, Elder, 1904), p. 276.

33. Bullwer Lytton, *The Peer's Daughters,* 1:132.

34. *Lady Cheveley; or The Woman of Honour. A New Version of Cheveley or, The Man of Honour* (London: Churton, 1839).

35. *Cheveley's Donkey; or, The Man in the Ass's Hide: a Roman Fable* (London: James Pattie, 1839).

36. Sadleir, *Bulwer and His Wife,* p. 403.

37. Bulwer Lytton, *Clumber's Chase,* 3:264.

38. For further discussion see Marie Mulvey-Roberts, "Fame, Notoriety and Madness: Edward Bulwer-Lytton Paying the Price of Greatness," *Critical Survey* 13, no. 2 (2001): 115–34.

39. The character of Varney in Lucretia is based on that of the poisoner Thomas Wainewright. See Helen Small, *Love's Madness: Medicine, the Novel and Female Insanity, 1800–1865* (Oxford: Clarendon Press, 1996), p. 144.

40. From a letter from Benjamin Disraeli to his sister, 29 January 1833, in *Lord Beaconsfield's Correspondence with His Sister 1832–1852*, ed. Ralph Disraeli (London: John Murray, 1886), p. 15.

41. See Sandra Dijkstra, *Flora Tristan: Feminism in the Age of George Sand* (London: Pluto Press, 1992), p. 161. The messianic madman, despite his verbal assault on Wheeler, professed to support the rights of women.

42. These are my italics. In 1824, James Mill's article on government, written for the annual supplement to the *Encyclopaedia Britannica*, gave philosophical credence to the first statutory act to disenfranchise and disempower women.

43. Quoted by William Thompson and Anna Wheeler, *Appeal of One Half of the Human Race, Women, Against the Pretensions of the Other Half, Men,* ed. Michael Foot and Marie Mulvey[-]Roberts (Bristol: Thoemmes Press, 1994), p. 9.

44. Anna Wheeler's name did not appear on the original title page. In view of Thompson's acknowledgment of Wheeler's collaboration, I have included her name on the title page of two editions. See note 43 and *Sources of British Feminism*. Ed. Marie Mulvey-Roberts and Tamae Mizota (London: Routledge Thoemmes, 1993).

45. See second Earl of Lytton, *Bulwer-Lytton* (London: Home and Van Thal, 1948), p. 40. I am not suggesting that Rosina actually wrote any part of the book but only that she helped imbue it with its particular brand of wit and outrageousness.

46. Another area in which both authors wrote was that of domesticity. In his early years of married life, Bulwer wrote many essays on domestic life such as "Domesticity, or a Dissertation upon Servants," "House-hunting," "Peculiarities of London Tradesmen," "The Kitchen and the Parlour, or Household Politics," "Long Journeys with Short Purses," and so on. See second Earl of Lytton, *The Life of Edward Bulwer, First Lord Lytton, by his Grandson*, 2 vols. (London: Macmillan, 1913), 1:217. These essays may have been influenced by Rosina who later in life wrote a treatise on servants and domesticity entitled *The Household Fairy* (London: Hale, 1870).

47. Edward Bulwer, *Richelieu; or, The Conspiracy* (London: Saunders and Otley, 1838), act 2, scene 2, p. 29.

48. Rosina Bulwer Lytton, *A Blighted Life: A True Story*, ed. Marie Mulvey[-]Roberts (Bristol: Thoemmes Press, 1994), p. 45.

# Bulwer Lytton and
# "The Cult of the Colonies"

## Charles W. Snyder

BACK IN 1910, T. H. S. ESCOTT COMMENTED ABOUT THE COLONIAL enterprise in his biography of Edward Bulwer Lytton: "The English People rose somewhat slowly to a right appreciation of the priceless treasure possessed by them in their settlements beyond the seas. . . . The true cult of the colonies at home was founded by Bulwer-Lytton in *The Caxtons*."[1] "Settlements beyond the seas," was just the right phrase, for it was the settlement colonies, rather than those populated primarily by native peoples, that captured Bulwer Lytton's imagination. The settlement colonies, in his view, represented hope for the future, both for those who would actually settle there and for those who would remain at home. The themes he emphasized when it came to the colonies were opportunity and durability. As to both, he was an optimist, if a cautious one. Still, in an era generally pessimistic about the prospects of the Empire, even cautious optimism set Bulwer Lytton apart from most.

Escott, to be sure, overstated Bulwer Lytton's role, and his reference to the English people coming slowly to an appreciation of the colonies reflects the largely discredited idea that the mid-Victorian era was one of indifference or even hostility to the Empire. The conventional wisdom when Escott wrote his biography was that the mid-Victorians regarded the Empire as an expensive burden from which Britain should free itself—"millstones around our neck," in Disraeli's famous phrase.[2] More recent scholarship has swept away the notion that the Victorians were hostile to the Empire. There were a few, like Richard Cobden, who at least sometimes maintained that Britain would be better off without any colonies;[3] or who anticipated, in Goldwin Smith's phrase, "the concession of independence to adult colonies, so that England might become indeed the mother of free nations."[4] But most Victorians were not separationists, and the statesmen of the era

174

oversaw, with varying degrees of enthusiasm, a considerable expansion of the Empire.[5]

If Victorian anti-imperialism has been exaggerated, there was nonetheless widespread pessimism about the prospects of the Empire. The division of opinion about the colonies tended not to be between Imperialists and Little Englanders but between optimists and pessimists, with the latter predominant in the mid-Victorian era. The pessimism largely stemmed from Britain's bitter experience with the American Revolution, for it was widely assumed that other colonies also would eventually break away. As C. C. Eldridge put it, the optimists and the pessimists divided over "whether any formal bonds of empire would last. And bearing in mind the American War of Independence, the collapse of the old colonial system and the ever-increasing sphere of colonial self-government, the practical possibility of continuing imperial unity did indeed seem remote."[6] In short, if Disraeli's likening the colonies to "millstones around our necks" did not really reflect the general opinion, there was a consensus that Turgot had been correct in saying that settlement colonies were like fruit that would drop away once it was ripe.

Bulwer Lytton did not regard the colonies as fruit that would fall away, but as saplings that, once planted, would flourish in the future. To establish a colony, he once wrote, is an act "more sure of fame a thousand years hence than anything we can do in the old world. It is carving our names on the rind of a young tree, to be found with enlarged letters as the trunk expands."[7]

It was once said of Bulwer Lytton that he never wrote so much as an invitation to dinner without an eye to posterity.[8] When he spoke of assuring future fame through establishing colonies, he meant business. He primarily addressed himself to posterity as an author, but he expected his endeavors on behalf of the Empire also to prove enduring. Such endeavors were undertaken in both his political and literary careers. Enthusiasm for the Empire was thus truly a unifying theme in Bulwer Lytton's life.

His political career was not insignificant, as he was a Member of Parliament for twenty-four years. Less than a decade after his novel *The Caxtons* featured emigration to Australia, the fortunes of politics carried him briefly into the cabinet. He served as Colonial Secretary, a post for which he was deemed fit at least in part because of his popularizing of the colonies as a novelist.[9]

The Empire not only linked Bulwer Lytton's literary and political careers, it helped provide a measure of continuity to the latter. In outline, his political career appears a steady migration from left to right along the political spectrum, from being too Radical for the Whigs, to becoming too conservative for the Tories. But there were points of consistency, and support for the Empire was one.

He began to take an interest in the Empire early in his Parliamentary career, when, as a young Radical M.P., he was allied with the colonial reformers. By the mid-1830s, he counted himself as a supporter of Lord Durham, whose report on Canada would become the leading state paper on responsible government for the colonies.[10] All along, whether as Radical or as Tory, whether as popular novelist or as practical politician, Bulwer Lytton's approach to the colonies stressed opportunity and durability.

Opportunity meant that British people of all classes might make better lives for themselves by emigrating to the settlement colonies: Canada, Australia, South Africa, and New Zealand. It was in these colonies that Bulwer Lytton expressed his interest, and not in ruling places unsuitable for European settlement. In the colonies of settlement, he saw a solution for the social problems of Britain herself. A disciple of Bentham and a reader of Malthus, the young Bulwer studied the effect on Britain of overpopulation, poverty, and the so-called "sturdy beggar." He supported the New Poor Law and saw in emigration a means to create new opportunities for those who could not find work. In *England and the English* (1833), the finest expression of Bulwer's Benthamite phase, he wrote of the benefits of emigration, albeit in a rather clinical style. He cited as his authority the prominent colonial reformer Edward Gibbon Wakefield, who

> takes the British population at twenty millions; he supposes that their utmost power of increase would move at the rate of four percent per annum, the constant yearly removal of the percentage, viz. 800,000, would prevent any domestic increase. But of these 800,000 you need to select only those young couples from whom the increase of population will proceed—these amount to 400,000 individuals— the expense of removing them at 10$L$ a head, is four millions a year. *We now therefore know exactly what it will cost to prevent too great a pressure of population on the means of subsistence!* But what individual emigration-companies can . . . persuade the people to accede to it? Is not this clearly the affair of the state . . . ?[11]

In time, Bulwer Lytton's youthful Benthamite belief in a strong, directing state gave way to a Burkean conservatism. His detached analysis of emigrants as mere statistics, reducing the excess population, was in like manner supplanted by a positive opinion of the colonists as part of an extended family of British nationality. His aim, he wrote, was to strengthen "the old English cordial feeling" and bind together the classes that the Manchester School was trying to separate.[12]

The role of the colonies in this binding together of the classes receives its best expression in Bulwer Lytton's novel *The Caxtons* (1848–49). The young narrator of the story, impoverished but idealistic, goes off to Australia in search of opportunity. In its essentials, the message about the benefits of emigration resembles the one so coldly expressed sixteen years before in *England and the English*—but what a difference in tone! The author of *The Caxtons* speaks through the character Albert Trevanion, an older man who advises the novel's hero as follows:

> "Yes, how many young men there must be like you, in this Old World, able, intelligent, active, and persevering enough, yet not adapted for success in any of our conventional professions. . . . For my part, in my ideal of colonization, I should like that each exportation of human beings had, as of old, its leaders and chiefs, not so appointed from the mere quality of rank; often, indeed, taken from the humbler classes; but still men to whom a certain degree of education should give promptitude, quickness, *adaptability*—men in whom their followers can confide. . . . And when the day shall come (as to all healthful colonies it must come sooner or later) in which the settlement has grown an independent state, we may thereby have laid the seeds of a constitution and a civilization similar to our own, with self-developed forms of monarchy and aristocracy, though of a simpler growth than old societies accept, and not left a strange motley chaos of struggling democracy. . . . Depend on it, the New World will be friendly or hostile to the Old, *not in proportion to the kinship of race, but in proportion to the similarity of manners and institutions*—a mighty truth to which we colonizers have been blind. . . .
>
> "I sympathize with your aspirations . . . ; looking to your nature and to your objects, I give you my advice in a word—EMIGRATE! . . . Australia is the land for you." (XII:vi)

It is the land, indeed, not merely for young Caxton, but for a troop of emigrants recruited to accompany him, men likewise "able, intelligent, active and persevering enough," but ill-suited for success in the Old World. For them Australia offers *opportunity*—not only for financial but more importantly for moral redemption. They include, among others, Guy Bolding, whose career at Oxford has foundered through profligate indulgence in the "fast" life; a country poacher known as the "Will of the Wisp"; Miles Square, a disabled mechanic and radical agitator against private property and the social order; and a Caxton cousin called "Vivian," whose scandalous misdeeds have caused his own father to disown him (XIII:iv).

Their first years in Australia are a time of struggle and privation. It will take about five years, spent mainly raising sheep, before Caxton and Bolding achieve financial success. That is not all they gain. Bolding, who has wasted the academic opportunities laid before him at Oxford, relishes in the Bush, where books are scarce, his hitherto latent love of literature. Miles Square, the erstwhile radical, undergoes an even greater transformation. After working his way up from shepherd to landowner, he eventually publishes a tract entitled "Sanctity of the Rights of Property"! (XIII:iv; XVII:i).

For Vivian, however, the opportunity for moral and material success in Australia is not enough. Another part of the Empire provides the kind of opportunity he requires to redeem himself for his past misdeeds. His personal redemption and service to the Empire culminates in a hero's death on the frontiers of India. "He died, as I knew he would have prayed to die, at the close of a day ever memorable in the annals of that marvelous empire, which valour without parallel has annexed to the Throne of the Isles" (XVIII:viii).

But the most striking aspect of the Australian interlude in *The Caxtons* is young Caxton's abrupt decision to return to England. After making enough to pay his family's debts, and coming away with a few thousand more, he disdains the genuine prospect that his hard work over five years has earned him, the chance to make a far more substantial fortune. He thus dismisses the notion of remaining: "The object is achieved: why should I stay?" (XVII:vi). His return suggests that the author does not want emigration to mean a permanent breach with Britain. Bulwer Lytton obviously sees the mother country as the sun around which the colonial planets revolve, even after they have attained responsible government. If that relationship is to endure, the colonies will have to create institutions modeled on those of the mother country, suitably adapted to circumstances of the New World. Above all, the emigrants must not forget the place from which they have come.

If Bulwer Lytton the novelist suggests that lesson in *The Caxtons*, Bulwer Lytton the statesman makes it explicit as Colonial Secretary. He instructs the Governor of the new colony of

Queensland: "Do your best always to keep up the pride in the mother country. Throughout all Australia there is a sympathy with the ideal of a gentleman. This gives a moral aristocracy. Sustain it by showing the store set on integrity, honour and civilised manners; not by preferences of birth, which belong to old countries."[13]

Through *The Caxtons*, Bulwer Lytton not only aided the development of Australia, he contributed to the creation of an image of Australia in British minds. Regardless of whether he actually created a "cult of the colonies," he did help popularize a notion of Australia as a land of opportunity for those Englishmen deprived of a fair chance at home.[14] That image also affected how Australians saw themselves. In the words of Coral Lansbury, who has explored this issue in *Arcady in Australia*, Bulwer Lytton, along with Charles Dickens and Charles Reade, created an "Arcadian Australia [that was] to become the most favoured interpretation in English literature; in turn it dominated the thought and traditions of writing in Australia."[15] As Allan Christensen has put it: "Given enormous popular currency in *The Caxtons* (1848–1849), the Australian myth . . . came profoundly to affect the Australian consciousness of identity. It was as an author, then, rather than as Colonial Secretary that Bulwer exerted his most important influence upon Australia."[16]

But as Colonial Secretary in 1858–59, he did his best to enhance not only the image of the Australian land of opportunity but also the practical durability of the Empire. Of course, he held office for so short a time that it would be vain to try to make too much of his accomplishments. Still, he did set out some definite lines of policy calculated to serve the long-term durability of the Empire. To do so, he had to counteract the attitude of pessimism discussed above: the attitude that colonies were too expensive and would eventually become independent anyway. He had also to be concerned with the growing spirit of independence within the colonies themselves. To foster enthusiasm for the Empire at home without offending colonial sensibilities required considerable tact and good judgment.

To Bulwer Lytton's annoyance, he had to deal early in his ministry with a proposal by Sir Edmund Head, Governor of the Colony of Canada, for the confederation of the British North American colonies (a plan for grouping several colonies in a single jurisdiction).[17] Probably inevitable, a confederation might even prove advantageous, and Bulwer Lytton knew that to oppose it openly would make the idea more attractive to some Canadian politicians. He decided that the best way to slow the drift toward confederation, with the attendant risk of more extreme demands for independence, was to quiet the controversy and await the formulation of a plan calculated to strengthen "the link between the Provinces and the Crown." Without such a plan, he warned, confederation might soon cost the Crown these colonies.[18] He was wary of confederation because, as he once noted, it is the "object of the mother country to keep alive distinctions between the colonies—in order that all links of union between them might centre in the bosom of the parent state."[19] Thus he wrote to Lord Derby, then prime minister, that confederation, if inevitable, should be accomplished in such a manner that "the only way to give some moral strength to the executive would be to preserve to it the prestige of the British Crown."[20] The idea of confederation was shelved for the time being, only to be achieved in 1867.

Not an outright opponent of confederation, Bulwer Lytton found that in certain circumstances, like those of South Africa, it might even be encouraged. His exploration of the possibility of confederation of the British colonies in South Africa had unexpected results, however, that shed considerable light on his approach to assuring the durability of the Empire. Besides a concern to preserve the central role of the British Crown, that approach was influenced by an awareness that the colonies cost too much money. To meet this financial objection and so improve the chances of the Empire's enduring, he made every effort to minimize imperial expenditures. But in South Africa his economical approach brought him into conflict with Sir George Grey, Governor of the Cape Colony. He wrote to Grey asking whether costs could be reduced by withdrawing troops and by uniting the Cape Colony with other nearby *British* colonies. Grey's non sequitur response was to put forth his own pet project of annexing the independent *Boer* republics, the Transvaal and the Orange Free State. Soon afterward, in defiance of Colonial Office policy, Grey actually recommended the annexation of these Boer republics to the Cape Colony Parliament. Bulwer Lytton reacted by sacking Grey.[21]

In evaluating Bulwer Lytton's reining in of his aggressive subordinate, one cannot help but compare his actions with those of his successors. Lord Carnarvon, formerly Bulwer Lytton's Under-Secretary, accomplished the annexation of the Transvaal in 1874. The consequences—Zulu wars, a Boer rebellion, British defeat, and an end to the confederation—fully justified Bulwer Lytton's earlier opposition to annexation.

If his controversy with Grey is to be seen as the classic confrontation between the "Man on the Spot" and the distant political figure in Britain, score one for the distant political figure. The experience of Disraeli's government of 1874–80 proved the folly of permitting "Men on the Spot" to ignore the policies of the government and so to commit the government to the support of unwanted colonial conflicts. The defeat of the Conservatives in the general election of 1880 can be blamed in large part on unpopular wars precipitated by "Men on the Spot" in South Africa and in Afghanistan.[22] (Ironically, the "Man on the Spot" that provoked the Afghan war was none other than Bulwer Lytton's own son, the first Earl of Lytton, then Viceroy of India.)[23]

The colonies of settlement, to summarize Bulwer Lytton's views, could offer a solution to Britain's social problems as lands of financial and moral opportunity for all levels of society. By encouraging the colonies to model their institutions upon those of the mother country, he also hoped, as the colonies achieved responsible self-government, to ensure the endurance of their connection with Britain. His wish to keep the colonial enterprise economical, and thereby popular, was similarly related to the value of duration. For "Duration," as he wrote in one of the *Caxtoniana* essays, "is an essential element of all plans for happiness, private or public, and conservatism looks to the durable in all its ideas of improvement."[24]

The Empire that Bulwer Lytton sought to preserve has witnessed profound changes since his day. But the basic idea of a community of English-speaking nations, sharing the best traditions of their British heritage, while adapting to changing times and conditions, continues to prove its worth. As Bulwer Lytton foresaw in a speech to departing colonists, the builders of Empire in his day have laid the foundations for a flourishing posterity: "Ages hence industry and commerce will crowd the roads that you will have made; travellers from all nations will halt on the bridges you will have first flung over solitary rivers, and gaze on gardens and cornfields that you will have first carved from the wilderness."[25] And the names that were inscribed on the trees of Empire planted long ago are indeed writ large today.

## NOTES

1. T. H. S. Escott, *Edward Bulwer, First Baron Lytton of Knebworth* (London: George Routledge & Sons, 1910), pp. 276–77.
2. Cited in C. C. Eldridge, *England's Mission—The Imperial Idea in the Age*

*of Gladstone and Disraeli 1868–1880* (Chapel Hill: University of North Carolina Press, 1974), p. 178.

3. Ibid, p. 2; see also Nicholas C. Edsall, *Richard Cobden, Independent Radical* (Cambridge: Harvard University Press, 1986), p. 312.

4. Goldwin Smith, *Reminiscences* (New York: Macmillan, 1910), p. 168.

5. C. C. Eldridge, "The Myth of Mid-Victorian 'Separatism': The Cession of the Bay Islands and the Ionian Islands in the Early 1860s," *Victorian Studies* 12 (1969): 331–46; John S. Galbraith, "Myths of the 'Little England' Era," *American Historical Review* 67 (1961): 34–48; John Darwin, "Imperialism and the Victorians: The Dynamics of Territorial Expansion," *English Historical Review* 112 (June 1997): 614–42.

6. Eldridge, *England's Mission*, p. 35.

7. Edward Bulwer Lytton to Sir George Bowen, 12 August 1860, unpublished letter in the Hertfordshire County Record Office [hereafter Hertford], D/EK C26.

8. Helen M. Swartz and Marvin Swartz, eds., *Disraeli's Reminiscences* (New York: Stein and Day, 1976), p. 61. But see also Bulwer Lytton's essay on the futility of seeking posthumous reputation: "Posthumous Reputation," in *Caxtoniana: A Series of Essays on Life, Literature and Manners*, 2 vols. (London: William Blackwood and Sons, 1863): 2:173–212.

9. Charles W. Snyder, *Liberty and Morality—A Political Biography of Edward Bulwer-Lytton* (New York: Peter Lang, 1995), p. 156.

10. Ibid., pp. 58–62, 155.

11. Edward Lytton Bulwer, *England and the English* [1833], ed. Standish Meacham (Chicago and London: University of Chicago Press, 1970), p. 142n.

12. Snyder, *Liberty and Morality*, p. 119.

13. Letter to Sir George Bowen, April 29, 1859, printed in second Earl of Lytton, *The Life of Edward Bulwer, First Lord Lytton*, 2 vols. (London: Macmillan, 1913), 2:286.

14. Bulwer Lytton as novelist dealt a second time with emigration to Australia in *A Strange Story* (1862). To be sure, in this "alchemical novel," the scene shifts to Australia in an atmosphere of gloom and foreboding, very different from the adventurous and even light-hearted spirit of *The Caxtons*. Dr. Fenwick, the hero of *A Strange Story*, seeks to leave behind his home and his profession and to get as far away as possible. It seems that he goes to Australia not because it is a land of opportunity but because it is at the ends of the earth. Still, there remains a hint of the attraction that drew the Caxton emigrants. Fenwick encounters a young German aristocrat who is going to join a college friend in a nearby German settlement. A wastrel in his own land, he now has high hopes of making a better life in Australia: "He owned himself to be good for nothing. . . ; and, withal, the happy spendthrift was so inebriate with hope,—sure that he should be rich before he was thirty" (lxxiii).

15. Coral Lansbury, *Arcady in Australia: The Evocation of Australia in Nineteenth-Century English Literature* (Carlton, Victoria: Melbourne University Press, 1970), p. 2.

16. Allan Conrad Christensen, *Edward Bulwer-Lytton: The Fiction of New Regions* (Athens: The University of Georgia Press, 1976), p. 229.

17. The Colony of Canada included the present provinces of Quebec and Ontario. Confederation would join with these the then separate colonies of Nova Scotia and New Brunswick (and others later on). For a full discussion of the controversy over confederation, see A. R. M. Lower, *Colony to Nation: A History of Canada* (Toronto: Longmans, Green, 1946), pp. 309–24.

18. Edward Bulwer Lytton to Lord Derby, September 7, 1858, Hertford, D/EK C27.

19. Edward Bulwer Lytton, undated memorandum, Hertford, D/EK/WC1.

20. Edward Bulwer Lytton to Lord Derby, September 7, 1858, Hertford, D/EK C27.

21. Snyder, *Liberty and Morality*, pp. 169–74.

22. Robert Blake, *Disraeli* (New York: Anchor, 1968), pp. 626–32, 634–42.

23. John Lowe Duthie, "Lord Lytton And The Second Afghan War: A Psychological Study," *Victorian Studies* 27 (Summer 1984): 461–75.

24. Bulwer Lytton, "On the Spirit of Conservatism," *Caxtoniana,* 2:342.

25. Address of 1858 to colonists departing for British Columbia, printed in second Earl of Lytton, *Life of Edward Bulwer*, 2:293.

# Between Men:
# Reading the Caxton Trilogy as
# Domestic Fiction

Peter W. Sinnema

ORIGINALLY PUBLISHED IN SERIAL FORM IN *BLACKWOOD'S*, EDWARD Bulwer Lytton's Caxton trilogy—*The Caxtons* (1849), *"My Novel," or, Varieties in English Life* (1853), and *What Will He Do with It?* (1859)—were aimed at a middle-class readership that purchased a periodical known to be "liberal in literature and conservative in politics."[1] If for no other reason, the trilogy deserves renewed attention because of its immense popularity with Victorian book buyers, whose infatuation with Bulwer Lytton's fiction made his novels the most extensively published in Britain between 1830 and 1870.[2] This essay, however, contextualizes the Caxton trilogy within the generic framework of domestic fiction. Specifically, it seeks to foster renewed appreciation for the ways in which the Caxton novels interrogate questions of empire, male education, and women's "place" at midcentury within a narrative framework preoccupied with the ideology of hallowed domesticity. Engaged, simultaneously, with the importance of male-male apprenticeship to moral development (and thereby signaling its participation in the bildungsroman tradition), the hopes and vexations of colonial expansion, and changing definitions of proper womanly conduct, the Caxton trilogy locates in the domestic sphere the promise of a resolution to various anxieties associated with these social and political issues.[3] Bulwer's Caxton novels guarantee his legacy as a central figure in the rise and popularity of domestic fiction. It should, ultimately, be apprehended as a relatively cohesive, if also textually labyrinthine, articulation of an ethics by which young Victorian men and women can live in an era heavily inflected by the affiliated realities of Empire and hearth.

The phrase "domestic fiction," however, is not employed to

184

refer solely to literature about the private sphere of the bourgeois home. Rather, in Bulwer's trilogy the domestic also designates the relation between an imperial center—the "home" country and its various coordinates (the domestic market, domestic population, and domestic social problems)—and its colonial margins. In fact, a focus on the latter definition has produced some of the most provocative Bulwerian scholarship. Considered in isolation from its companions, for example, *The Caxtons* has been read almost exclusively as a novel advocating the "true cult of the colonies."[4] Coral Lansbury traces the profound influence of Samuel Sidney's best-selling *Australian Handbook* (1848) on *The Caxtons*, which manifests not only a "belief in a Golden Age which could be regained by a return to the plough and a furrowed field beneath a clear sky," but also defines Australia "in the English literary tradition of Arcadianism."[5] Patrick Brantlinger follows Lansbury's example by situating *The Caxtons* within colonialist discourse and commenting on its superlative imagining of the Australian Bush as a "realm of potential redemption" for Britain's "superfluous" population: "If Bulwer perceives the home country as deluged, overcrowded with a redundant population to the extent that members of the middle and upper-classes are themselves becoming superfluous, Australia is virtually empty, a desert."[6] According to this reading, *The Caxtons* is of interest primarily for its figural "negation" of the Australian landscape through "rhetorical strateg[ies] by which Western writing conceives of the Other as absence, emptiness, nothingness, or death."[7]

Pisistratus ("Sisty") Caxton, the novel's central protagonist, serves as the ideological focal point of such a reading in his perception of Australia as unobstructed space. Shortly after his arrival in Australia, he rhapsodizes about the beauty and potential of his new home:

> "And this land has become the heritage of our people! . . . How mysteriously, while Europe rears its populations, and fulfils its civilising mission, these realms have been concealed from its eyes,—divulged to us just as civilisation needs the solution to its problems; a vent for feverish energies, baffled in the crowd; offering bread to the famished, hope to the desperate; in very truth enabling the 'New World to redress the balance of the Old.'" (XVII:ii)

In Sisty's optimistic paean, Australia is envisaged as an anodyne to the ills of superannuated, European civilization. *The Cax-*

*tons* can therefore be apprehended in part as a trial run for the aggressively expansionist policies that its author was to advocate in 1858 when he became secretary for the colonies in the Derby-Disraeli cabinet; it articulates more explicitly than any of Bulwer's other novels an ideal model for colonization. Construed simultaneously as wide-open, yet well-governed lands of opportunity for ambitious young men constrained by the economic realities of midcentury England, the colonies come to represent a ready solution-in-waiting: "The world is wide," Sisty's father, Austin, advises his son at one point late in *The Caxtons*; "go into a state that is not so civilised. The disparities of the Old World vanish amidst the New!" (XVI:x).

As Brantlinger has astutely pointed out, in this "colonial novel" men down on their luck in England "can discover roles for themselves in the colonies, fighting the wild animals and the wild blacks, taming the wilderness, turning deserts into Arcadias."[8] But Brantlinger fails to emphasize that these roles are invariably played out in ultimate service to what Sisty calls "that marvelous empire, which valour without parallel has annexed to the Throne of the Isles" (XVIII:viii). England—Empire's dead center, the national home—always remains central to the consciousness of characters in *The Caxtons*. A useful homology thus suggests itself: the mother country is to the remote colony what the hearth is to the public sphere—an idealized center for which exiles long, yet in relation to which they construct their political and economic identities. "Novel after novel" in the Victorian era "suggests that it is the daily construction of the home country as the location of the colonizer's racial and moral identity and as the legitimization of the colonizer's national subjecthood that made possible the carrying out of the work of the Empire."[9]

Despite the priority it is given in present-day Bulwer criticism as an element of cultural situatedness in an otherwise hoary narrative, Australia is really just one of numerous spheres of opportunity, one relatively brief stop in quest plots that prepare young men for public service and domestic contentment in the "hardy air of the chill Mother Isle," England (XVIII:i). The dramatic contrast between the span of time Sisty spends in Australia and the duration of that span's textual narration—to put it crudely, less than one-seventeenth of Sisty's narrative is devoted to roughly one-third of his life as it unfolds up until the ending of *The Caxtons*—should, on its own, signal a problem with denominating this text a colonial novel. Bulwer himself insisted that the Caxton trilogy was to "apeal [*sic*] to domestic Emotions";[10] it is "in those supreme domestic values [that] all men may find their interests converging, and when fought on behalf of them, the Battle of Life becomes an instance not of life fractional but of life integral."[11]

This is not to suggest, however, that domesticity (figured as a feminine sphere) and occasionally violent, masculinized, public activity (colonialism in particular) exist in states of splendid isolation. Rather, each may be said to presuppose and rely upon the other for its own sense of identity and the containment of its own distinct values. Sisty's radical freedom as a vivacious bachelor in a largely unregulated, "open" colony is meaningful only in relation to the structured home he has temporarily left behind and to which he returns with the hope of marrying. "Manly" colonial activity requires an image of the passive, domestic woman as its ideological antithesis and, more importantly, as the point of return.

Each Caxton novel, to borrow the phrasing of Nancy Armstrong, records "a struggle to individuate" on the part of characters that can self-identify as being masculine or feminine, but only in an unpredictable world that occasionally reveals the tenuousness of such identities and the consequent need to shore them up. Sexual stability is secured only because Bulwer's novels "evaluate these [processes of individuation] according to a set of moral norms that exalted the domestic woman" while also reifying her.[12] Although state diplomacy and party intrigue are central to all three of the Caxton novels, the political arena exists primarily as a vaguely defined public space, one in which male characters are given the opportunity to develop professionally but from which they must habitually retire to enjoy the morally reinvigorating climate of the domicile, presided over by affectionate wives and mothers. Comprehended as narratives that construct a field of knowledge for proper domestic living, the novels in the Caxton trilogy provide evidence of a gendered division in fiction that Armstrong argues began in the eighteenth century: "To gender this field, things within the field itself had to be gendered. Masculine objects were understood in terms of their relative economic and political qualities, while feminine objects were recognized by their relative emotional qualities."[13] Armstrong's oppositional model is, perhaps, too rigid to account adequately for the occasional confusion and anxiety about gender roles that arise in Bulwer's domestic fiction, particularly when young men defer to the superior knowledge and experience of older mentors. But this model is useful as a vehicle to demonstrate how "home" is the ideological focal point of Bulwer's narratives, connoting seclusion from the turbulence of Victorian politics.

Home, however, does not function as a contestatory space in which female characters attain representational depth. Just as home is consecrated as the serene antipodes of the Bush or the city, so "woman"—more properly, the womanly presence—is made the middle-class home's essential piece of furniture. Even when home lacks a literal mother or wife, it maintains the aura of a distinctly female presence. An old bachelor's cottage in *What Will He Do with It?*, for example, because well-tended and suffused with the occupant's love for his granddaughter, "is the Presence of Home,—that ineffable, sheltering, loving Presence,—which, amidst solitude, murmurs 'not solitary'" (V:x).

Not surprisingly, then, *The Caxtons* ends happily a year after Sisty's marriage to his cousin Blanche—a girl who, during the narrator's sojourn in Australia, had been nurtured by her father to become "the ornament and joy of the one that now asked to guard and cherish it" (XVIII:viii). More frequently in the trilogy, however, this sort of nurturing is practiced between men. Bulwer positions his central male characters as protégés to experienced and worldly mentors. In their various struggles to achieve independence and earn a name, ambitious young men in the Bulwerian universe invariably submit themselves to one or more preceptors, men highly adept and steeped in the knowledge of politics, high art, journalism, military discipline, practical industry, or academia. Eager for renown, patient under duress, Bulwer's young heroes undergo prolonged tutelage to become valiant and successful Englishmen. They mature into representatives of masculine courage and fortitude, attributes fundamental to Bulwer's conception of essential Englishness.

The logic governing these mentorships, however, is not that of pure imitation. Several of the men who function as preceptors are clearly inadequate to the task; their occasional moral failures can be spectacular, including, among other vices, drunkenness, pride, insincerity, and betrayal. Bulwer, therefore, does not advocate unthinking discipleship, but draws instead on the conventions of picaresque narratives. The episodic structure of such narratives is mirrored by the adventures of those male novices who end up as exemplars in their own right after wandering from one mentor to another, patterning themselves after the good and learning to identify and reject the vicious. Mentorship in Bulwer's fiction can be understood as the narrative organization of a series of privileged relationships through which young men move, and from whose vicissitudes and contradictions these men learn how to be, or not be, in the world.

Sisty Caxton is a particularly fast learner. In contrast to his aimless father, Austin, who years before had lost "all motive for exertion" to complete his Great Work on "The History of Human Error," Sisty is very early in life "animated by the practical desire to excel" (VII:viii; II:i). Along with two of the boy's uncles, Austin carries out a comfortable homosocial experiment in home education for Sisty. By the time the Caxton family moves to London from their modest provincial estate in order to expedite the publication of the Great Work, Sisty has been well prepared by his several male pedagogues to recognize and seize upon advantageous situations. The journey to London, which Sisty makes on foot, is itself an important educational experience for a boy reared in rural isolation, and it foreshadows a binary opposition between city and country central to the subsequent Caxton novels. In Bulwer's imaginative world, London is axial, emphatically more significant than Australia as a site of opportunity (and, predictably, of potential ruin for the unwary or corrupt). Sisty finds that the "vast wilderness of London" is a place of "active energy all around, at first saddening . . . soon exhilarating, and at last contagious" (V:iv). In the teeming metropolis Sisty begins to "sigh for toil, to look around . . . for a career" (V:iv); there, he becomes better acquainted with Mr. Trevanion, an old college friend of his father, who in turn introduces the young man to a dignified bachelor and "true fine gentleman," Sir Sedley Beaudesert. These two men come to function as Sisty's most influential mentors next to his father and Uncle Roland. Trevanion takes the lad on as a secretary and eventually lends him £1500 to emigrate. Beaudesert, in turn, is to Sisty a practical adviser and paragon of calm refinement.

Sisty gradually but unequivocally assumes a masculine, English identity. Whereas previously he could only admire and emulate "men who have won noble names, and whose word had weight on the destinies of glorious England" (VIII:iv), by the conclusion of *The Caxtons* he can legitimately claim to have joined ranks with such men. This assumption of a definite identity can best be apprehended as the desired result of an informal but rigorous training that inducts him into a male camaraderie and makes of him a suitable mentor in his own right. Sisty's personal sense of being, above all else, an Englishman is secured through an unequal relation of tutelage with the half-barbarous (and only half-English) Francis Vivian, an irascible adventurer who ultimately turns out to be his cousin, Herbert de Caxton. Midway through his narrative Sisty claims to have "gained a sort of ascendancy over [Vivian's] savage nature" (VIII:iv). Vivian's taste for fashionable French novels, in particular, is anathema to Sisty, who locates in such literature "the confusion of all wrong and right in individual character . . . the hatred, carefully instilled, of the poor against the rich" (X:i). Vivian's refractory books are evidence of a mind perversely vulnerable to un-English ideas.

Raised by a Spanish mother whose Catholicism, bold principles, and national prejudices negated the lessons about honor and duty his English father tried to instill in him, Vivian remains for much of his life the victim of a pernicious home education carried out on the Continent. He is only redeemed when he is convinced to accompany Sisty to Australia; in that New World, he is transformed into a member of the "master race," one of those English "lords of the land" (XVII:i). In effect, Vivian is Anglicized through emigration: what Sisty sees as the baleful influences of Spanish blood and French literature are nullified entirely when, near the end of the novel, Vivian dies fighting for the British Empire in India. Bravery under the colors of the Union Jack in far-flung corners of the empire salvages a flawed domestic education. Australia and India are literally *and* conceptually extensions of home and home education. If Vivian's eventual salvation is indicative of Bulwer's conviction that colonial possessions have enormous potential to regenerate the nation's youth, it also impresses upon readers the importance of the domicile as the nurturing ground for individual and national morality.

Seditious literature is again implicated as a primary corrupting force in *"My Novel."* Lenny Fairfield, this text's counterpart to Sisty, is a pupil to a series of moralizers and employers, eventually becoming a successful novelist in London and marrying his childhood sweetheart, Helen Digby. Like Sisty, Lenny is contrasted throughout *"My Novel"* to an outright villain, Randal Leslie, avaricious heir to a diminished fortune. Early on it seems as if Lenny's career might follow the path forged by Vivian or Leslie. When still a young boy, Lenny is hired by Signor Riccabocca as a gardener's assistant. Although in the service of a generous and humane man, Lenny's discontent with his lowly position in the world is fueled by "poisonous tracts" that begin to circulate through the village. He purchases a number of these incendiary tracts, what the narrator calls the "aqueducts and sewers" of literature. Fortunately, Riccabocca discovers the boy's penchant for such literature and expostulates successfully with him on its dangers: "Now, Lenny, take this piece of advice. You are young, clever, and aspiring: men rarely succeed in changing the world; but a man seldom fails at success if he lets the world alone, and resolves to make the best of it" (IV:viii). By the time Lenny reaches the age of independence and moves to London, he has achieved the moral fortitude to resist the great city's temptations.

Lenny's original flirtation with revolutionary tracts, however, is adumbrated in a seemingly insignificant, but analogous, scene much later in *"My Novel."* By this point Lenny has benefited from the material help or worldly tutelage of no fewer than five men: Riccabocca, his mercenary uncle Richard Avenal, the dissolute essayist John Burley, Waterloo veteran Harley L'Estrange, and Mr. Norreys, a professional author who takes Lenny on as his literary amanuensis. Lenny's final maturation is signaled by his capacity to demur from the philistinism and debauchery of men like Avenal and Burley, while simultaneously imbibing useful knowledge about the ways of the world. His prolonged conditioning under the watchful, if occasionally delinquent, eyes of such mentors molds him into a defender of the "public spirit," which, as he proclaims at a Tory party meeting, "augments the manly interest in all that affects the nation" (XII:xxxii). The mentorships that benefit Lenny, therefore, do not produce in him merely a vague appreciation for the values of Victorian conservatism, but inspire a commitment to high Tory politics. This midcentury Toryism, although flourishing "the public spirit" as its ideological banner, insulates "manly interests" from all that might threaten its exclusive integrity—especially women and social parvenus.

When the bluff Squire of Hazeldean, then, encounters Lenny on a West End street, the anecdote he tells the latter about a boy back in the shire who became addicted to subversive propaganda no longer has any deep resonance with the reformed young novelist. "Why," Hazeldean blusters in reference to the unnamed insurrectionary,

"he was a village genius [like Lenny himself in his childhood], and always reading some cursed little tract or other; and got mighty discontented with King, Lords, and Commons, I suppose, and went about talking of the wrongs of the poor, and the crimes of the rich, till, by Jove, sir, the whole mob rose one day with pitchfork and sickles, and smash went Farmer Smart's thrashing machines; and on the same night my ricks were on fire! . . . The village genius, thank heaven, is sent packing to Botany Bay." (XI:ii)

Whereas Austin Caxton reads Australia as "a safer field" for a potential criminal like Vivian, the Squire of *"My Novel"* refers, with the self-satisfied air of an aggrieved landowner, to the infamous penal colony in New South Wales where British convicts were transported after 1788. In both interpretations, however, *property* is the weighty concept that grounds equivocal signification. The Squire's property, as well as his right to its private enjoyment, is protected with the insurgent's swift transportation, while Sisty quickly develops the proprietary disposition in a colony where land is readily available.

This disposition, as already suggested, is something inculcated in the young through male-male apprenticeships. Australia *may* be the ground on which it is fostered, but veneration for property takes on a kind of universal conviction in Bulwer's domestic novels; it is a value preserved across the generations as a trust between seasoned men and receptive proselytes. Indeed, this trust can itself be read as a propertied relation, the most valorized territory preserved between men. It is a relation that benefits Lionel Haughton of *What Will He Do with It?*, who experiences a conditioning in conservative values similar to that of Sisty and Lenny. An ambitious but indigent seventeen-year-old near the beginning of the novel, he eventually inherits an enormous fortune from his uncle and chief benefactor, Guy Darrell. As a result of this inheritance, he can marry Sophy Waife, whose true identity as the daughter of an aristocrat, Arthur Branthwaite, is only revealed in the final pages of the narrative.

During a brief residence at Fawley Manor House, Darrell's country seat, Lionel adds to his noble ambitions a deep appreciation for the value of ancient lineage. He digests Darrell's own reverence for birthright and home. He also escapes being contaminated by his patron's intense bitterness: Darrell's youthful, unrequited love for Caroline Montfort is a tragedy that continues to mark his life, although the lady herself has long suffered from self-reproach and still adores Darrell. Unlike Lenny and Sisty, however, who settle on writing careers, Lionel never joins a profession. Instead, his central achievement involves a reversal of the initial mentor/apprentice relationship, demonstrating his inauguration into patriarchy: Lionel helps to reintegrate the reclusive Darrell with the active world. In turn, Lionel is aided by Morley and his cousin, George, in overcoming the hurdles of prejudice so that he can marry Sophy.

Lionel, in short, is schooled for nothing more than marriage and inheritance, and in the complex series of transactions between men that bring the novel to a close, his only trial is to be patient while others clear the way for his engagement. When Sophy's true, aristocratic identity is discovered, all difficulties evaporate. Darrel happily consents to Lionel's petition for Sophy's hand, and he is suddenly able to recognize that his own marriage to Caroline Montfort would "give at least noble occupation and lasting renown to a mind that is drowning itself and stifling its genius" (XII:xi).

Sophy's sudden change of class identity, however, also operates as a condensation of the sexual and class politics that lie at the root of the three narratives of male growth traced above. Whereas protagonists such as Pisistratus, Lenny, and Lionel "set to the task of fixing themselves, their Selves, and their interests"[14] through apprenticeships that are, fundamentally, processes of masculine individuation, female characters like Sophy are always already "fixed" in Bulwer's domestic fiction. Sophy, Blanche, Violante, Helen, Caroline Montfort—each plays a one-dimensional role, familiar to any reader of Victorian fiction as that of the domestic(ated) angel.

Bulwer's angelic woman finds her acme, perhaps, in the cipher-like Nora Avenal, Lenny's deceased mother in *"My Novel,"* whose talents as an unpublished poet are doubly sublimated by womanly attributes clearly more admirable to the narrator than those of the female artist; Nora is praised for her "docile, yielding temper—her generous, self-immolating spirit" (XI:xvi). The death of Nora long before *"My Novel"* begins is emblematic of other, metaphorical "deaths": female characters in Bulwer's domestic fiction are caught up in a system of representational stasis so inflexible that any possibility of their development threatens to undermine the stories about male growth and maturation central to the novels. Nora's poetic aptitude must await its full expression in her son, whose posthumous adoration of his mother as a personal muse enacts a reifying, if pathetic, idealization.

The cultivation of masculine identity in Bulwer's domestic novels, therefore, requires, along with lengthy mentorships and an expansive field of action, an antithetical conception of invariable, universal womanhood. Men can "become" precisely because women simply "are." Male subjectivity evolves and secures itself in contradistinction to a particular construction of "woman," and in this process constitutes itself as everything contrary to the feminine: impelled by ambition, physically vital, aggressively patriotic, characters such as Sisty, Lenny, and Lionel appear to be driven by desires that by definition exclude (if paradoxically and incompletely) women from the field of action.

Sisty, who at one point in *The Caxtons* rejects the monotony of college for the heady life of the colonist, provides one of the most striking examples of this exclusion. His own aspirations as a fortune-hunting emigrant are tied solely to the renewal of the Caxtons' patrilineal heritage, a redemption of glory that quarantines male prerogative from the interruption of womanly claims, especially claims to property. Referring to his father's inertia and Uncle Roland's decrepit ancestral home, Sisty is filled with longing prior to his departure for the colonies: "To restore my father's fortunes, re-weave the links of that broken ambition which had knit his genius with the world, rebuild these fallen walls [of Roland's medieval tower], cultivate these barren moors, revive the ancient name, glad the old soldier's age, and be to *both* the brothers what Roland had lost—a son" (XII:v). The patrilineal nature of these desires indicates that Sisty's quest for a vocation is itself intricately linked with the search for an independent, masculine identity. As his father cautions Sisty earlier in the novel, recalling his own impossible infatuation for Lady Ellinor when a young man, such a quest risks failure if influenced by sexual desire: "Great was the folly . . . of linking the whole usefulness of my life to the will of a human creature like myself" (VII:viii). The masculine exclusivity of the mentorship by which Sisty benefits is a guarantee that he will not suffer Austin's emasculation.

The gendering of the field of sexual relations in Bulwer's domestic fiction, to return to Nancy Armstrong's argument, thus means the rigorous segregation of roles for male and female characters. Admission into productive manhood via homosocial mentoring, in particular, re-emphasizes the cultural potency for mid-Victorians of a belief in what Ruskin was to call the "separate characters" of the sexes, which retain their immaculate, "natural" difference through a balancing act of reciprocity. If, as Ruskin contended, "each [sex] has what the other has not: each completes the other, and is completed by the other," then it follows that apprenticeship into this rightful sphere-sovereignty is best accomplished between members of the same sex. Bulwer's boys are trained to recognize that "man's power is active, progressive, defensive," whereas his girls learn (although it is unclear precisely how and under whose tutelage this gender education takes place) that "woman's power is for . . . sweet ordering, arrangement, and decision." *Both* sexes, however, come to appreciate "the true nature of home—it is the place of Peace;

the shelter, not only from all injury, but from all terror, doubt, and division."[15] If Bulwer's male heroes are homosocialized by being (to put it somewhat awkwardly) mentored into masculinity, the educational process itself presupposes that, as the author intoned in an earlier quotation, the "Battle of Life" is ultimately waged in defense of "supreme domestic values."

Bulwer, then, focuses almost solely on male-male apprenticeships: despite a professed veneration for the virtues of the domicile that rivals Ruskin's tribute, the relegation of women to marginal roles indicates that mentoring itself is a privilege of men, solidifying their central status in his fiction and, implicitly, in the real world—at least as Bulwer would like to see it. But there are two notable exceptions, both contained in the last of the Caxton novels, which seem to threaten this centering praxis. If Bulwer's domestic fiction attempts to reconcile social differences through sexually exclusive mentorships that rescue young men from "life fractional" and move them towards "life integral," then the possibility of female characters themselves becoming legitimate mentors profoundly disrupts what Allan Christensen calls Bulwer's "vision of humanity,"[16] humanization through *paternal* instruction. These two potentially disruptive moments can be turned to by way of conclusion because they are symptomatic of the fundamental tenuousness of male identities. "Generous, self-immolating" wives and daughters, like the "wild blacks" of Australia, function as eternal Others over and against whom young Bulwerian men define themselves—as chivalric protectors of the home and its virtues or as rightful defenders of newly staked territory. The possibility of successful resistance to sexual or racial colonialism threatens to undermine the masculine project itself, the coming-into-being of virile Englishmen.

Whereas there is no significant congress between women in *The Caxtons* and *"My Novel"*—no attention given to modes of gender indoctrination that, readers are left to assume, gradually fashion girls into "the quiet, serene, unnoticed, deep-felt excellence of woman" so cherished by Bulwer (*"My Novel,"* IX:viii)— *What Will He Do with It?* presents two instances in which male prerogative seems to be usurped by female characters. Firstly, Caroline Montfort informally adopts Sophy when she is temporarily abandoned by her grandfather, William Waife. As a lonely widow, Caroline's determination to secure the girl's protection and complete her education offers the only real counterpart in the Caxton trilogy to similar relations between boys and men: the adoption is a twist on male-male apprenticeships, a relationship that intimates the possibility of a closed, feminine sphere in which gendered knowledge is produced and inculcated, an alternative "space" to that created between Darrell and Lionel.

A second, rather bizarre, codependent relationship between the novel's degraded desperado, Jasper Losely, and his one-time fiancée, Arabella Crane, presents a version of the jilted-lover plot. Like Darrell, Arabella suffers under the weight of past injustice: "some memory in her past had poisoned the well-springs of her social being" (IV:iv). It turns out that Jasper failed to fulfill an earlier promise to marry Arabella, and compounds the insult with malicious denials of attachment or obligation. Jasper's indulgence in bawdy pleasures and physical excess, however, make him financially vulnerable. With increasing frequency he is forced to petition Arabella for funds to pay off gambling debts and keep himself in drink. She, in turn, gains a mysterious power over the once-dandiacal wretch and devotes herself to his redemption.

In the end, Arabella's reformational project for Jasper rests on an undignified compulsion that the text implies is peculiar to her sex. "Her own life," Bulwer's narrator explains, is "a barren sacrifice, but a jealous sentinel on his" (IV:xix). Recognizing that the once-suave object of her passionate devotion has become a muddled drunkard, Arabella seems unable to purge herself of ruinous affection. In the very moment of her ultimate triumph, while she nurses an incapacitated Jasper as he falters on his deathbed, Arabella indulges in an outburst that transforms her from the repressed victim of desires to a dupe of bathetic yearning: "You heard," she cries out to the visiting Caroline when Jasper pleads for attention shortly before he dies, "*he misses me*! He can't bear me out of his sight now,—me, me!" (XII:x).

An unscrupulous reading of Arabella, then, might suggest that her career as a potent femme fatale—a vengeful figure, tragically misled in her youth, who comes to wield monstrous power over Jasper—parallels that of Guy Darrell, who must wrench himself free of morbid obsessions with the past in order to prove that he is not a lifelong "brilliant failure." Deftly consolidating her mastery over the once-menacing Jasper, Arabella could be viewed as yet another projection of male, Victorian anxiety about the viraginous woman, a more fortunate version of Lady Audley (or a less defiled precursor of Wilde's Salomé), who does not have to pay the price of death for encroaching on male prerogative. Arabella's unilluminated devotion to an insolent reprobate, however, seriously dilutes the force of such a reading. Ultimately, she remains a victim to impulses that are underscored by the novel as being essentially feminine. Because Arabella's constancy, however vexed and acrimonious it may be, never receives the type of psychological exploration that helps readers make sense of Darrell's choler, she represents a perversion of ideal femininity rather than an alternative vision of womanhood.

Caroline Montfort, too, experiences a direct and abrupt negation of any authority that her role as guardian might initially have lent her. Lionel's marriage with Sophy is a transaction expedited only by Darrell and Waife. Significantly, prior to the engagement, these men grow to appreciate each other after a long period of mutual distrust and misunderstanding: Waife falls ill at Fawley Manor House and must endure a long recuperation under Darrell's increasingly affectionate care. The pact made for the "poor young lovers," as Waife calls them, can therefore be comprehended as the final legitimation of patriarchal ascendancy in domestic matters. By giving his granddaughter to Darrell's heir, Waife engages in a triangular exchange that cements an already-strong homosocial relation. Sophy's surrogate mother, Lady Montfort, is notably absent from this exchange; her agreement is not solicited.

Arabella's self-erasure and Caroline's acquiescence to male privilege reveal that male insularity and self-sufficiency are idealized states that can only be maintained through constant narrative vigilance. Bulwer curtails Caroline's participation in Sophy's education and enervates Arabella to the point that her emotional addiction is preposterous. Adequately subdued—Lady Montfort will become Mrs. Darrell, while Arabella retires into dejected but comfortable solitude—these women leave traditionally public responsibilities to men.

Bulwer's female characters, it seems, must on occasion be reminded of their natural, domestic calling. This is one of the lessons that lies at the heart of the Caxton trilogy, and if it is fundamental to an appreciation of the novels as works of domestic fiction, it is not unrelated to Bulwer's interest in matters of Empire. After all, in a similar vein, *The Caxtons* recalls young men to their colonial duty: at midcentury, entire continents still awaited the benefits of the civilizing, Anglicizing mission. But if Australia must be represented as a "negative" space in order to justify its colonization, such a conceptual refusal to acknowledge the physical presence of indigenous peoples, let alone their history and culture, is expressive of intense anxiety about colonialism itself. Sisty's and his companions' heroic "rituals of militarized masculinity [spring] not only from the economic lust for . . . silver and gold, but also from the implacable rage of paranoia." Apprehensiveness about intruding onto the "edges and blank spaces" of colonial territory, fears about native reprisal "and hence [about] the tenuousness of possession"[17] are repressed through acts of chasing and killing "the blacks." The violent *creation* of empty space is converted into the myth of an originary, vacant landscape, ripe for the taking and taming.

An equally intense paranoia frequently defined the terms of confrontation between male Victorian writers and that other "dark continent," Woman. This familiar metaphor, however, is not wholly appropriate as a diagnosis of the anxieties that plague the trilogy. In Bulwer's domestic fiction, women are not creatures of mystery lacking an explanatory code; rather, they remain objects of male knowledge, comprehended without difficulty as being either self-effacing, and hence suitable, overseers of the domicile, or as libidinal offenders in need of moral reclamation. It is safe to assume that the certainty underwriting Bulwer's identification of such female types contributed in no small degree to the popularity of his fiction with *Blackwood*'s conservative readership.

And perhaps, in the end, this popularity is the most intriguing aspect of Bulwer's domestic fiction for present-day readers interested in the ideological persuasions of an earlier book-buying public. It is easy to dismiss Bulwer's moral project as banal or predictable; the Victorian propensity to eulogize the home and family is now very much a given, as one scholar of the nineteenth century intimates when writing of an era that "regarded it as axiomatic that the home was the foundation and the family the cornerstone of . . . civilization."[18] Such dismissal, however, would originate from a position of hindsight that fails to appreciate the enormous resonance "home" was coming to acquire for a "domestic" people actively engaged in the expansion and management of Empire. I have attempted to trace some of the interrelations between home, Empire, and masculinity and, in the process, reopen for ongoing investigation a textual terrain that had obvious appeal and import for the Victorians.

## NOTES

1. Walter Graham, *English Literary Periodicals* (New York: Octagon, 1966), p. 280.
2. "Victorian readers discerned in the Caxton novels the summit of Bul-

wer's fictional achievement," Allan Christensen notes, "and perhaps that contemporary judgment also deserves, with some reservation, the ratification of the ages" (*Edward Bulwer-Lytton: The Fiction of New Regions* [Athens: University of Georgia Press 1976], p. 136.)

3. Both the title of this paper and my discussion of male-male apprenticeships find much of their impetus in Eve Kosofsky Sedgwick's now well-known proposition in *Between Men: English Literature and Male Homosocial Desire* (New York: Columbia University Press, 1985): that patriarchal heterosexuality "can best be discussed in terms of one or another form of the traffic in women: it is the use of women as exchangeable, perhaps symbolic, property for the primary purpose of cementing the bonds of men with men" (pp. 25–26).

4. James L. Campbell, Sr., *Edward Bulwer-Lytton* (Boston: Twayne, 1986), p. 98.

5. Coral Lansbury, *Arcady in Australia: The Evocation of Australia in Nineteenth-Century English Literature* (Carlton, Victoria: Melbourne University Press, 1970), pp. 44, 90.

6. Patrick Brantlinger, *Rule of Darkness: British Literature and Imperialism, 1830–1914* (Ithaca: Cornell University Press, 1988), p. 122.

7. David Spurr, *The Rhetoric of Empire: Colonial Discourse in Journalism, Travel Writing, and Imperial Administration* (Durham, N.C.: Duke University Press, 1993), pp. 92–93.

8. Brantlinger, *Rule of Darkness*, p. 123.

9. Rosemary George, "Homes in the Empire, Empires in the Home," *Cultural Critique* 26 (1993–94): 107.

10. Malcolm Orthell Usrey, ed., "The Letters of Sir Edward Bulwer-Lytton to the Editors of *Blackwood's Magazine*, 1840–1873, in the National Library of Scotland," (Ph.D. diss., Texas Technological College, 1963), p. 132.

11. Christensen, *Edward Bulwer-Lytton*, p. 157.

12. Nancy Armstrong, *Desire and Domestic Fiction: A Political History of the Novel* (New York: Oxford University Press, 1987), p. 5.

13. Ibid., pp. 14–15.

14. Donald E. Hall, *Fixing Patriarchy: Feminism and Mid-Victorian Male Novelists* (New York: New York University Press, 1996), p. 3.

15. John Ruskin, *Sesame and Lilies*, in *The Complete Works of John Ruskin* 11 (New York: Kelmscott, n.d.): 59.

16. Christensen, *Edward Bulwer-Lytton*, p. 162.

17. Anne McClintock, *Imperial Leather: Race, Gender and Sexuality in the Colonial Contest* (London: Routledge, 1995), p. 28.

18. Anthony S. Wohl, introduction to *The Victorian Family: Structures and Stresses*, ed. Anthony S. Wohl (London: Croom Helm, 1978), p. 10.

# Writing and Unwriting in *The Caxtons,* *"My Novel,"* and *A Strange Story*

Allan Conrad Christensen

Many FICTIONAL NARRATIVES OF THE NINETEENTH CENTURY TELL not only of human characters but of texts that the reader does not contemplate directly. Carlyle's *Sartor Resartus*, which is constructed in its relationship to the fictitious *Die Kleider, ihr Werden und Wirken*, provides an especially complex example. It has surely influenced Bulwer's presentation of *Zanoni* as an editor's imperfect effort to translate into comprehensibility a manuscript composed in a daunting cipher.[1] Described in *Zanoni* only in the supposed editor's introductory account of his task, the unseen other text acquires greater prominence in *The Caxtons* and *A Strange Story*, which are narrated throughout in the first person. In *The Caxtons* the other text is a monumental "History of Human Error" on which the autobiographer's father is laboring throughout the story. In *A Strange Story* the narrator-physician describes in some detail his own authorship of the ambitious "Inquiry into Organic Life." In progress throughout the autobiographical narratives in which they figure, these fictitious texts become defining countertexts to the autobiographies as well as alter egos of the autobiographers themselves. "The History of Human Error" is always the father's "other son," whom the narrator therefore recognizes as "my brother." The narrator of *A Strange Story* asserts a still fuller identity with his fictitious text: "The work was I myself!—I, in my solid, sober, healthful mind" (lxxiv).

As its title suggests, "The History of Human Error" traces the flaws that have undermined the human condition since the beginning of time. The scholarly author examines the heritage of original sin, which has always thwarted longings for a peacefully productive and just social order. Yet the great work, the fruit of immense research, tells its sinful story "with an arch, unmalignant smile" (IV:ii) and in a hopeful perspective: "From this record of error, [my father] drew forth the grand eras of truth. He showed how earnest men never think in vain, though their thoughts may be errors. He proved how, in vast cycles, age after age, the human mind marches on—like the ocean, receding here, but there advancing" (IV:ii).

While successfully mastering human error in this vast perspective, the book nevertheless typifies the particular erroneous weakness of its author, who has not mastered his own fate. After an early disappointment in love, Mr. Caxton's taking refuge in scholarship has implied an existential defeat. "We dreamers," he sadly tells his son, "solitary students like me, or half-poets like [my] poor [brother] Roland, make our own disease. How many years . . . have I wasted! . . . I took no note of time. And therefore, now, you see, late in life, Nemesis wakes. I look back with regret at powers neglected, opportunities gone" (VII:viii). Despite a wish to see scholarly inclinations in his son Pisistratus, he therefore urges him while a schoolboy to avoid his own mistake: "Master books, but do not let them master you. Read to live, not live to read. One slave of the lamp is enough for a household: my servitude must not be a hereditary bondage" (II:i).

In Mr. Caxton's view, that servitude has indeed been "a hereditary bondage." Although his brother Roland disputes the matter, he has decided to trace their ancestry back to William Caxton the printer, which explains his own absorption into the world of books. Because of this ancestor, whom the narrator himself apostrophizes as "William Caxton, William Caxton!—fatal progenitor!" (XI:i), Mr. Caxton cannot distinguish between the life of flesh and blood and the life of books. The story frequently suggests that his books—in particular his own "Great Book"—are alive for him, whereas the life continuing outside those books lacks reality. He does not go into society, preferring with respect to contemporary authors to "meet them in their books [rather] than in a drawing-room" (VI:iv). And ancient writers too live for him in their printed versions in the library of the British Museum: "My father spends his mornings in those *lata silentia*, as Virgil calls the world beyond the grave. And a world beyond the grave we may well call that land of the ghosts, a book collection." The library, says Mr. Caxton, "is an Heraclea"—"the city of necromancers, in which they raised the dead. Do I want to speak to Cicero?—I invoke him. Do I want to chat in the Athenian marketplace, and hear news two thousand years old?—I write down my charm on a slip of paper, and a grave magician calls me up Aristophanes. And we owe all this to our ancest[or]" (V:ii).

For Pisistratus the heritage of this ancestor has become a nightmare: "We can never escape the ghosts," he remarks to his uncle: "They haunt us always. We cannot think or act, but the soul of some man who has lived before, points the way. The dead never die, especially since . . . our great ancestor introduced printing" (IV:i). Pisistratus must assert his own right to life against the suffocating power of those ghosts, a struggle in which Uncle Roland sometimes assists him. With vehemence, indeed, Roland reproaches Mr. Caxton for his oblivion to the crisis through which his living son is passing: "Look up from those cursed books, brother Austin! What is there in your son's face? Construe *that*, if you can!" (IX:i).

As an alternative to the "cursed books," Uncle Roland proposes a more potentially violent way of life. Recalling what Andrew Brown considers "the most famous words [Bulwer] ever wrote" (in *Richelieu*)—"the pen is mightier than the sword"[2]—the two Caxton brothers prosecute a continuing debate. Roland is a retired soldier and claims that the family descends not from the great printer but from a swordsman, Sir William de Caxton, who fell at Bosworth. But in the case of Roland's son Vivian, the heritage deriving from that hypothetical ancestor proves as disastrous as that stemming from the printer. A rebellious and violent personality, Vivian forcibly abducts the woman for whose affections he and his cousin Pisastratus are rivals. Caught after a chase, Vivian is eventually disarmed and disowned.

The Caxtonian curse strikes Pisastratus himself most damagingly with the failure of a publishing venture in which his foolish father has risked their patrimony. Needing now to make his own way in life, Pisistratus also recognizes that beyond his particular family the curse afflicts the whole culture. Whereas "the mere book-life," as he has long known, "was not meant for me," the state of contemporary culture offers his entire generation little else but the "book-life": "All the professions are so book-lined, book-hemmed, book-choked," his epistle to a possible patron observes, "that wherever these strong hands of mine stretch towards action, they find themselves met by octavo ramparts, flanked with quarto crenellations." Recoiling from the heartbreaking prospect of having to waste years to enter a "book-choked" profession, he concludes with an anguished appeal: "In short, barring the noble profession of arms"—since Uncle Roland's profession too is clearly not meant for him—

> can you tell me any means by which one may escape these eternal books, this mental clockwork, and corporeal lethargy? Where can this

passion for life that runs riot through my veins find its vent? Where can these stalwart limbs and this broad chest grow of value and worth, in this hot-bed of cerebral inflammation and dyspeptic intellect? . . . There has been a pastoral age, and a hunting age, and a fighting age. Now we have arrived at the age sedentary. Men who sit longest carry all before them: puny, delicate fellows, with hands just strong enough to wield a pen, eyes so bleared by the midnight lamp that they see no joy in that buxom sun. (XII:vi)

The solution is to emigrate, for having exhausted its *élan vital*, British civilization must now, according to Bulwer's colonial theory, undergo its rejuvenating ordeal in the colonies. The ordeal will erase many accumulated refinements and stultifying accretions to the manners of an overly self-indulgent, dyspeptic, and now decaying culture. The mentor of Pisistratus urges upon him a regime that corresponds, in the context of the present argument, to the activity of unwriting: "*De-fine-gentlemanise* yourself from the crown of your head to the sole of your foot, and become the greater aristocrat for so doing" (XII:vi). So Pisistratus spends ten years in the Australian Bush, raising sheep in a land that contains very few books. Yet like other colonists he comes to miss books, and his hand itches to wield the pen in the service of a new cultural vision. Having repaired the family fortunes, he returns to England and initiates a literary career by writing the autobiography that we have been reading.

Like the proliferation of books belonging to the "book-life" against which Pisistratus has rebelled, this new book too possesses a power that may be "mightier than the sword." But unlike all those other books that have "hemmed" in and "choked" a more genuine sort of life, the book of Pisistratus is evidently meant to reintroduce fresh air into the ghostly *lata silentia*. It would release and express the "passion for life that runs riot through my veins," thereby using the medium of writing itself to counteract or, in effect, to unwrite other texts. To this end the autobiography develops, like other works in this mode, a double narrative perspective—involving, besides the tale of the author's growth towards maturity, the story of the writing of that story. In what Bulwer evidently considered the manner of Laurence Sterne,[3] the narrator frequently pauses with pen in hand, reflecting engagingly upon his own authorial task as he encounters distractions or introduces a digressive "Chapter on Housetops." A contrast emerges between the scholarly writing project of the father, desirous of correcting human error but mastered by the erroneous "book-life," and the easygoing, liberating, unliterary project of the son. The writing of the son's story seems amusingly to undermine, or to unwrite, the more serious paternal project.

The father will finally complete his "Great Book," and in the last chapter he announces to his family, "there—the work is done!—and now it may go to press as soon as you will." But sending the work to press depends on the will of the son and narrator, who evidently does not wish to report publication of his father's work. The final pages of the narrative present an inconclusive discussion of the problem of evil and other matters. When the narrative of the Caxton family then resumes in the opening chapter of *"My Novel,"* there is still no indication that the father's book has been published. "With the recollection of The Great Book rising before him," Pisistratus resists the suggestion that he, or anyone, might commence another long Caxtonian book: "Indeed, sir, I should think that that would just finish us!" Ironically, considering the Caxtonian heritage, Pisistratus cannot allow his father's book in particular to be published. For despite pious professions of devotion to his father, his own autobiography demonstrates its success precisely by implying the unpublishable longueurs of the paternal book. In supplanting the "other son," the living son also wrests the empowering pen from the paternal hand.

The Caxton fortunes depend henceforth upon Pisistratus, as he continues to write their story in *"My Novel."* While an instance of texts breeding ever new texts, the new work evidently represents a further stage in the endeavor to make writing release rather than suffocate the "passion for *life.*" Involving the genre of fiction, this new stage may also enable the Caxtonian potentiality to fulfil itself more completely. For the author of "The History of Human Error" has been himself recognized as an inadequate novelist—a *romancier manqué*: "What a writer of romances [my father] would have been . . . if he had had as sad an experience of men's passions, as he had the happy intuition into their humours" (*Caxtons* IV:ii). Now that the father has discovered that talent in his son, he will subordinate his own scholarly bent to the cause of the new fictional project. "Novels have become a necessity of the age," he tells Pisistratus in the first chapter of *"My Novel"*: "you must write a novel," and he proceeds to offer suggestions. It must be "the romance of real life . . . [that] puts you chiefly among scenes with which you are familiar, and furnishes you with characters which have been very sparingly dealt with since the time of Fielding" (I:i).

"Real life," then, rather than the "book-life." Yet Pisistratus observes in his reflections upon the developing novel that it treats chiefly the *intellectual* dimension of contemporary reality. The protagonists "belong to that species which we call the INTEL-LECTUAL . . . [and] through them are analysed . . . human intellect, in various forms and directions. . . . This history, rightly considered, is a kind of humble familiar Epic . . . upon the Varieties of English Life in this our Century, set in movement by the intelligences most prevalent" (VIII:i). Unlike the diachronic analysis of "The History of Human Error," this work analyses the synchronic interactions of currently active human "intelligences." By intelligences are meant, I believe, discourses such as the sociological, economic, political, military, literary, religious, and philosophical. In these various fields the characters are shown to be interacting, arguing, struggling for power, in what may seem a convincing vision of realities. The unifying theme is the power that accompanies *knowledge* in these various discourses. Reminding us indeed of Michel Foucault, the phrase "Knowledge is Power" reverberates throughout the immense work.[4] Although the narrator may not like the situation, knowledge is possibly mightier than both the pen and the sword.

Between the generations of the Caxtons, the power struggle continues in the initial chapters, of each of the twelve books into which the novel is divided, which resemble those of *Tom Jones*. At first Pisistratus accepts advice from both his father and Uncle Roland and accords them—and implicitly the rival ancestors that they represent—a share in the paternity of the novel. But he comes thereafter to resist their conditioning. "I plunged my pen into the ink, and my thoughts into the 'Fair Shadowland,'" he reports as his private demon leads him into a new book (V:i). The work is ever more *"My"* novel, and from the initial chapters of Books VIII, IX, X and XI, which contain authorial reflections, the rest of the family is completely exiled. When the family then noisily reappears in Book XII, eager to interfere in the management of the denouement, Pisistratus reduces them again to silence. They too, he ironically reminds us, are only fictional characters at the mercy of a higher authorial control:

"Silence!" cried Pisistratus, clapping his hands to both ears. "I can no more alter the fate allotted to each of the personages whom you honour with your interest than I can change your own; like you, they must go where events lead them, urged on by their own characters and the agencies of others. Providence so pervadingly governs the universe, that you cannot strike it even out of a book. The author may beget a character, but the moment the character comes into action, it escapes from his hands—plays its own part, and fulfils its own inevitable doom." (XII:i)

Whereas Pisistratus has taken over the pen from his father, the novel escapes in its turn the control of its author. With his last pen stroke, the author dismisses it: "Go forth to the world, O MY NOVEL!"

Writing does not simply project, then, the power of the pen-holding author. It subjects the author himself to a power in the text, which rather than with the suffocating "book-life" may, in a novel, be identified with a providential vitality informing the real world. The speculation continues in *A Strange Story*, as Allen Fenwick, the scholarly protagonist, encounters in another genre of writing the vital powers at work in reality. Instead of Pisistratus's "romance of real life," which depicts the motivating "intelligences" of cultural power struggles, he aspires to analyze the human struggle for survival at the biological level. His promising treatise, "The Vital Principle; Its Waste and Supply," has aroused the respectful attention of the scientific community before the opening of the story. (The functions of wasting and replenishment that it observes in the life process may also correspond, in the textual dimension, to an activity of unwriting and rewriting.) Thereafter, for most of the length of his autobiography, Fenwick's work on a more boldly ambitious "Inquiry into Organic Life" constitutes one of the principal lines of the plot. Unlike the experience of the novelist, however, the power that the scientific author comes to recognize may again be that of the smothering "book-life." Fenwick may resemble Wordsworth's bookish Matthew or the Wordsworthian scientist that fails really to live as he writes about a life that has been murdered for dissection.

Years must nevertheless pass before Fenwick will confess that the text so lovingly described has mastered him. His truest life, he believes, passes at the desk in his study, where in choosing to admit or exclude material he exercises a superb power over "the work [that] was I myself!" During one especially productive long night of composition, the exhilaration of establishing his firmly human identity may even imply wrestling successfully against God. In his own writing he is unwriting a ghostly divine text:

I wrote on rapidly, warmly. I defined the properties and meted the limits of natural laws, which I would not admit that a Deity himself could alter. I clamped and soldered dogma to dogma in the links of my tinkered logic, till out from my page, to my own complacent eye, grew Intellectual Man, as the pure formation of his material senses, mind, or what is called soul, born from and nurtured by them alone. (xx)

That night, Fenwick does not discern the imprisoning implications of his clamping, soldering, linking construction. Nor does he detect a possible similarity between the creature of his own production, the "Intellectual Man," and the monster of Frankenstein that will later threaten his maker. In growing "from my page," the creature also becomes like a fictional protagonist and has qualities in common after all with the embodiments of "human intellect, in various forms," in the novel of Pisistratus.

Eventually Fenwick must come to acknowledge, like Pisistratus, that there is a higher power in the text to which he himself must submit. In this case, the power is not that of a "Providence [that] so pervadingly governs the universe" but that of a tyranny inherent in the discursive "system" that writes itself through Fenwick's pen:

When [a writer] settles himself back into the phase of his being as author, the mere act of taking pen in hand and smoothing the paper before him restores his speculations to their ancient mechanical train. The system, the beloved system, re-asserts its tyrannic sway, and he either ignores, or moulds into fresh proofs of his theory as author, all which, an hour before, had given his theory the lie in his living perceptions as man. (lxxiv)

The living man, as in the nightmare of the young Pisistratus, suffocates within the "book-life," to which the duped Fenwick nevertheless continues to remain loyal. His writing becomes liable to the menace of two other books in particular. Called upon to edit the memoir of the murdered Sir Philip Derval, a more imaginatively daring scholar than himself, he fears the insinuation of Derval's dangerous, undermining, but tempting speculations into his own text. The sense of the threat emerges especially during one night passed in the seemingly haunted library of Derval, another important site of the "book-life." Still more ominously, the older physician Dr. Faber attacks Fenwick's materialism and thrusts into his hands the Bible—a text that would annihilate that of Fenwick's "Intellectual Man." Faber urges him indeed to burn his "Inquiry" and to give up writing altogether in favor of humble reading of Holy Scripture. But Fenwick stubbornly re-

Footnote, page 119.

"Besides the three great subjects of Newton's labour, the fluxional calculus, physical astronomy and optics, a very large portion of his time was devoted to researches of which scarcely a trace remains. Alchemy which had fascinated so many eager & enthusiastic minds seems to have tempted Newton with an overwhelming force.

What theories he formed, what experiments he tried in that laboratory where it is said the fire was scarcely extinguished for weeks together will never be known. — It is certain that no sacrifice attended his labours, & Newton was not a man — like Kepler — to detail to the world all the hopes & disappointments, all the subtle & mystical fancies which mingled themselves up with his career of philosophy. — —

"Many years later we find Newton in correspondence with Locke, with reference to a mysterious red earth by which B——e who was then recently dead had asserted that he could effect the grand desideratum of multiplying gold. By this time however Newton's faith had become somewhat shaken by the unsatisfactory communications which he had himself received from Boyle on the subject of the golden recipe; tho' he did not abandon the idea of giving the experiment a further trial as soon as the weather should become suitable for furnace experiments

From the manuscript of *A Strange Story,* Chapter LXXV: a scholarly footnote relevant to the scientific treatise that Fenwick, in effect, "unwrites." Courtesy of Hertfordshire Archives & Local Studies, Ref. D/EK W25.

sists and prosecutes—even in the Australian Bush, where like Pisistratus he has taken refuge—the scientific endeavor.

Fortunately his story has also contained an attractive alternative to the "book-life." Recalling the two rival sons of Mr. Caxton in the earlier novel, a rivalry exists in *A Strange Story* between Fenwick's beloved book and his beloved fiancée Lilian. In her soulful ethereality she recognizes his book as something hostile to herself, and she has somehow the power to struggle with the book for the loyalty of Fenwick. At the end of the night in which Fenwick complacently defines his material self as "Intellectual Man" and demonstrates the impossibility of the soul and an afterlife, her reproachful presence invades the fortress of his study:

> Suddenly, beside me I distinctly heard a sigh,—a compassionate, mournful sigh. The sound was unmistakable. I started from my seat, looked round, amazed to discover no one,—no living thing! The windows were closed, the night was still. That sigh was not the wail of the wind. But there, in the darker angle of the room, what was that? A silvery whiteness, vaguely shaped as a human form, receding, fading, gone! Why, I know not—for no face was visible, no form, if form it were, more distinct than the colourless outline,—why, I know not, but I cried aloud, "Lilian! Lilian!" My voice came strangely back to my own ear; I paused, then smiled and blushed at my folly. (xx)

"There are more things in heaven and earth," clearly, "than are dreamt of in [Fenwick's materialist] philosophy." Lilian represents Fenwick's own soul, from which he has been alienated. After his neglect of her and other events have driven her into insanity and almost to the point of death, he becomes desperate to save her. All of his scientific knowledge has proved unavailing, and the only hope now lies in relinquishing his intellectual arrogance and his materialistic self-definition. As if to echo the process whereby Pisistratus has *"de-fine-gentlemanise[d]"* himself, he must humbly undo the tendencies of a lifetime: "All my past, with its pride and presumption and folly, grew distinct as the form of a penitent, kneeling for pardon before setting forth on the pilgrimage vowed to a shrine" (lxxxix). Returning to the simple faith of childhood, he becomes like little Amy, the young orphan who has accompanied them to Australia and whose prayers Dr. Faber has held up for his emulation. The act of praying restores him to union with his immaterial soul. Lilian rather than the "Intellectual" Me has always typified his fundamental identity.

Without his knowing it, his whole life has been an indirect pilgrimage towards the shrine that he now sees before him. So in undoing the false version of his life—his scientific career—he must also abandon or unwrite the "Inquiry into Organic Life" that he had wrongly thought to be "I myself." Instead of the scientific treatise, he now drafts the *Strange Story* that we have been reading, which takes us in the last lines beyond the fictionally present moment of Lilian's recovery: "even . . . now, at the distance of years from that happy morn, while I write the last words of this Strange Story, the same faithful arms close around me, the same tender lips kiss away my tears." The long tale of the writing of Fenwick's great "Inquiry" turns out to have been all along (although not confessed until the end) the story of its abandonment, its unwriting, its kissing away. The text eventually published derives its significance, as in *The Caxtons*, precisely by supplanting or overwriting another, unseen text that has been engaging our interest for most of the book.

In the figure of writing and unwriting, which suggests the "double writing" of Jacques Derrida as well,[5] it may be possible to discern Bulwer's metaphor for all the power struggles "set in movement" "in this our Century." The ongoing struggles in the various discourses are forever enacting new texts not out of nothing but by undoing the old ones. Although the liberation of a renewed vitality occurs in the phase of unwriting, the written materials of the old "book-life" prove necessary for the process too. Without the writing, the unwriting cannot be performed.

## NOTES

1. The comparison between *Zanoni* and *Sartor Resartus* is developed further in Allan Conrad Christensen, *Edward Bulwer-Lytton: The Fiction of New Regions* (Athens: University of Georgia Press, 1976), pp. 108–9.

2. See the Chronology prepared for this volume by Andrew Brown.

3. Regarding the influence of Sterne, see Joseph I. Fradin, "The Novels of Edward Bulwer-Lytton" (Ph.D. dissertation, Columbia University, 1956), pp. 196–216.

4. Foucault's identification of "power" and "knowledge" would not seem to require a particular source, although he and his commentators sometimes refer the notion to Sir Francis Bacon. The source may be in Bacon's brief essay, "De Hæresibus," one of the "Meditationes Sacræ" published in *Essayes. Religious Meditations. Places of Perswasion & Disswasion* (London: Humfrey Hooper, 1597), pp. 13–14. Among the three degrees of heresy, the third and most perverse uses true statements for bad purposes, and Bacon remarks, noticing the element of power, "(nam & ipsa scientia potestas est)" [in parentheses in text]

Bulwer, as I have observed in *Edward Bulwer-Lytton*, p. 246, n. 14, commented to Blackwood about his own frequent use, in connection with the story of Randal Leslie in *"My Novel,"* of the aphorism "Knowledge is Power": "I al-

ways suspected that Bacon could not [have] been the author of that silly aphorism Knowledge is Power & Resolved to hunt him all thro' to see if I could find
it—And certainly it is not in Bacon. Thinking it might possibly have Escaped
my search I then applied to Macaulay's Wonderous Mermory & to a gentleman
who has taken Bacon as his one study Both bear me out." Malcolm Orthell
Usrey indicates, however, in his edition of "The Letters of Sir Edward Bulwer-
Lytton to the Editors of *Blackwood's Magazine*, 1840–1873, in the National Library of Scotland" (Ph.D. dissertation, Texas Technological College, 1963), p.
89, that the phrase may occur not only in "De Hæresibus" but in *Novum Or-
ganum*.

5. Both Derrida (in terms of "double writing") and Foucault contemplate
the simultaneous deconstruction of one text and enactment of a new one, according to Edward W. Said, *The World, the Text, and the Critic* (London and
Boston: Faber and Faber, 1983), p. 186.

# Bulwer Lytton and Imperial Gothic: Defending the Empire in *The Coming Race*

Lillian Nayder

MIDWAY THROUGH BRAM STOKER'S NOVEL *DRACULA* (1897), THE English Hero, Jonathan Harker, takes a stroll from Hyde Park Corner down Piccadilly with his wife, Mina, on his arm. To his horror, Harker catches a glimpse of Count Dracula outside a shop, having last seen him lying in a coffin in Transylvania. Terrified and amazed, Harker realizes that the Eastern European vampire has arrived on England's shores, prepared to conquer that imperial nation. Turning to view the object that has so frightened her husband, Mina Harker sees a tall, thin man intently watching a "pretty girl." Recording the scene in her journal, she notes that the face of the stranger "was not a good face"; in particular, she is troubled by the sight of "his big white teeth, . . . pointed like an animal's."[1]

In a novel written nearly three decades before *Dracula*, another invader with notably sharp teeth enters a foreign land, animated by dreams of empire. This figure is the unnamed narrator of Edward Bulwer Lytton's *The Coming Race*, first published in 1871. Soon after his arrival in the subterranean regions of the Vril-ya, the narrator is placed in an unconscious state and carefully examined by the highly civilized vegetarians whose domain he has entered. He later learns that his teeth nearly proved his destruction. As his host, Aph-Lin, explains:

> "During your unconscious state your teeth were examined, and they clearly showed that you were not only graminivorous, but carnivorous. Carnivorous animals of your size are always destroyed, as being of dangerous and savage nature. Our teeth, as you have doubtless observed, are not those of the creatures who devour flesh . . . like beasts of prey. . . . [Thus] it was proposed to dissect you." (xxii)

The narrator of *The Coming Race* is not a vampire but a carnivore, and he meets with a happier fate than does Count Dracula, who is ultimately destroyed. Nonetheless, he shares the Count's imperial appetite, as his dental formation suggests. Dracula travels to England hoping to "create a new and ever widening circle of semi-demons" from amongst its "teeming millions,"[2] with vampirism a grotesque metaphor for empire building; Bulwer's narrator imagines eating elk steak rather than herbs and fruit as he dreams of becoming an emperor and conquering the subterranean territories of those tribes less civilized than the Vril-ya: "One might invade them without offence to the vril nations, our allies, appropriate their territories, extending, perhaps, to the most distant regions of the nether earth, and thus rule over an empire in which the sun never sets. (I forgot, in my enthusiasm)," he hastens to add, "(that over those [subterranean] regions there was no sun to set)" (xxv).

Bulwer's joke here is twofold. Not only is the image of an empire's eternal daylight ill-suited to the underground regions of the Vril-ya, where the sun never shines; this familiar image of the British Empire in all its greatness is appropriated by a narrator who is not British but American.[3] If the catchwords of Britain's imperial glory ring hollow beneath the surface of the earth, they also resonate ironically when spoken by Bulwer's narrator—a proud citizen of the United States who endorses the Monroe Doctrine, who "rall[ies] round the Stars and Stripes" (xxvi), and who proudly reminds us that his ancestors fought in the American Revolution—on what some readers might consider the "wrong" side (I). Speaking of the "destined spread" of "American democracy . . . over the world," the narrator of *The Coming Race* looks ahead to a "magnificent future": one in which "the flag of freedom should float over an entire continent, and two hundred millions of intelligent citizens, accustomed from infancy to the daily use of revolvers, should apply to a cowering universe the doctrine of the Patriot Monroe" (vii). Clearly, then, Bulwer has the Americans as well as the Vril-ya in mind when he speaks of "the coming race."[4]

With its futuristic treatment of the science and technology of the Vril-ya, their energy source "vril," and their classless and equitable society, Bulwer's novel is usually understood as an example of utopian, dystopian, or science fiction.[5] But the novel's concern with empire building and with the interconnection between the primitive and the civilized, as well as its anxieties about colonization by a "coming race," also identify it as a work of imperial gothic, a subgenre in which the tables are turned on an ostensibly civilized, imperial power, whose people find themselves threatened with colonization, usually at the hands of a "barbarous" race. At one and the same time, writers of imperial gothic express their fear that the British Empire is declining and suggest that this decline may be well deserved because of acts of barbarism committed in the name of imperialism. Thus Stoker's Count Dracula is both a primitive, foreign invader and a monstrous mirror image of the English themselves. However briefly, Dracula teaches Harker and his compatriots how it feels to be the member of a so-called "subject race."[6]

To those familiar with such novels as *The Caxtons* and with Bulwer's service as a colonial secretary, it may seem hard to imagine him as a critic of imperialism. In *The Caxtons*, serialized in *Blackwood's* from April 1848 until October 1849, Bulwer valorizes imperial expansion. When "Sisty" Caxton emigrates to Australia, he "plant[s] in the foreign allotments all the rudiments of a harmonious state analogous to that in the mother country" and "give[s] life to a desert" (XII: vi). With such passages in mind, T. H. S. Escott argues that "the true cult of the colonies . . . was founded by Bulwer-Lytton in the *Caxtons*" and that Bulwer taught Disraeli that "the upholding of England's empire [was] the great object of Conservative policy."[7] Patrick Brantlinger finds Escott's idea of Bulwer's influence "exaggerated" yet agrees that his "stance toward the Empire was aggressively expansionist."[8] Bulwer's work as Colonial Secretary in 1858 and 1859 supports this view. At a time in which British claims to Western Canada seemed especially valuable but also especially vulnerable, when the United States seemed ready to challenge British authority in what had become a gold-rush region, Bulwer introduced the bill to establish the colony of British Columbia (1858), which he envisioned as "a second England on the shores of the Pacific."[9] In 1871, the year in which he published *The Coming Race*, Bulwer was no doubt relieved to learn that British Columbia, faced with a dire financial crisis, chose to join the new Dominion of Canada, rejecting a proposed annexation to the United States.[10] As the Earl of Elgin had warned his countrymen at midcentury, while serving as Governor General of Canada (1847–54), "Let the Yankees get possession of British North America . . . [and] who can say how soon they may dispute with you the Empire of India and of the Seas?"[11]

As such warnings suggest, American rather than British expansionism leads Bulwer to write his imperial gothic novel, in an attempt to teach Americans their proper, subordinate, place. "I felt a thrill of horror," the narrator of *The Coming Race* confesses after learning that the Vril-ya routinely exterminate resistant "barbarian" tribes, "recognizing much more affinity with 'the savages' than [he] did with the Vril-ya [themselves]" (xvii). Despite this affinity, which effectively equates the American with the primitive, the threat of America's rise to imperial power and Britain's decline informs Bulwer's story, even as the novelist attempts to defuse this threat by turning the tables on the American and making his grandiose claims about his nation seem comical under the disempowering circumstances in which he is placed. In a statement that typifies his arrogance (and Bulwer's ridicule), the narrator describes the current state of affairs on earth:

> Desiring to represent in the most favourable colours the world from which I came, I touched but slightly, though indulgently, on the antiquated and decaying institutions of Europe, in order to expatiate on the present grandeur and prospective pre-eminence of that glorious American Republic, in which Europe enviously seeks its model and tremblingly foresees its doom. (vii)

In *The Coming Race*, Bulwer discredits the brash American, who is by no means ready to assume what Kipling would soon term "the white man's burden" (1899). At the same time, Bulwer displaces—or rather submerges—his imperial anxieties by identifying "the coming race" as an unfamiliar and subterranean one. The Vril-ya often appear other and inhuman to the narrator, and they express contempt for the democratic form of government that he extols—the "government of many," which they term a "Koom-Posh" (xvii).

Nonetheless, Bulwer models the society of the Vril-ya, in part, on American ideals, which are taken to a dehumanizing extreme in their classless but unheroic culture.[12] Among the Vril-ya, the narrator explains, there is neither crime nor virtue and "all occupations hold the same equal social status"; thus the brother of the chief magistrate chooses to become a shoe salesman (xv). Such social features lead critic Geoffrey Wagner to describe the Vril-ya as "pseudo-America[ns]" while Jon Thiem traces them back to Tocqueville's *Democracy in America*.[13] Perhaps most importantly, both the Americans and the Vril-ya share a sense of manifest destiny. Anticipating what W. T. Stead would later term "the Americanization of the World" (1901), the Vril-ya see themselves as "destined to return to the upper world, and supplant all the inferior races now existing therein" (xv), while the narrator

believes in the "destined spread" of "American democracy . . .
over the world" (vii).

Countering such beliefs, British readers and consumers eagerly
identified *themselves* as members of "the coming race," although
they modified the diet of the Vril-ya in the process, infusing it
with meat: hence the popularity of the beef drink Bovril, inspired
by Bulwer's "vril." Swilling their Bovril, Britons could imagine
themselves rather than their imperial rivals reflected in the
highly evolved race whose technological and physical supremacy
makes them remarkably efficient, if deadly, colonists. Advertisements for Bovril played on the parallel between British supremacy and the Vril-ya variety: for example, one showed that the
South African route followed by Lord Roberts in his 1900 campaign against the Boers actually spelled the word "Bovril." Bulwer himself connects the Vril-ya to the British on at least one
occasion, when the narrator compares their state to the England
that the original American colonists left behind (xviii).

Yet Bulwer's portrait of the Vril-ya is an oddly composite one,
and parallels between the Vril-ya and either the British or the
Americans prove incomplete. Although the Vril-ya are repeatedly
compared to Anglo-Saxons, they are also compared to the "red
man" (iv). Despite their cutting-edge technology, their architecture is described as early Egyptian in style and their facial "out-

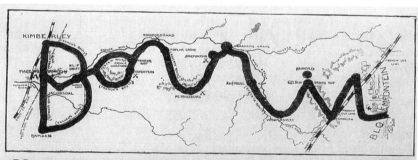

**"The Event of the Year. How Lord Roberts wrote Bovril." Reproduced
with kind permission of Unilever Bestfoods from an original in
Unilever Corporate Archives.**

line and expression" as sphinx-like (iv), while some of their habits recall those of the ancient Roman empire in its "luxurious age" (xxv). Hybrid creatures, highly civilized yet tigerish and serpent-like (iv), the Vril-ya embody Bulwer's sense that the relation between the colonized and the colonizer has become thoroughly unstable; that civilizations decline and fall, while barbarians rise to power; that those who are civilized may also be barbarian.[14] Thus the analogies that Bulwer draws between the Vril-ya and those living on the earth's surface are various, shifting, and contradictory. The Vril-ya are compared to "Anglo-Saxon emigrants" in America and to the "citizens of New York" (xxvi, iv) but also to Native Americans (iv); the narrator compares Anglo-Saxon Americans to the Vril-ya—both imperial races—but also likens himself and his Anglo-Saxon countrymen to Native Americans and "negroes" (xxvi, xv). He associates the Vril-ya with the British, and Vril-ya emigrants with American settlers (xviii); at the same time, he suggests that the Americans wish to colonize the British, just as the Vril-ya colonize barbarous, subterranean tribes. Ultimately, the Vril-ya threaten to colonize the Americans and the British alike.

An odd composite of the very old and the very new, the imperial and the aboriginal, the Vril-ya are perhaps most closely aligned with the British when Bulwer evokes images of past imperial glory. England is, after all, "the old country" (i), at least from the American's point of view, and British Victorians were wont to compare their empire with its ancient antecedents. "Comparisons have often been drawn between the Roman and the British empires," a writer in Dickens's *All the Year Round* noted in 1866, "and the question asked: 'Will Britain lose its strength and fade away, as Rome faded?' That it is natural that every nation should have its periods of youth, of maturity, and of decay, the records of ancient nations would lead us to infer."[15]

I began this essay by comparing the narrator of *The Coming Race* to Count Dracula, yet Bulwer's American more closely resembles a second, more youthful, imperialist in Stoker's novel: the Texan Quincey Morris. Armed with his Bowie knife and his pistol, a pioneer from the American West, Morris joins the band of English heroes who battle with Dracula, but poses a greater, if more subtle, threat to their power than does the Eastern European invader. Stoker leaves it to the madman Renfield to envision the day "when the Pole and the Tropics may hold allegiance to the Stars and Stripes,"[16] but Renfield's view is shared by his English psychiatrist: "If America can go on breeding men like that,"

Dr. Seward says, referring to Quincey Morris, "she will be a power in the world indeed."[17] Such observations help to explain why Morris—like Dracula—is finally killed off by Stoker. As Stephen Arata argues in his reading of the novel:

> If *Dracula* is about how vigorous races inevitably displace decaying races, then the real danger to Britain . . . comes not from the moribund Austro-Hungarian or Ottoman empires, but from the rising American empire. Without at all dismissing the powerful anxiety that the Count produces, we can say that Stoker's attention to Dracula screens his anxiety at the threat represented by Morris and America. Stoker insistently directs our gaze East, all the while looking back over his shoulder.[18]

In *Dracula*, Stoker assuages these imperial anxieties by redefining the crisis that his heroes face: he confronts them with a female vampire whose sexual aggression and whose violence against children tie the monstrous invader to the so-called "New Woman"[19] rather than the new empire in the West. Demonstrating their solidarity as members of an embattled male sex, the American and the Englishmen join forces in a metaphoric rape scene that restores the transgressive woman to her proper place.

Bulwer's novel is neither as sexually explicit nor as violent as *Dracula*, but it anticipates Stoker's strategy nonetheless. Midway through the novel, its focus shifts, as Bulwer redefines racial and imperial relations in terms of gender difference: the narrator finds himself imperiled by the romantic advances of his host's daughter, Zee, not by the imperial advances of her people. Among the Vril-ya, the narrator learns, Victorian gender norms are inverted; each female of the race is called a "Gy" (for "guy" as well as "gyno"), with some reaching nearly seven feet in height. "I recognized at once the difference between the two sexes," the narrator observes: "the . . . females were of taller stature and ampler proportions than the males; and . . . were devoid of the softness and timidity of expression which give charm to the face of woman as seen on the earth above" (v).[20] Stronger and more intelligent than their fathers, brothers, and sons, "armed not only with the rights of woman, but with the powers of man" (xxiii), they direct the "College of Sages" (vi), court the "demure" and "prudish" males, and decide when to pop the question (xxv, x). To his dismay, the narrator finds himself pursued by Zee and placed in a sexually subordinate and feminized position. Terrified of a female "eminently superior to himself" (xxi), the American is now threatened with colonization of a different sort, at the hands of a female "Caesar" (xvi). As he fearfully observes, a "Gy" "can not only defend [herself] against all aggressions from the males, but could, at any moment when he least suspected his danger, terminate the existence of an offending spouse" (x). For as Zee and her sisterhood proudly contend, "females are generally large enough to make a meal of their consorts if they so desire" (x).

This may seem an odd boast for vegetarians to make, but it serves an important function in the novel, redefining the dangers posed by an unruly, carnivorous appetite and providing imperial rivals with common ground. "Except [for] England and America," the narrator reminds us, "young ladies" are "demure and shy . . . in . . . civilized countries" (xxv). Using his female "Gy"s in much the same way that Stoker uses his female vampires, Bulwer reiterates his theme that Britons and Americans face a common threat but he does so with a significant variation: the greatest danger to both empires may lie at home, he suggests, among women uncivilized enough to hunger for the rights of their fathers and husbands.

## NOTES

I would like to thank Lesley Owen-Edwards, Senior Archivist at the Unilever Corporate Archives, for providing me with a scan of "How Lord Roberts wrote Bovril."

1. Bram Stoker, *Dracula*, ed. A. N. Wilson (Oxford: Oxford University Press, 1989), p. 172.

2. Ibid., p. 51.

3. The description of Britain's "dominions" as a region "on which the sun never sets" originated with "Christopher North" (John Wilson) in his "Noctes Ambrosianae," no. 42, published in October 1826 in *Blackwood's Magazine*.

4. Focusing on the treatment of social leveling and individualism rather than empire building, Geoffrey Wagner identifies the Americans as "the coming race" in Bulwer's novel and suggests that "his utopia is set within the bowels of America itself" ("A Forgotten Satire: Bulwer-Lytton's *The Coming Race*," *Nineteenth-Century Fiction* 19, no. 4 [March 1965]: 381). A number of other critics discuss this parallel as well.

5. See, for example, Hans Seeber, "Bulwer-Lytton's Underworld: *The Coming Race* (1871)," *Moreana* 30 (1971): 39–40, which identifies the novel as a warning against utopian socialism and scientific materialism; B. G. Knepper, "*The Coming Race*: Hell? or Paradise Foretasted?" in *No Place Else: Explorations in Utopian and Dystopian Fiction*, ed. Eric S. Rabkin, Martin H. Greenberg, and Joseph D. Olander (Carbondale: Southern Illinois University Press, 1983), pp. 11–32; James L. Campbell, Sr., "Edward Bulwer-Lytton's *The Coming Race* as a Condemnation of Advanced Ideas," *Essays in Arts and Sciences*

16 (May 1987): 55–63, which approaches the novel as a "conservative dystopia" (p. 62); and Darko Suvin, "The Extraordinary Voyage, the Future War, and Bulwer's *The Coming Race*: Three Sub-Genres in British Science Fiction, 1871–1885," *Literature & History* 10, no. 2 (Autumn 1984): 231–48.

6. For a discussion of imperial gothic fiction and its political implications, see Patrick Brantlinger, *Rule of Darkness: British Literature and Imperialism, 1830–1914* (Ithaca: Cornell University Press, 1988), pp. 227–53; and Stephen D. Arata, "The Occidental Tourist: *Dracula* and the Anxiety of Reverse Colonization," *Victorian Studies* 33 (Summer 1990): 621–45. As Brantlinger explains, "the three principal themes of imperial Gothic are individual regression or going native; an invasion of civilization by the forces of barbarism or demonism; and the diminution of opportunities for adventure and heroism in the modern world" ( p. 230).

7. T. H. S. Escott, *Edward Bulwer, First Baron Lytton of Knebworth* (London: George Routledge, 1910), p. 273 (quoted by Brantlinger, *Rule of Darkness*, p. 28).

8. Brantlinger, *Rule of Darkness*, p. 28.

9. Second Earl of Lytton, *The Life of Edward Bulwer, First Lord Lytton*, 2 vols. (London: Macmillan, 1913), 2: 293. As his grandson and biographer explains, Bulwer introduced the bill on 8 July 1858. On its second reading, he expressed his "humble trust that the Divine Disposer of all human events may afford the safeguard of His blessing to our attempt to add another community of Christian freemen to those by which Great Britain confides the records of her empire, not to pyramids and obelisks, but to states and commonwealths whose history shall be written in her language" (2:290–91). Addressing a group of engineers leaving Portsmouth for the new colony later that year, Bulwer praised their "English valour and English loyalty, . . . English intelligence and English skill," characterized them as "Pioneers of Civilization" rather than "common soldiers," and envisioned "our national flag . . . wav[ing] in peaceful triumph . . . from walls and church towers": "children unborn will, I believe, bless the hour when Queen Victoria sent forth her sappers and miners to found a second England on the shores of the Pacific" (2:291–93). As Colonial Secretary, Bulwer also oversaw the separation of Queensland from New South Wales in Australia.

10. Robert Shadle, "British Columbia," in *The Historical Dictionary of the British Empire*, ed. James S. Olson and Robert Shadle, 2 vols. (Westport, Conn.: Greenwood Press, 1996), 1:170–71, 171.

11. Quoted by Ronald Hyam, *Britain's Imperial Century, 1815–1914: A Study of Empire and Expansion* (New York: Barnes and Noble, 1976), p. 181. As A. P. Thornton writes of the 1867 British North America Act, which created the Dominion of Canada, "the fact of Canada denied the facts of North American geography, denied the fact of what many in the nineteenth century held to be the manifest destiny of the growing United States: to become territorial sovereign of the whole continent. It was the link with the British Empire that . . . saved [Canada] from absorption by her powerful southern neighbour" (*The Imperial Idea and Its Enemies: A Study in British Power* [London: Macmillan, 1966], p. 253).

12. Perhaps most notably, the Vril-ya have no contemporary literature or history; having eliminated conflict within their culture, and with nothing to strive for, they have no forms of greatness and "no events to chronicle": "What more of us can be said than that they were born, they were happy, they died?" Aph-Lin asks (xvii).

13. Wagner, "A Forgotten Satire," p. 383; Jon Thiem, "The American Woman in *The Coming Race* (1871): Bulwer-Lytton's Fictional Rebuttal to Tocqueville," in *Portrayal of America in Various Literatures*, ed. Wolodymyr T. Zyla (Lubbock, Tex.: Texas Tech University, 1978), pp. 19–28.

14. Clare A. Simmons overlooks the instability of racial identity in *The Coming Race* when discussing "Anglo-Saxonism" in the novel. Arguing that Bulwer sees "English speakers . . . destined to rule the world," she downplays the imperial rivalry between the Americans and the British in the name of their shared Anglo-Saxon "kinship" ("Anglo-Saxonism, the Future, and the Franco-Prussian War," *Studies in Medievalism* 7 [1995]: 133, 140).

15. "Touching Englishmen's Lives," *All the Year Round* 15 (30 June 1866): 582.

16. Stoker, *Dracula*, p. 244.

17. Ibid., p. 173.

18. Arata, "The Occidental Tourist," p. 642.

19. Stoker, *Dracula*, p. 89.

20. Wagner claims that Bulwer "was principally objecting to the new woman in *The Coming Race*" ("A Forgotten Satire," p. 384), an argument fully developed by Thiem, who notes that America was seen as "a land of sexual equality" by British Victorians ("The American Woman," p. 19). Thiem approaches *The Coming Race* as a rebuttal to Tocqueville's *Democracy in America*, which attributes the strength and prosperity of Americans to what Tocqueville terms "the superiority of their women" (quoted by Thiem, p. 23).

# The Last Days of the Second Empire:
## *The Parisians* and *La Débâcle*

Philip Rand

Aʙᴏᴜᴛ ᴀʟʟ ᴛʜᴀᴛ ʙᴜʟᴡᴇʀ ʟʏᴛᴛᴏɴ ᴀɴᴅ ᴇᴍɪʟᴇ ᴢᴏʟᴀ ᴍɪɢʜᴛ ѕᴇᴇᴍ ᴛᴏ have in common is the fact that they wrote novels. Certainly the crude, graphic descriptions characteristic of Zola and the much politer rhetorical style of the English novelist would make an association between the two seem highly improbable. Yet near the end of their respective careers, Bulwer in 1871–72 and Zola in 1892, they both found in the debacle of France following the Franco-Prussian War a worthy subject for an ambitious work. In the twenty years separating Bulwer's *The Parisians* from Zola's *La Débâcle,* no other novels of similar scope were written on the subject. There are only these two significant works of nineteenth-century fiction to provide interestingly diverse perspectives on the same events. The one by the English reporter reflects the immediate shock of the French military defeat and the subsequent Parisian rebellion while the other work retrospectively fits the events into a Darwin-inspired representation of history. We have, in a sense, both a synchronic and a diachronic analysis, with their respective virtues and limitations, of the history of nations in action. For the purposes of the present volume, the analysis of Zola may prove especially useful insofar as it can provide a foil for Bulwer's ideas about history and the historical cataclysms that so often engage his attention. The French novel, as well as the French nation, becomes in this context the Other, to borrow the term that Joachim Mathieu uses in his discussion of *England and the English,*[1] against which the English work and the English nation can be measured.

The focus of Zola's narrative is the crucial battle of the Franco-Prussian war, Sedan, which marked a turning point in the conflict and the beginning of the French defeat. The novel portrays war, physical suffering, struggles to survive as they affect a cross-section of French society—especially the peasantry and the bourgeoisie, as well as women and the military treated as categories of their own.

Peasants in *La Débâcle* are represented by Jean and Maurice, the two main protagonists, and by the sister of Maurice and the Père Fouchard. They are intimately connected with the soil and preoccupied with "charrue, travail, épargne" (plow, labor, savings),[2] which determines their instincts and their reactions to suffering and privation. Old Fouchard evinces a more negative characteristic of the peasantry, their slyness and avarice. War for him offers an opportunity for speculation, and the impulse to defend his property almost prevails over a human concern for the safety of Jean and of France itself. Jean's peasant virtues, including knowledge of the land and common sense, often come to the rescue during the grueling conflict, especially as his more volatile companion, Maurice, loses self-control in dangerous situations.

The factors that help explain Maurice's behavior are both physiological—an incipient madness, determined by heredity, which is an important theme throughout the *Rougon-Macquart* novels—and socially determined. Maurice has been educated, and consequently estranged from the simpler and more single-minded perceptions of people like Jean. Imperfectly grasped and extraneous ideas easily carry him away. At the end of *La Débâcle*, his association with the extremist Commune uprising leads to his downfall.

The two young men, whose initial hostility gradually turns into affection as they face hardship together, suggest the double-sided personality of France itself.[3] The rugged common sense and patriotic loyalty of Jean typifies the stability, continuity, and strength of the identity rooted in the French soil. The often neurotic Maurice figures the unreliable instability of a nation that can be carried away by undigested ideologies. The disharmony between the two companions is not fully resolved until the destructive fury of the Communards (Maurice among them) has run its course. The loyalist Jean then kills a Communard who turns out to be Maurice. Although tragic in a personal sense, the killing signifies on the allegorical level the elimination of a national flaw. After an almost fatal illness, the nation may proceed along the road to recovery.

If the peasants cling to their property and soil for their livelihood and seek to protect and conserve their fruits, the bourgeois see in their estates not only the generating source of their wealth but the symbol of their personal distinction. In this attitude toward property, as René Pernous points out, the bourgeoisie emulate the nobility.[4] The bourgeois figures in *La Débâcle* thereby conform more or less to the well-established values and patterns of behavior of their class. A small property owner named Weiss, a "gros bourgeois"[5] with no military experience, is so provoked by the Prussian threat to his country house that he dies a hero's death defending his property. A wealthy property owner, Delaherche, faced with the threat of damage to his sumptuous estate in Sedan is similarly stricken with the "peur de perdre dans la catastrophe sa fortune et sa vie" (the fear of losing his wealth and his life in the catastrophe).[6] For him, the fall of the emperor and even the surrender of France are lesser evils than the destruction of his property would be.

Women are treated as a distinct social category in *La Débâcle*. As heroically devoted wives and nurses, they play a subordinate role to their men. In the peasant context, Maurice's sister faces great risks while protecting Jean during his recovery from war wounds. In bourgeois households like that of the Delaherche, charity is similarly a virtue practiced by women who do not generally perform more professional activities.[7] The female propensity for charity transcends class differences, as if it were physiologically determined.

Those most directly involved in the war, the soldiers and officers, form a separate social microcosm in a hierarchy ranging from peasant soldiers to superior officers, with elements of lesser or greater integrity at every level.[8] At the lowest level, traffickers and malcontents in the infantry sow the seeds of discontent and corruption, whereas more loyal soldiers like Jean doggedly and unquestioningly pursue the goal of defending France. In the higher echelons, some officers are not fully committed to the war effort; disorganization and disagreement prevail in various examples of incompetence and failure to elicit respect.[9] In contrast, a wounded officer being treated in the Delaherche home exemplifies great conscientiousness. Clearly appalled at how the war is being conducted, he unexpectedly dies from not normally fatal wounds. His death demonstrates that the essential values of professional conduct and military honor have vanished.

Napoleon III, the former leader of brilliant Parisian society, is also portrayed in the military context of *La Débâcle*. At Sedan his entourage is prepared to provide him with abundant meals, unlike the undernourished soldiers struggling nearby under physically repulsive conditions. Silent and pale, weakened by his bladder ailment, the emperor is usually seen at a distance or through windows. This frail embodiment of the French state has come to Sedan in the vain hope of dying a hero's death.[10] Hardly able to touch his food, he is pathetically portrayed, on one occasion, seated on a chamber pot. Once a symbol of glory, his image now represents the illness and decay of the country itself in this critical historical moment. (Although the fact is not mentioned in Zola's novel, Napoleon was actually reading at Sedan Bulwer's *The Last of the Barons*: he must have been relating the end of his own empire to one of Bulwer's stories of the end of things.)[11]

The conception of history, for the author of *La Débâcle,* derives from a Darwin-inspired myth of a species threatened by extinction struggling to readapt—of the French social body in this case. Zola's observation about Maurice, to the effect that he is "corrompu par le règne du plaisir"[12] suggests the decadence affecting French society during the regime of Louis Napoleon.[13] We learn that the "éducation brillante" received by Maurice has brought him into contact with ideologies from foreign sources, which he and others like him have embraced for emotional reasons. Various soldiers too, whom *La Débâcle* portrays as using revolutionary language out of frustration and desire for revenge against those perceived to be the source of their suffering, are evidently symptoms of the national corruption. Since the *règne du plaisir* is associated with the speculation and grandiose building projects of Baron Haussmann, it is easy to see in them as well a contribution to the social decay. The workers, who have become idle when the bubble of prosperity bursts, become a source of discontent and thus one of the socioeconomic factors in the debacle. In other words, the debacle has begun with the moral corruption of the nation preceding the actual defeat at Sedan.

Yet Zola's final message is one of hope. This emerges in the tour de force of the final scene, which is as spectacularly apocalyptic as the fiery eruption of Vesuvius in *The Last Days of Pompeii*. The dying Maurice, his sister, and Jean are at a window, witnessing the flames that are consuming the Paris of the Commune. The narrator insists not on the tragic aspect of the scene but rather on the cleansing and regenerating effect of the fires. The burning of Paris suggests the natural process of degeneration and rebirth that nations undergo. While the newly created German nation now enjoys the vigor of youth, France will come one day to recover her own strength. As the disease associated with the negative characteristics of the French identity burns itself out, a rejuvenated France better adapted for the struggle for survival will rise from the ashes. Beneath the ashes the healthy French soil will once more nourish the sturdy values of the peasant. But as the metaphor suggests, the process occurs as blindly as do the cycles of growth, decay, and rebirth in nature. Human protagonists may contribute to the phase of decay but cannot initiate through their own will the phase of rebirth.

The retrospective stance must have helped Zola to perceive the enduring value of virtues associated with the peasantry and with the biological basis of life. Engulfed in the horrors of the moment, Bulwer could not discern such reasons for hope, and the peasantry and the biological dimensions evidently did not strike him with their virtuous aspects. Whereas Zola offers graphic portrayals of human beings engaged in the most basic physical functions and focuses upon Sedan, Bulwer leads his readers through the salons of Parisian society and relates only the essentials of the crude military battles. In avoiding Paris, Zola also perceives the fiery catastrophe from without—from a distance not only in space but, implicitly, in time—while Bulwer registers the sense of disintegration as it is felt within Paris, from 1869 to the German siege and the start of the Commune.

The works differ with respect to the organizing principles of their plotting too. Conceiving his work with Cartesian rigor, Zola creates tightly knit scenes that allegorically demonstrate a Darwinian impression of a poorly adapted species, the French nation, in its apparent decay towards extinction. Improbable episodes like Jean's unwitting shooting of Maurice acquire the force of logic in the theoretical pattern of natural selection. Instead of organizing *The Parisians* in terms of such a thesis, Bulwer represents French politics and social classes within the framework of a conventional plot structure and traditional fictional devices. A love story, for the outcome of which the reader is in suspense, provides the unifying plot element. One of the lovers, an English aristocrat named Graham Vane, pursues a quest for a missing heir in loyal service to his late guardian. While not strictly relevant to the sociopolitical theme, the quest interests us as it offers obstacles to his union with the beloved Isaura Cicogna. Other conventional devices are coincidences that do not seem to bear allegorical significance as in Zola (the heir sought by Graham is related to the Vicomte de Mauléon, and Mauléon himself becomes the benefactor of a woman who turns out to be the heir's daughter). There are disguises and mistaken identities, and, quite inconceivable in the novel of Zola, there is even humor related to attempts made to conceal a little pet dog, appetizing to hungry Parisians, from their avid gazes. In *La Débâcle* the order of things is such that while Jean and the sister of Maurice love one another, fate wills that they cannot be united, whereas happy or, at least, suitable matches do come to pass in *The Parisians*.

Although all of the characters are embedded in the plotting and serve to advance the action, the novel is of course concerned not just with plot but with reporting on the sociopolitical situation in Paris. "The author's son" points out in the prefatory note to the second volume that *The Parisians* is "a work of dramatised observation" (as opposed to the "pure fancy" of *The Coming Race* or "the more distinctly drawn outline" of *Chillingly*). Bulwer has scrupulously studied the Parisian scene and systematically describes the various parties and factions. Representative characters such as Savarin, a journalist, and Rameau, likewise a journalist and a "Red Republican," along with the various salons visited by his protagonists, and commented on by various witnesses, present the significant political orientations or shades of opinion concerning current events. Circulating among the upper echelons of French society there are also an educated and somewhat brazen American wife and her husband. In their comments on the French scene, they also represent the young American republic.

Into the fabric of plots, subplots, and commentary, Bulwer does also weave his own ideological component, in favor of a conservative vision of class-articulated human solidarity and in opposition to Darwinism and Marxism. As Walter Göbel notices in this context, an "affirmative ideology" goes hand in hand with the "melodramatic" structure of *The Parisians*.[14]

For Bulwer, as for Zola, Paris is the *règne du plaisir*, and he likewise perceives an historical moment in which an obsession with money has dominated society. Zola sees this as a pathology, described especially in another of his late novels, *L'Argent*, whose protagonist, in a sort of madness, engages in frantic speculation for speculation's sake. For Bulwer, money and the corruption associated with money are less a pathological degeneration than a moral guilt or a religious heresy. He describes the *bourse* of Paris as the temple at which people worship today, whereas churches are frequented by few people (at least before Paris has been placed under siege). Thoughts of material gain apparently outweigh spiritual considerations for Parisians, until disaster strikes.

In analyzing the situation in terms of representative classes and components of society, the two novelists also manifest a temperamental difference. Zola concentrates on the provincial bourgeoisie and especially the peasants in whom he can embody his myth of the soil. Bulwer deals with the aristocracy, as well as the urban middle and working classes.

Before noticing Bulwer's characterization of these classes, we should observe the two figures that stand apart as points of reference for the other components of the French panorama. The first is Isaura Cigogna, an artist of extraordinary sensitivity and skill who belongs to a company of fascinatingly unconventional heroines in Bulwer's novels.[15] Uncompromising when it comes to developing her art, she can allow only genuine love or a spirit of compassion to deflect her from this commitment. *Paris corrupteur,* with its fashion-conscious society, its avid speculators, and those who preach revolution, does not affect this creature who, significantly, would prefer to live outside the city, if this were possible. Isaura stands for the "higher regions" of ideas,[16] and possesses a platonic belief in ideals and a sort of religious mysticism. Not only does she provide the focus of the plot, in her relationship with the English aristocrat, but she is also a goddess figure, embodying the Truth that Bulwer wants to represent, an idealist vision of history based on human solidarity.

The second figure is her lover Graham Vane, the English counterpart to corresponding personages from the French aristocracy. He demonstrates the sense of honor of the nobility, as he pursues his demanding quest and as his relationship with Isaura provides the main thread of the plot. The fact that neither of them is French suggests that they may represent within the story the foreign viewpoint of the author. In this respect, Zola's temporal detachment from the material may be compared to Bulwer's indication of a cultural detachment from the Parisian scene.

Bulwer's tale of moral fall and recovery in French society (as opposed to Zola's biological metaphor) is perhaps most clearly traced in the treatment of the aristocracy. That class has begun to fall in a moral sense as it has already fallen in a financial sense. Forced to recognize its precarious financial situation after the revolution, it must now deign to become more directly involved in the task of providing for its own subsistence—to seek out, in other words, sources of income. The noblemen in *The Parisians* are, to varying degrees, tainted by *Paris corrupteur,* directly or indirectly because of considerations of money. A young Breton, Alain de Rochebriant, of monarchist convictions and noble bearing, pursues the mission of finding a way of saving his family's property from bankruptcy and thus the honor of the family. The narrator points out that his pride is that both of his class and of the French in general. He resists the idea of doing military service side by side with lower-class soldiers. When Alain consults a powerful speculator, the action of *Paris corrupteur* commences. The capitalist knows he can ruin the Breton first by gaining control over his investments and then by advancing him some money in order to tempt him to acquire the expensive taste for luxury characteristic of Parisian society. So he starts Alain off on the road to insolvency.

The father of another family, the Vandemar, represents a class of aristocrats that has become imbued with Voltairian ideas. An agnostic and cynic, he devotes more attention to the pleasures of Paris than to the pursuit of ideals. One of his sons, Enguerrand de Vandemar, shares a similar taste for Parisian luxury, until the impact of the war is felt, while the other son, Raoul, is more religious and devotes much of his time to performing acts of charity. Both sons, however, must also deign to manage a commercial enterprise because of their need to keep up the tenor of Parisian life in the face of failing family finances. The fact that they run a shop is kept secret for fear of the dishonor it could bring down upon the family.

The Vicomte de Mauléon is another representative of the aristocracy. When first introduced, he is seen as an intriguer, involved in a plot to overthrow the government of Napoleon III. His political action (contemptible to Bulwer's way of thinking) is motivated by desire for revenge against his peers, who, because of his involvement in a scandal, have turned their backs on him.

When disaster strikes with the siege, the subsequent battles with the Germans, and famine, each of Bulwer's aristocrats rises morally to the occasion, and this suggests that regeneration is possible.[17] Alain, his fortunes saved thanks to a rival of the capitalist who had intrigued to take over his estates, can easily withdraw from the trials inflicted upon the Parisians and marry his benefactor's daughter. Yet he insists upon plunging into battle, casting aside his qualms about fighting side by side with common soldiers. (Perhaps conveniently, the author sees to it that he is wounded and consigned to the relative safety of a field hospital.)

Enguerrand de Vandemar, originally interested in the brilliant salons of Paris, likewise becomes a commander of troops and, indeed, makes the ultimate sacrifice. His brother Raoul, already religious and charitable, exposes himself to every possible danger rescuing the wounded (including Alain and his own brother) on the battlefield. As a result of his experiences—in particular, the death of his brother—he becomes a sort of religious mystic. Of the bereaved Raoul's transformed physiognomy the narrator observes that it was "that of a man who has sorrowed[;] . . . perhaps it was more sweet,—certainly it was more lofty" (XII:iii).

The formerly scheming and vindictive Mauléon likewise responds in a commendable way to the disasters. Having recognized the senselessness of his revolutionary activity, he distinguishes himself for heroism and abnegation in battles against the Germans. The human side of this otherwise Vautrin-like figure becomes apparent at the end. Having been wrongly condemned in the scandal, as it turns out, he emerges as a social benefactor.

All these examples support Bulwer's conclusion that the "higher classes, including the remnants of the old *noblesse* had, during the whole siege, exhibited qualities in notable contrast to those assigned them by the enemies of aristocracy" ( XII:i).

In Bulwer's middle classes, the triumph of goodness over potential corruption comes out, in a similar pattern, as a result of the catastrophe. The novel briefly covers the "tradesfolk," but concentrates on two aggressive speculators who are characteristic figures in Second Empire society. Louvier, wolflike as his name in French suggests and with legitimist sympathies, and Duplessis, who favors the imperial regime, vie with one another to acquire ever more property, prestige, and power over others. Louvier's desire to take over the Rochebriant property is abetted by the class hatred of the rising bourgeoisie against the aristocracy. (Past rivalry with Alain's father over a woman adds a further dimension to the drama.) Political differences between the two capitalists exacerbate their bitter competition.

The debacle of France means the end of the speculation set off by Napoleon's campaign to rebuild Paris, and the speculators must await better days. The events bring out good-hearted instincts in the ruthless Louvier. After he has been foiled by Duplessis, he magnanimously accepts his defeat, and with the passing of the crisis the two agree to forget their competition for bigger and better estates and to work together. Duplessis fulfills his fatherly duties by smoothing the way for the marriage of Alain to his beloved daughter. The narrator puts in a good word for other representatives of the middle classes as well: The " 'thrifty tradesfolk' and the small *rentiers*, not known for their courage when face to face with an angry mob," he points out, "have faced the siege and privation with great courage" (XII:i).

The working-class figures in *The Parisians* represent danger, the uncontrolled forces of a Darwinian vision, which (in contrast with Zola's impressions) must always imply a bleak view of things. Polish and Italian revolutionaries, two minor figures that reflect the great interest of the French public in the independence movements of those two nations, are menacing in the violence of their language. An artisan, Armand Monnier, is, however, the main representative of the lower classes. Inspired by the ideas of Fourier, he is perhaps the most avid of the participants in Mauléon's conspiracy. At the outset he possesses some virtues: although a vociferous opponent of the institution of marriage, he is a good father in his common-law family unit. But when disaster strikes, he suffers a fate very different from that of the characters in the upper classes. He obsessively devotes all his efforts to the revolutionary conspiracy and to defending the "honour of his class" (XI:ix). As a result, he ends up neglecting his consort and child, and, the ultimate sign of degeneration in *The Parisians*, he resorts to alcohol, which was indeed the case for many workers during the siege. To get revenge for Mauléon's abandonment of the conspiracy (in an incident beyond the Vicomte's control), Monnier kills his former mentor.

The intellect of this proletarian, strong but "so estranged from practical opinions, so warped, so heated, so flawed and cracked in parts" (XI:ix), is the cause of his downfall. The author sees in Monnier's fate (similar to that of Maurice in *La Débâcle*) that of "many an honest workman," the change into a "wild beast," and, toward the end of the novel, he associates this phenomenon with the "civil war of the Communists" (that is, the Communards). The implication is that an improperly developed intellect means uncritical acceptance of ideologies, and blind devotion to persuasive leaders such as Mauléon. As the narrator comments, "each man has in him a portion of the wild beast, which is suppressed by mild, civilising circumstances, and comes uppermost when self-control is lost" (XI:ix). The fall of the uneducated classes, an easy prey to the ideologies of socialism and communism that Bulwer so deplores, thus entails as well the decay of civilization into a Darwinian struggle among wild beasts.

Rameau belongs to another category, that of the *poète engagé* and the journalist so characteristic of the Second Empire. This "spoiled child of that Circe, imperial Paris," inspired, perhaps in part, by Victor Hugo,[18] fares poorly in Bulwer's scale of values before and after the debacle. His unforgivable sin in the author's mind, above and beyond his lamentable "red republican" leanings, is his willingness to allow his art and his ideals to be contaminated by baser considerations—financial gain, vanity, ambition. Despite the would-be *poète engagé*'s exalted opinion of himself, he is a mere tool in the hands of the scheming Mauléon, who creates for him a political journal as an organ for the propagation of the ringleader's subversive ideas. Rameau's willingness to adapt his own hotly proclaimed ideas to the dictates of Mauléon in return for a handsome income, shows his corruptibility, and, presumably, that of the entire class of journalists. Physically attractive in some respects, he also possesses certain unpleasant traits, like the uncontrollable appetite for absinthe that hints at his degeneration. Significantly, he fails in his attempt to win the hand of Isaura. The goddess of transcendent art and ideas cannot be tainted by this representative of *Paris corrupteur*.

After the farewell of Isaura, Rameau settles for an actress, who is indeed a generous and devoted person,[19] cynically rationalizing: "This is love! No preaching [his interpretation of Isaura's words of wisdom] here! *Elle est plus digne de moi que l'autre.*" Predictably, the poet is already dreaming of creating a new journal where he can express his "scorn of the miserable *banalities of the bourgeoisie*" (XII:ix), although, as he uses this phrase, his lucidity is clouded by the inevitable glass of absinthe, the sign not just of physical but of moral poison.

Whereas Zola's microcosm is acted upon by uncontrollable natural forces, there is in Bulwer's Paris a power in coherent ideas and moral ideals that constitute antidotes to the poisonous notions arising from irrational, passionate, and beastly instincts. At the highest level of society are those classes that possess the intellectual ability to perceive and to act upon the ideas and ideals upon which a nation's destiny depends. On the lower levels, where an underworld of chaos lurks, those classes incapable of transcendent thought are obsessed with their own immediate physical instincts (like Rameau), and passions such as a desire for revenge. (The class difference emerges when the proletarian Monnier's vindictiveness wreaks havoc while the aristocratic Mauléon is able to transcend his vengeful instincts.) Those Parisians who can rise above base instincts must become the guides of their nation through the disasters of political unrest, economic collapse, and the war itself.

In the uneducated classes remains, as the Mauléon-Monnier relationship suggests, a perpetual potentiality for instability and destructiveness. The killing by the inebriated Monnier of his former chief is indicative of the hazard of manipulating the working classes for selfishly partisan interests. As Monnier, called the "miscreant . . . Red Republican," himself says, "he [Mauléon] has duped me. But in moving me he has set others in movement; and I suspect he will find he has duped himself" (XI:ix). The Vicomte has set forces in motion that he has not reckoned upon. Not only do they cost him his own life, they threaten the fabric of the entire society.

The conclusion is that social coherence and stability are to be achieved through the efforts of those classes capable of unselfish reasoning. Their judgment naturally leads to the growth of virtuous instincts—to self-control, generosity, the pursuit of ideals. The lower classes are to be guided but not exploited and manipulated.

Awareness of the force of ideas is suggested in Isaura's remarks at the end of *The Parisians.* She and Graham are in Sorrento, the land of Tasso, where she has grown up, and she is speaking to the Englishman of the country "in which the romance of Christian heroism has ever combined elevation of thought with silvery delicacies of speech." Isaura, "forever seeking in the unseen and the spiritual the goals in the infinite which it is their instinct to divine" (VII:vi), has also exemplified through her art and her selfless acts during the siege "Christian heroism." This is the supreme, visionary exaltation to which a character in *The Parisians* may aspire. The vision has ennobled, says the narrator, especially "women, and the priesthood," who have emerged as the most "beautiful elements" in the Parisian ordeal of the siege (XII:i).

Bulwer's own vision of the ideas operating behind the noisy surfaces of history comes out in his narrator's answer to observations made by the seasoned and cynical journalist Savarin. Hearing the rumblings of street mobs, the prelude to the Commune uprising, Savarin predicts that Paris with its extravagance, frivolity, and irrationality will never change. The narrator, however, goes on to comment: "For my part, I believe that throughout the whole known history of mankind, even in epochs when reason is most misled and conscience most perverted, there runs visible, though fine and threadlike, the chain of destiny, which has its roots in the throne of an All-wise and an All-good" (L'Envoi).

For Bulwer, history is guided by a divine idea of wisdom and goodness which naturally leads to morally positive actions in the framework of a social-class structure. Whereas Zola perceives history as the Darwinian functioning of physical, biological, and social mechanisms that individuals must obey rather than control, Bulwer discerns a situation in which human beings, properly educated, can exercise the faculty of free choice. They bear responsibility for redeeming their culture and directing the course of history towards a more just and stable society.

The novel *is* incomplete, however, and at the end mobs are

roaming menacingly through the streets of Paris. Perhaps Bulwer did not finish *The Parisians*, as Allan Christensen has suggested, because of "a sort of failure of nerve": in dismay he may have doubted the tendency of contemporary civilization towards "some divine culmination."[20] Could a condition of amoral, blind, natural forces—such as we have seen prevailing, although in an ultimately redemptive sense, in the novel of Zola—actually be undermining the foundations of civilization? What the mid-nineteenth-century narrator of Bulwer's *The Caxtons* had observed in French novels of an earlier day may still be characterizing the French scene: a "damnable demoralisation" is, in the society of those novels, "painted in colours so hideous that if true, instead of a revolution it would draw down a deluge" (X:i). If not quite yet in that period of *The Caxtons*, France is possibly approaching in the last days of the Second Empire a deservedly apocalyptic deluge. In the debacle of 1871 the French cultural identity may well find, like that of Pompeii in 79 A.D., not its moment of regeneration but its destiny of extinction. As it fails, in contemplating that possibility, to go beyond the moment, *The Parisians* may convey a more just impression than does *La Débâcle* or Bulwer's own previous novels the very atmosphere of history being experienced during the last days.

## NOTES

1. Joachim Mathieu, *Edward Bulwer Lytton's* England and the English: *A Description of England in the "Age of Reform"* (Hamburg: Verlag Dr. Kovač, 2001), p. 179, and Mathieu's article in this volume. Mathieu places the novelist in the tradition of literature using the "comparative approach."

2. Emile Zola, *La Débâcle*, in *Les Rougon-Macquart*, ed. Henri Mitterand, 5 vols. (Paris: Bibliothèque de la Pléaïde, 1960–67), 5: 716.

3. The allegorical significance of the Jean-Maurice pair is treated by Henri Mitterand in his discussion of the novel in the Pléaïde edition, 5: 1400–04.

4. For a full treatment of the French bourgeoisie, see Régine Pernoud, *Histoire de la bourgeoisie en France: 1. Des Origines aux Temps modernes; 2. Les Temps modernes* (Paris: Editions du Seuil, 1981)—especially "La Société bourgeoise," 2: 373–88.

5. Zola, *La Débâcle*, p. 577.

6. Ibid., p. 664.

7. According to Pernoud, *Histoire de la bourgeoisie*, 2: 388.

8. For the details of Zola's portraits of the military, see Georges Lote, "Zola historien du second [*sic*] Empire," *Revue des Etudes Napoléoniennes* 3 (Jan.–Jun. 1918): 39–87.

9. Semi-anonymous witnesses of the events underscore this state of affairs in the military: Hozier, F.C.S., F.G.S., and Captain H.M., *The Franco-Prussian*

*War: Its Causes, Incidents and Consequences* (London: William Mackenzie, n.d.), p. 66.

10. Theo Aronson, *The Fall of the Third Napoleon* (London: Cassell, 1970), p. 136, mentions the expectation in imperial circles that it would be appropriate for the emperor to die heroically.

11. Aronson reports (*Fall of the Third Napoleon*, p. 181), that on the night after the emperor had notified the Empress Eugénie of his surrender to the Germans, his bedtime reading was Bulwer's *Last of the Barons*.

12. Zola, *La Débâcle*, p. 715.

13. Brian Nelson deals with the matter in greater detail in *Zola and the Bourgeoisie: A Study of Themes and Techniques in "Les Rougon-Macquart"* (London and Basingstoke: Macmillan, 1983).

14. Walter Göbel, *Edward Bulwer-Lytton: Systemreferenz, Funktion, literarischer Wert in seinem Erzählwerk* (Heidelberg: Universitätsverlag C. Winter, 1993), p. 95.

15. James L. Campbell, Sr., *Edward Bulwer-Lytton* (Boston: Twayne, 1986), p. 4, comments on the source of the inspiration for "young, idealized, fairylike girls, innocent and pure yet made interesting by the freedom from conventional social behavior."

16. The phrase is a translation of the "heitern Regionen" in a poem by Schiller that fascinated Bulwer. Allan Conrad Christensen discusses the way in which the concept of these "higher regions" functions in the late novels of Bulwer in *Edward Bulwer-Lytton: The Fiction of New Regions* (Athens: University of Georgia Press, 1976), pp. 198–210.

17. According to Göbel (*Edward Bulwer-Lytton*, p. 96), the aristocrats of *The Parisians* are the "heroes" while democrats and socialists are the "villains."

18. John Sutherland, *The Stanford Companion to Victorian Fiction* (Stanford, Calif.: Stanford University Press, 1989), p. 489, suggests the possible connection with Victor Hugo. Of course Hugo in exile on Jersey was not a "spoiled child of . . . imperial Paris." The character type might also refer to some of the *poètes maudits*, who, if not politically involved, were fond of absinthe.

19. This character Julie plays an historically documented role in Parisian life. As Hozier et al. comment (*Franco-Prussian War*, p. 311): "Many a poor actress accustomed to lively society, played constantly for charitable objects, receiving nothing but a franc or two for the necessary gloves or other trifles, and returned home weary and famished." Julie's presence in *The Parisians* once again suggests Bulwer's desire to paint a complete and representative portrait of the society of Paris.

20. Christensen, *Edward Bulwer-Lytton*, p. 174.

# Kenelm Chillingly:
# The Bildungsroman Revoked

Walter Göbel

Besides Thomas Carlyle (according to Carlyle's own admission), Edward Bulwer Lytton can be regarded as one of the most important mediators of German culture in England.[1] He translated Schiller's poems and added a short biography of him; he was familiar with many contemporary German authors and frequently praised and emulated Goethe, especially his *Wilhelm Meister*. The bildungsroman formula of that work is applied and modified in at least six of Bulwer's novels, among them *Pelham*, *Ernest Maltravers*, and *Kenelm Chillingly*. In the preface to *Ernest Maltravers* Bulwer acknowledged his debt.[2] In *The Pilgrims of the Rhine*, which also uses elements of the bildungsroman,[3] he attempted to captivate the spirit of German romanticism in novellas and ballads with such success that a German critic spoke of an "assimilation of Germany."[4] It is little wonder that a contemporary literary history regarded Bulwer as more popular in Germany than in his home country.[5] He was the most admired author besides Scott, sometimes preferred to the latter or even appropriated as "somewhat of a German author."[6] The affection was obviously mutual, as the dedication of *Ernest Maltravers* "To the great German people, a race of thinkers and critics" shows. Bulwer saw the Germans—rather stereotypically—as a nation of philosophers, men of letters and explorers of the metaphysical, a realm which many of his novels, and especially *Zanoni*, paired with the occult in a peculiar mixture of humanitarian idealism and mysticism.[7]

The concept of the *metaphysical novel*, which Bulwer had linked with *Wilhelm Meister* in an essay,[8] incorporates elements of a late romantic, mystic search for the good, true, and beautiful, for a "divine Priesthood of the Beautiful" that is to provide initiation into the "sublimest mysteries of our being" and into "all the powers that eternally breathe and move throughout the universe of Spirit.''[9] In the *apprenticeship novels*, however, the mystic element is not quite so pronounced as it is, for example, in *Zanoni*. Susanne Howe, who has investigated the influence of the bildungsroman formula upon Bulwer, has thus emphasized the structural parallels between *Wilhelm Meister* and Bulwer's works rather than the romantic mysticism. In accord with the Goethean pattern, Bulwer's young hero leaves home, experiences one or two abortive love affairs, goes on an extended journey and is by a mentor figure (comparable to Goethe's Jarno and Abbé) pushed towards an active, more useful life, finally choosing a political career that is appropriate for a person of his social status. While Bulwer's heroes are distinguished by a somewhat Byronic melancholy, they choose, as did Wilhelm Meister, to turn from "idle dilettantism to action for others."[10] Pelham, Algernon Mordaunt (*The Disowned*), Ernest Maltravers, and Kenelm Chillingly all move from a search for individual fulfillment, mainly in love, to some sort of social service. For Susanne Howe, *Kenelm Chillingly* simply offers Bulwer's most mature example of the bildungsroman formula, but a detailed analysis of the novel will be able to show a number of significant modifications of the formula defined by Howe.

From the very beginning there are significant differences: Kenelm is of aristocratic, not bourgeois descent. His father is a rich landowner from an old family, he himself a blasé young aristocrat characterized by ennui and a melancholy mind, without any specific interests or marked feelings, somewhat timid and governed by a "kind of tranquil indifferentism" (I:xi). Howe glosses over these basic differences when she observes that Bulwer's heroes, "in common with their German prototype," go on a Grand Tour. This term may be applied to the somewhat aimless vagaries of Kenelm, but hardly to the various quite specific missions Wilhelm sets out on in order to discover his own interests, to find a place in society and finally to earn money—a much more modern and middle-class enterprise than Kenelm's rambling adventures. While Kenelm's initial state is characterized by "idle dilettantism," Wilhelm's love for the theater and for art is inspired by a serious and heartfelt youthful enthusiasm. The primary aim of Wilhelm's journey is to visit his father's business partners and, among other things, to learn about the world of commerce and merchandizing, though he is quite often led astray on various missions of the heart and by his passion for the theater. Kenelm, in contrast, sets out to cure his *ennui* in the disguise of a tenant farmer—and he travels on foot, not in a coach, as would become his status.

The initial situation of the hero is thus decisively changed: Wilhelm goes on a quest for self-fulfillment, during which he challenges the world to meet his demands, and finally moves towards a compromise between individual desires and interests and the laws of society. Kenelm sets out in a disguise which makes self-realization difficult. Apparently the blasé young aristocrat Kenelm can only experience excitement and adventure in disguise; in a coach he would be little more than a distant observer. Adventures, deep feelings, and excitement appear in this age of aristocratic decline into exclusivism, emotional starvation, and ossification to belong to the lower orders. It is the age of which Villiers de l'Isle-Adam's dandy Axël will remark: "As for living, our servants will do that for us." Kenelm, perhaps unintentionally, offers an early caricature of the type of the effete decadent:

> "It is," soliloquised Kenelm Chillingly, "a strange yearning I have long felt,—to get out of myself, to get, as it were, into another man's skin, and have a little variety of thought and emotion. One's self is always the same self; and that is why I yawn so often. . . . Myself is Kenelm Chillingly, son and heir to a rich gentleman. But a fellow with a knapsack on his back . . . may take a livelier view of things: he can't take a duller one." (I:xv)

Feeling like a modern picaro, Kenelm compares himself to Amadis, Don Quixote, and Gil Blas. In as early a novel as *Godolphin*, another of Bulwer's characters had envisaged a metaphysical *Gil Blas*-type narrative with a different kind of hero, a "man of a better sort of clay than the amusing laquey was, and the product of a more artificial grade of society" (xx). The playful transgression of borders between classes in *Kenelm Chillingly*, which in a way parodies the picaresque formula, allows for the better sort of man and, as he disguises himself, for vicarious episodic adventures, but not for the self-realization typical of the bildungsroman hero. In the utopian ending of *Wilhelm Meister*, which Schiller admired, Wilhelm seems to achieve that self-realization by moving beyond his bourgeois social station, a movement that represents, however, an assimilation of middle class and aristocratic values. It is the moment in which progressive social utopian ideas of the eighteenth century meet nineteenth-century tendencies towards restoration. Bulwer's hero, in contrast, returns to his aristocratic milieu—in a circular movement that encompasses the entire novel—at the very moment when a love affair with an aristocratic lady demands it, by simply removing his yeoman clothing. Class boundaries are playfully transgressed but never endangered.

Kenelm's disguise is in any case largely ineffective, because his educated language and noble behavior give him away. His superiority is especially striking in the many scenes in which he preaches to members of the lower classes with the austerity and condescension of a second Sir Charles Grandison. In the following scene he addresses the son of a farmer. The preference he shows for ancient learning as opposed to progress and enlightenment is characteristic of his basically conservative views:

> "In the first place," answered Kenelm, "since you value yourself on a superior education, allow me to advise you to study the English language, as the forms of it are maintained by the elder authors, whom, in spite of an Age of Progress, men of superior education esteem. . . . In the second place, since you pretend to the superior enlightenment which results from a superior education, learn to know better your own self before you set up as teacher of mankind." (II:xxi)

Kenelm's inborn nobility is exhibited in many episodes. Like the stereotype of the *bel inconnu*, he can be recognized by his elevated style, his noble deeds, and his gentlemanly behavior. From the very beginning his similarity to the mythic or the epic hero is noted: "Adventure on foot is a notion that remounts to the age of fable. Hercules, for instance—that was the way he got to heaven, as a foot traveller" (II:i). Kenelm's various good deeds display a catalogue of traditional, usually genteel or knightly virtues, once he is actually called "a knight-errant of . . . gallant conduct" (III:iv). At school he already demonstrates his valor and his honesty in fights with a bigger boy: in order not to violate the laws of fair play, he even informs him that he has taken boxing lessons before he teaches him a lesson himself. Chivalry is shown early on his journey when he hurries to the aid of a weaker person: "The chivalry natural to a namesake of the valiant Sir Kenelm Digby was instantly aroused" (II:ii); "there was one way that went straight to his heart—you had only to be weaker than himself, and ask his protection" (II:iii).

When Kenelm discovers that he has actually been helping a girl in disguise, he shows his good sense and responsibility by persuading her to return to her family. In an encounter with the attractive peasant girl Jessie Wiles, Kenelm proves his chastity and again his valor by beating up an impertinent and unwelcome admirer. Finally he displays his generosity by promoting the union of Jessie and her beloved Will, a handicapped young man, and devoting all his ready money to this cause. When we recall the doubtful situation we find Wilhelm Meister in at the very beginning of the novel—his liaison with the unchaste actress Marianne—it is evident how stereotypically idealized Kenelm is as the exponent of a chivalrous catalogue of virtues. The bildungsroman is transformed into the chivalrous adventures of a somewhat Byronic, but nevertheless exemplary hero. Unlike the weak and erring Wilhelm, he may even appear as a pompous deus ex machina who can restore order to the world: "Providence," answered Kenelm solemnly, "sent me to this village for the express purpose of licking Tom Bowles. It is a signal mercy vouchsafed to yourself, as you will one day acknowledge" (II:xii). What may appear comic in its pomposity is, however, in accord with Kenelm's general behavior. As an example of virtue Kenelm is often as unrealistic a character as Samuel Richardson's Sir Charles Grandison and as unchangeable, because, in his own words, "Nobility, like genius, is inborn" (VIII:vii).

While his virtuous behavior remains invariably exemplary, Kenelm's social and political views do undergo a marked change, which is at the same time a process of unlearning. At the beginning of the novel Kenelm has already come under the influence of his uncle Chillingly Mivers. The disillusioned and agnostic editor of a satiric journal, Chillingly has acquainted him with the "new ideas" of a utilitarian and democratic age, in which traditions are despised and reform for the sake of reform is popular. Under his influence Kenelm holds a speech on the festive occasion of his twenty-first birthday, enlightening his father's household and friends to the effect that neither traditions nor landowners like his father are honorable or valuable for themselves. For the sake of the welfare of the community, the most efficient tenants will aim at securing the maximum profit, favoring modern improvements instead of respecting old loyalties and family ties: "It is not, my friends, a question whether a handful of farmers like yourselves go to the workhouse or not. It is a consumer's question. Do you produce the maximum of corn to the consumer?" (I:xii). Kenelm has become a convinced utilitarian; man and nature are regarded from a rational and mechanical point of view: "If to an artist Nature has a soul, why, so has a steam-engine" (I:xiv).

The main aim of Kenelm's further education, or rather de-education, is to purge him of such poisonous ideas. His noble and sympathetic heart soon teaches him how inadequate and often inhumane utilitarian principles can be. When he uses his money to help Jessie Wiles and her beloved Will to acquire a shop, he sets aside the market principles according to which a richer bidder should have been favored. His chivalric heart, which must incline towards the values of a nobler age, rejects the ideas of a rational modern age of economists and sophisters—to use Carlyle's terms. Instead of the maximization of profits, Kenelm slowly returns towards the older patriarchal ideals that have characterized a traditional economy of large households with many superfluous hands to make labor easy, as the oxymoron "lazy occupation" indicates in a description of the labor force on the Chillingly estate. Kenelm's father Sir Peter, who is too generous to count his pennies or to exploit his tenants, seems indeed to be the benevolent patriarch of a more traditional economy. The upkeep of the family home and grounds of Exmundham is thus quite costly, as a modern visitor reproachfully observes:

> Leopold Travers . . . lectur[ed] Sir Peter on the old-fashioned system of husbandry which that good-natured easy proprietor permitted his tenants to adopt, as well as on the number of superfluous hands that were employed on the pleasure-grounds and in the general management of the estate. . . . Exmundham, indeed, was a very expensive place to keep up. . . . There were paths and drives through miles of young plantations and old woodlands that furnished lazy occupation to an army of labourers. No wonder that, despite his nominal ten thousand a year, Sir Peter was far from being a rich man. Exmundham devoured at least half the rental. (VII:vii)

Most of the characters in the novel fit either into the category modern/egoistic or into that of old fashioned/altruistic, and Kenelm's aimless wanderings—as well as the vagaries of his sometime companion, a "wandering minstrel"—can be understood implicitly to question the teleological style of life of the careerist and the profit-seeker. Whereas Wilhelm Meister learns to accept the necessity of a mundane calling when he finally becomes a doctor, Kenelm learns to despise all utilitarian reasoning. His counterpart is the political careerist Chillingly Gordon, who buys a seat in Parliament and weighs every word he utters carefully and opportunistically. In a letter to his father, Kenelm unmasks Gordon as the soulless representative of modern times:

> "He said to me the other day, with a *sang-froid* worthy of the iciest Chillingly, 'I mean to be Prime Minister of England: it is only a ques-

tion of time.' Now, if Chillingly Gordon is to be Prime Minister, it will be because the increasing cold of our moral and social atmosphere will exactly suit the development of his talents. He is the man above all others to argue down the declaimers of old-fashioned sentimentalities—love of country, care for its position among nations, zeal for its honour, pride in its renown. (Oh, if you could hear him philosophically and logically sneer away the word 'prestige'!) Such notions are fast being classified as 'bosh'." (IV:vi)

Hegel's "poetry of the heart," which has utopian tendencies in *Wilhelm Meister*, is in *Kenelm Chillingly* directed towards honor, national pride, and a chivalric code of virtue. If Wilhelm moves from the poetic world of the theater towards a compromise with bourgeois humdrum existence—Friedrich Schlegel, somewhat disappointed, denied the novel any actual "poetic significance"[11]— Kenelm's de-education turns away from the modern world to rediscover a bygone aristocratic and also poetical world. Poetry is—in the spirit of conservative romantics—considered to have embellished a former, more humane age, in which landowner and tenant were bound by mutual respect and shared responsibilities. One of Kenelm's guides on this quest for former ideals is the wandering minstrel, surely influenced by Goethe's figure of the harpist, but with special retrospective medieval connotations, perhaps even reminiscences of Sir Walter Scott. Under the minstrel's guidance, Kenelm slowly turns from a mechanical concept of nature towards "nature idealised."[12] One of the wandering minstrel's drawings is interpreted by Kenelm as an emblem of the meaningful, inspired nature that belongs to romanticism and denies realist principles:

> KENELM.—"But I have a great reverence for poetry as a priesthood. I felt that reverence for you when you sketched and talked priesthood last evening, and placed in my heart—I hope forever while it beats— the image of the child on the sunlit hill, high above the abodes of men, tossing her flowerball heavenward, and with heavenward eyes." . . .
>
> Kenelm resumed. "I have been educated in the Realistic school, and with realism I am discontented, because in realism as a school there is no truth. It contains but a bit of truth, and that the coldest and hardest bit of it, and he who utters a bit of truth and suppresses the rest of it, tells a lie." (III:xii)

The image of the poet as priest, the innocent child, and the concept of divinely inspired nature link Kenelm's poetics with romanticism. With Wordsworth quoted as an authority, the forces of religion, the heart, and poetry fight against the modern age of the go-getters. Kenelm's infatuation with the elflike Lily, a reincarnation of Wilhelm's Mignon,[13] is similarly based on romantic ideas of innocence and pantheistic nature. When Lily remarks, "What an interchange of music there must be between nature and a poet!," the spellbound Kenelm replies:

> "The Creator has gifted the whole universe with language, but few are the hearts that can interpret it. Happy those to whom it is no foreign tongue, acquired imperfectly with care and pain, but rather a native language, learned unconsciously from the lips of the great mother. To them the butterfly's wing may well buoy into heaven a fairy's soul!" (V:v)

The order of a benevolent patriarchal society is, it seems, supported by the idea of an ordered cosmos, which may be accessible to the romantic, but not to the modern poet. Hegel's poetry of the heart and a traditional form of society seem to be interdependent and opposed to the prosaic nature of modern life. The empathy between the innocent, elflike Lily and the chivalrous Kenelm points towards a fusion of romantic and medieval ideas, which curbs romanticism of its utopian potential and emphasizes its retrospective tendencies. Already in *England and the English* Bulwer had suggested that Wordsworth had "an influence of a more noble and purely intellectual character than any writer of our age and nation," adding that "his ideas, too, fall into that refined and refining *toryism*, the result of a mingled veneration for the past—of a disdain for the pettier cries which float over that vast abyss which we call the public." Wordsworth's praise of the common speech of the common man is thus reinterpreted in the spirit of a generally antimodern and antidemocratic animus, whereas Shelley is described in contrast as "spiritualizer of all who forsake the past and the present, and, with lofty hopes and a bold philanthropy, rush forward into the future." Shelley is presented as the apologist of "dreamers of foolish dreams," whose "influence, both poetical and moral, has been far less purifying and salutary than Wordsworth's."[14] Such selective recanonization allows for a conservative interpretation of romantic literature in the spirit of the Young England movement.

In the idyllic setting of Moleswich, where Lily grows up, the benevolence and sensibility that the eighteenth-century culture of sensibility had interpreted as common to all men, are assimilated to the values of the nobly born. Valor, generosity, and chastity are

united with naïveté and poetic sensibility, *courteoisie* with freedom, modern sensibility with the Middle Ages. It is little wonder
that Kenelm, purged of his new utilitarian ideas, finally returns
to the family home of Exmundham with the intention of becoming a member of the society that accepts his father's patriarchal
values and of entering political life as a conservative Member of
Parliament. The revolutionary speech he has held on his twenty-
first birthday is now presented as a "bad joke on the new ideas"
(VIII:xv), and the circular process of Kenelm's de-education,
which seems to be patterned upon Bulwer's own movement away
from early political radicalism, is complete. Cured of his youthful
political enthusiasm as well as of his possibly too-idealistic love for
the untutored Lily—who can be seen as an example of uncivilized
and unspoilt humanity in the tradition of Rousseau[15]—Kenelm
finally turns towards old values and social responsibilities that
adorn the aristocrat and gentleman. Youthful enthusiasm and the
dangers of political radicalism have been left behind and Kenelm
has completed a circular journey towards the values of old. The
movement symbolically undoes the modern age and modern realistic art in favor of a romantically conceived traditional society,
which is ideologically linked with the Young England movement.
Programmatically, Kenelm finally announces: "the time has
come to replace the old Kenelm with the new ideas, by a new Kenelm with the Ideas of Old." (VIII: "Chapter the Last") In retrospect we can appreciate why Kenelm was named after Kenelm
Digby, the author of *The Broad Stone of Honour* (1822), a study
and eulogy of chivalry that influenced the Young England movement.[16]

Kenelm's de-education is highlighted by the careers of contrasting figures like the farrier Tom Bowles, whom the chivalrous
hero must beat up in order to liberate the young maiden, Jessie
Wiles. Subsequently Kenelm is able to win his friendship and to
awaken his sensibilities for poetry, for the beauties of nature, and
for books. Tom's education, however, also fires his ambition: he
soon becomes a prosperous young man and forgets his beloved
Jessie in favor of an elegant young lady further up the social
scale, whose father offers Tom an attractive business partnership. Kenelm is disappointed by Tom's worldliness and by his
easy "transfers of allegiance,"[17] while at the same time wryly
prophesying that he will become a successful man of affairs and
social climber: "you will marry the young lady you mention, and
rise, through progressive steps of alderman and major, into the
rank of member for Luscombe" (VII:iii). Although Kenelm had

begun to redeem Tom's heart and mind, the much despised age of progress has transformed him into an egoistic go-getter. This new age of progress, which Kenelm calls an age of prigs, causes commonplace ideas and egotism to prevail. So the mature Kenelm criticizes his uncle Chillingly Mivers, who has been responsible for his modern and atheistic education:

> "But the times now, my dear father, are so cold-blooded that you can't be too cold-blooded to prosper. What could Chillingly Mivers have been in an age when people cared twopence-halfpenny about their religious creeds, and their political parties deemed their cause was sacred, and their leaders were heroes?" (IV:vi)

The subplot, which concerns the angelic Lily, illustrates the pernicious influence of the new age of progress and mammon. Not knowing her parents, Lily lacks a family, traditions, and guidance. She appears to be an angelic poetic being, but she is doomed to die because involved at too early an age in tragic conflicts between family allegiances. As Kenelm later learns, her grandfather, a gentleman, had entered into a partnership with a banker, a Mr. Jones from Clapham, who went bankrupt and was convicted for embezzlement, thus throwing the entire family into disgrace and causing the parents' early death. The family history, which Kenelm first discovers because of a picture that has been removed from the portrait gallery of the Travers family, leads to one of his few emotional outbursts:

> "how common . . . is the discontent with competence, respect, and love, when catching sight of a money-bag! How many well-descended county families, cursed with an heir who is called a clever man of business, have vanished from the soil. A company starts—the clever man joins it—one bright day. Pouf! The old estates and the old name are powder. Ascend higher. Take nobles whose ancestral titles ought to be to English ears like the sounds of clarions, awakening the most slothful to the scorn of money-bags and the passion for reknown. Lo! In that mocking dance of death called the Progress of the Age, one who did not find enough in a sovereign's revenue, and seeks The Little More as a gambler on the turf by the advice of blacklegs! . . . In the old time it was through the Temple of Honour that one passed to the Temple of Fortune. In this wise age the process is reversed." (III:xvi)

Leopold Travers has hidden the portrait of his ancestress Arabella Fletwode in a corner because she is also an ancestress of

Lily's disgraced grandfather. In the absurdity of Travers's gesture, Kenelm discerns the failure of modern man, motivated by mercenary ambition, to understand what an appropriate sense of family honor entails:

> "What a speaking homily," soliloquized Kenelm, addressing the picture, "against the ambition thy fair descendant would awake in me, art thou, O lovely image! For generations thy beauty lived in this canvas, a thing of joy, the pride of the race it adorned. Owner after owner said to admiring guests, 'Yes, a fine portrait, by Lely; she was an ancestress—a Fletwode of Fletwode.' Now . . . thou art thrust out of sight. . . . The infamy of one living man is so large that it can blot out the honour of the dead." (III:xx)

Kenelm's turn towards traditions and old ideas and his return to the family property, which implies the honoring of the family line, is a logical answer to the disaster of the Fletwodes. Education has led Kenelm astray, and the modern democratic age with its utilitarian ideas can fascinate only for a short time, until he learns to understand that the old ideas and values of a patriarchal society are more humane. Communal responsibilities come finally to dominate over individual desires, and the modern nineteenth-century world is sharply criticized from a conservative point of view. Kenelm himself can be interpreted as an allegorical impersonation of the hopes of conservative cultural critics that democratic ideas and the power of the monied interest will prove to be mistaken but reversible modern tendencies. Whereas Edmund Burke had sadly proclaimed, "the age of chivalry is gone.— That of sophisters, oeconomists, and calculators, has succeeded; and the glory of Europe is extinguished for ever," Bulwer anticipates a restoration and embellishes it in the light of a more poetic, romanticized age.[18]

*Kenelm Chillingly* reinterprets the main features of the bildungsroman and revokes the central message: instead of a mediation between the interests of the enlightened, hopeful individual and the demands of society, the story shows Kenelm turning away from modern society and, rather than exploring his talents and desires, accommodating to venerable traditions. "Bildung" does not in *Kenelm Chillingly* mean a development of the individual's powers and abilities, which in Goethe's novel aims at an ideal of self-fulfillment, but simply the demonstration of inborn virtues as in the classical *aventures* of the knight. The formal transformation of the basically enlightenment genre of the bildungsroman is an indicator of the conservative message: the return of the "prodigal son in exile" to the father indicates a general restoration of partriarchal ideals.[19] This kind of transforming or "unwriting" of pre-existing models can surely be linked with Bulwer's technique of "unwriting" and replacing earlier versions of his own stories or of fictitious texts, the topic of Allan Christensen's analysis in this volume. But while that analysis of the unwriting of individual fictitious texts and the discourses they represent raises existential and epistemological questions, the revocation of the genre of the bildungsroman entails a more strictly ideological challenge.

## NOTES

1. Cf. T. H. S. Escott, *Edward Bulwer, First Baron Lytton of Knebworth* (London: George Routledge & Sons, 1910), p. 5.

2. "For the original idea which, with humility, I will venture to call the philosophical design, of a moral education or apprenticeship, I have left it easy to be seen that I am indebted to Goethe's *Wilhelm Meister*" (Bulwer, preface to the edition of 1840, *Ernest Maltravers*).

3. Edwin Eigner speaks of a failed adaptation of the formula in *"The Pilgrims of the Rhine*: The Failure of the German *Bildungsroman* in England," *The Victorian Newsletter* 68 (1985): 19–21.

4. "Anempfindung Deutschlands" (Heinrich Laube, *Moderne Charakteristiken*, 2 vols. [Mannheim: C. Löwenthal, 1835], 2:373).

5. Johannes Scherr, *Geschichte der englischen Literatur*, 2nd ed. (Leipzig: Wigand, 1874), p. 232.

6. Cf. Louise Sigmann, *Die englische Literatur von 1800–1850 im Urteil der zeitgenössischen deutschen Kritik* (Heidelberg: Carl Winter, 1918), pp. 232f., 251 [my trans.].

7. Allan Conrad Christensen has explored Bulwer's idealistic and antimimetic tendencies in detail in his *Edward Bulwer-Lytton. The Fiction of New Regions* (Athens: University of Georgia Press, 1976).

8. Bulwer Lytton, "On Moral Fictions. Miss Martineau's Illustrations of Political Economy," *New Monthly Magazine* 37 (Feb. 1833): 146ff.

9. Bulwer Lytton, dedicatory epistle and preface to the edition of 1853, *Zanoni*.

10. Susanne Howe, *Wilhelm Meister and his English Kinsmen: Apprentices to Life* (New York: Columbia University Press, 1930), p. 139.

11. F. Schlegel, *Literary Notebooks*, ed. H. Eichner (London: University of London Press, 1957), Nr. 1703.

12. Even from the beginning of the novel, however, there seems to be a tension between Kenelm's utilitarian ideas and his heartfelt and somewhat romantic sympathy for God's creation: "Up rose from the green blades of corn a solitary skylark. His voice woke up the other birds. A few minutes more and the joyous concert began. Kenelm reverently doffed his hat, and bowed his head in

mute homage and thanksgiving" (II:i). This tension seems to anticipate his conversion.

13. Lily is also a recasting of a fatal early love affair of Bulwer's: "Indeed the long episode of Kenelm's love for the ethereal Lily reproduces almost the precise details of the young Edward Bulwer's tragic love for the girl at Ealing" (Christensen, *Edward Bulwer-Lytton*, p. 207).

14. Edward Lytton Bulwer, *England and the English* [1833], ed. with an introduction by Standish Meacham (Chicago and London: University of Chicago Press, 1970), pp. 282–85. For Wordsworth's influence upon Bulwer see also Christensen, *Edward Bulwer-Lytton*, pp. 206–07.

15. Lily seems precariusly poised between, on the one hand, the asssimilation of romantic ideas to a retrospective evocation of a more poetic age and, on the other, the dangers of excessive sensibility and idealism—between, that is, two tendencies of the romantic spirit.

16. The seventeenth-century namesake is in this context perhaps of less importance.

17. The use of the old-fashioned term "allegiance" for matters of the heart is remarkable, as it has medieval connotations.

18. Edmund Burke, *Reflections on the Revolution in France*, in *The Works*, 12 vols. in 6 (London: John C. Nimmo, 1887 [rpt. Hildesheim: Olms, 1975]), 3–4:331.

19. Christensen indicates (*Edward Bulwer-Lytton*, pp. 209–10) that Bulwer evidently associated the story of the prodigal son's return from exile and the reconciliation of father and son in this, his last novel with the approach of his own death. In death, Bulwer speculated, one returns to "the father he has so often forgotten. It is to a father's judgment that he is to render the account of his wanderings—it is to a father's home that he returns" (stray note of the period printed in 2nd Earl of Lytton, *The Life of Edward Bulwer, First Lord Lytton*, 2 vols. [London: Macmillan, 1913], 2:488). Regarding restorative thinking in Bulwer's works and the conservative recasting of literary forms, see Walter Göbel, *Edward Bulwer-Lytton. Systemreferenz, Funktion, literarischer Wert in seinem Erzählwerk* (Heidelberg: Universitätsverlag C. Winter, 1993).

# Notes on Contributors

ANDREW BROWN is Director of Academic Publishing at Cambridge University Press. Among his more recent writings on Bulwer, on whom he has worked for thirty years, are "The Supplementary Chapter to Bulwer Lytton's *A Strange Story*" (*Victorian Literature and Culture*, 1998), and the standard entries in *The Cambridge Bibliography of English Literature* (3rd ed., 2000) and *The New Dictionary of National Biography* (2004). He has also edited George Eliot's *Romola* (1993).

ALLAN CONRAD CHRISTENSEN is Professor of English Literature at John Cabot University in Rome. Besides many articles on romantic and Victorian writers, he has published books on Bulwer Lytton (1976) and Giovanni Ruffini (*A European Version of Victorian Fiction*, 1996) and coedited *The Challenge of Keats: Bicentenary Essays* (2000). His current project is a book on nineteenth-century narratives of contagion.

DAVID LYTTON COBBOLD, 2ND BARON COBBOLD OF KNEBWORTH, is on his mother's side a great-great-grandson of Bulwer Lytton. Responsible since 1971 for the care and restoration of the Bulwer Lytton home in Hertfordshire, he has organized many theatrical and other cultural initiatives that have made Knebworth House a point of reference for Victorian studies. Rosina Bulwer, throughout his childhood "the ancestress we don't mention," has long intrigued him. He has rehung her portrait at the house, visited her family home in County Tipperary, placed a tombstone on her unmarked grave, and called his own daughter Rosina.

RICHARD CRONIN is Professor of English Literature at the University of Glasgow. His most recent books are *1798: The Year of the Lyrical Ballads* (1998) and *The Politics of Romantic Poetry: In Search of the Pure Commonwealth* (2000). He is editor of the forthcoming *Blackwell Companion to Victorian Poetry*.

ANGUS EASSON is Research Professor of English at the University of Salford. His publications include *Elizabeth Gaskell* (1979) and

*Elizabeth Gaskell: The Critical Heritage* (1991) and, among editions, Gaskell's *The Life of Charlotte Brontë* and *Wives and Daughters*. He is currently working on a *Companion to Nicholas Nickleby*.

WALTER GÖBEL, Professor of English and American Studies at the University of Stuttgart, has published books on Sherwood Anderson (1982), Edward Bulwer Lytton (1993), and the African-American novel of the twentieth century (2001), and he has co-edited *Modernization and Literature* (2000), *Renaissance Humanism: Modern Humanism(s)* (2001), and *Engendering Images of Man in the Long 18th Century* (2001). He is currently working on a volume of essays on Conrad in Germany and on eighteenth-century masculinities.

JONATHAN H. GROSSMAN is Associate Professor of English at the University of California, Los Angeles, and author of *The Art of Alibi: English Law Courts and the Novel* (2002). His current project continues his work on the transformation of novelistic form in the 1820s and 1830s.

JOACHIM MATHIEU teaches at the Gabrieli-Gymnasium in Eichstätt, Bavaria. He has published *Edward Bulwer-Lytton's England and the English: A Description of England in the "Age of Reform"* (2001), and his first play, *Mackerels Cannot Write*, has recently been produced.

MARIE MULVEY-ROBERTS, Reader in English at the University of the West of England, Bristol, is the author of *British Poets and Secret Societies* and *Gothic Immortals* and has edited over thirty books, including reprints of Rosina Bulwer Lytton's works. She is co-editor of the journal *Women's Writing* and is currently working on a triple biography of Anna Wheeler, her daughter Rosina Bulwer Lytton, and Rosina's granddaughter Lady Constance Lytton.

LILLIAN NAYDER, Professor of English at Bates College, has published *Wilkie Collins* (1997) and *Unequal Partners: Charles Dickens, Wilkie Collins, and Victorian Authorship* (2002). She is working on a biography of Catherine Dickens.

CATHERINE PHILLIPS is Fellow in English at Downing College, Cambridge, and Newton Trust Lecturer in the Faculty of English.

Her publications include *Robert Bridges: A Life* (1992), *"The Hour-Glass": The Manuscript Materials* (in the Cornell Yeats series, 1994), *John Donne: The Critical Heritage* (vol. 2, with A. J. Smith, 1996), and various editions of the works of Gerard Manley Hopkins—*Oxford Authors Hopkins* (1986, 2002), *Selected Poems* (1995, 1996), and *Selected Letters* (1990). She is presently writing about Victorian art and literature with special reference to Hopkins.

LAWRENCE POSTON is Professor of English at the University of Illinois at Chicago. He has published a number of articles on the romantic-Victorian transition in literature, of which one recent example is "Beyond the Occult: The Godwinian Nexus of Bulwer's *Zanoni*" (*Studies in Romanticism*, 1998). A current project is a monograph on Newman, and his broader interests include nonfictional prose more generally and late Victorian musical culture.

PHILIP RAND teaches at the Scuola Superiore per Mediatori Linguistici "Carlo Bo" in Rome. He has published textbooks regarding techniques of translation and the history of the English language. His research, beginning with his doctoral dissertation, has focused for many years on Paris during the Second Empire, and an article on the *Paris* of Maxime Du Camp is forthcoming in *The Writer and the City*, the papers of a recent conference at the University of Leiden.

ESTHER SCHOR, Associate Professor of English at Princeton University, teaches courses in nineteenth-century English literature and Jewish studies. She is the author of *Bearing the Dead: The British Culture of Mourning from the Enlightenment to Victoria* (1994) and co-editor of *Women's Voices: Visions and Perspectives* (1990) and *The Other Mary Shelley: Beyond "Frankenstein"* (1993). Her volume of poems, *The Hills of Holland*, has appeared recently (2002), and the *Cambridge Companion to Mary Shelley*, which she has completed editing, is forthcoming.

PETER W. SINNEMA, Associate Professor of English at the University of Alberta, is author of *Dynamics of the Pictured Page* (1998) and editor of Samuel Smiles's *Self-Help* (2002). He has published various articles on Victorian subjects, with emphases on the rise of illustrated journalism, questions of Englishness and national identity, and the fiction of Jules Verne. His current project is a study of mid-nineteenth-century representations of death and the spectacle of nationhood.

CHARLES W. SNYDER is an attorney in private practice in Savannah, Georgia. He is the author of *Liberty and Morality: A Political Biography of Edward Bulwer-Lytton* (1995) and of "An American Original: Theodore Roosevelt Jr." in *Theodore Roosevelt: Many-Sided American* (edited by Natalie Naylor, Douglas Brinkley, and John Allen Gable, 1992).

HEATHER WORTHINGTON is researcher and associate lecturer in the Centre for Critical and Cultural Theory at the University of Wales, Cardiff. Her recently completed doctoral dissertation concerns nineteenth-century crime fiction in the popular press, with emphasis on the emergence of the detecting figure. The early fiction of Bulwer Lytton was the subject of her M.A. dissertation, and she has written on topics as diverse as Val McDermid's serial-killer thriller *The Mermaids Singing* and T. H. White's *The Once and Future King* (*Arthuriana*, 2002).

# Index

Numbers in italics refer to illustrated pages.